12/11/96

To Bill—

POWER,
PASTA &
POLITICS

Keep fighting
the good fight —

Best Wishes

Al D'Amato

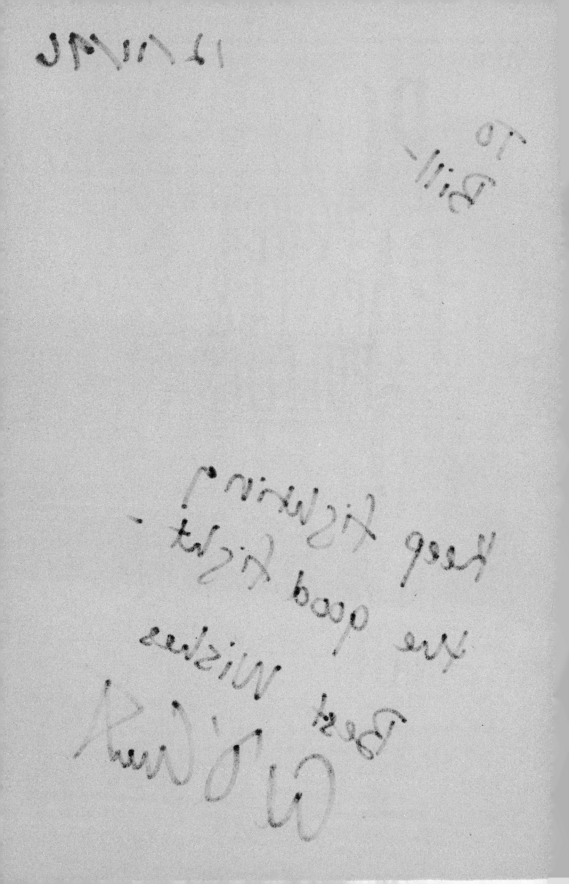

17/1/94

To Bill —

keep fishing]
the good fight —
Best Wishes

POWER, PASTA & POLITICS

THE WORLD ACCORDING TO SENATOR AL D'AMATO

FOREWORD BY SENATOR BOB DOLE

INTRODUCTION BY ED KOCH

HYPERION

NEW YORK

PHOTOGRAPH CREDITS

Page 1, all: Photos from the author's personal collection; Page 2, all: Photos from the author's personal collection; Page 3, left 1969, left 1981: Photos from the author's personal collection; Page 3, below: Courtesy of Senator D'Amato; Page 4, all: Courtesy of Senator D'Amato; Page 5, left 1984: Courtesy of Senator D'Amato; Page 5, below 1985: © Ronald L. Glassman; Page 5, left 1986: © Memo Zack; Page: 6, right: Courtesy of Senator D'Amato; Page 6, below: Courtesy of Senator D'Amato; Page 7, left: Courtesy of Senator D'Amato; Page 7, below: Courtesy of Senator D'Amato; Page 8, all: Courtesy of Senator D'Amato; Page 9, all: Courtesy of Senator D'Amato; Page 10, all: Courtesy of Senator D'Amato; Page 11, all: Courtesy of Senator D'Amato; Page 12, above and right: Courtesy of Senator D'Amato; Page 13, top: © Sender Schwartz; Page 13, center: © Ronald L. Glassman; Page 13, bottom: Courtesy of Senator D'Amato; Page 14, top: © *Newsday*; Page 14, center: © 1992 *Newsday*; Page 14, bottom: © Steven R. Brown; Page 15, opposite top: Courtesy of Senator D'Amato; Page 15, opposite bottom: Courtesy of Senator D'Amato; Page 16, top: © Tom A. Mike; Page 16, center: Courtesy of Senator D'Amato; Page 16, bottom: © Mike Guzofsky/Sygma.

A leatherbound signed first edition of this book has been published by The Easton Press.

Copyright © 1995 Senator Alfonse D'Amato

Design by Joel Avirom

Library of Congress Cataloging-in-Publication Data
D'Amato, Alfonse.
Power, pasta, and politics : the world according to Senator Al D'Amato / foreword by Bob Dole : introduction by Ed Koch. – 1st ed.
p.   cm.
ISBN 0-7868-6045-6
1. D'Amato, Alfonse.   2. Legislators–United States–Biography.   3. United States. Congress. Senate–Biography.
4. United States–Politics and government–1989–1993.
5. United States–Politics and government–1993–
I. Title.
E840.8.D36A3   1995
328.73′092–dc20
[B]   95-9429
CIP

FIRST EDITION

10 9 8 7 6 5 4 3 2 1

My Grandpa Alfonso always said that in America everything was possible. This book is dedicated to that spirit.

CONTENTS

V- LIFE IN BILL CLINTON'S WASHINGTON

*A**CKNOWLEDGMENTS***

I want to thank all of those who have inspired me throughout my life to achieve dreams I never thought were possible.

To my family who nurtured and stood by me–my Grandpa Alfonso; my parents, Armand and Antoinette; my brother and sister, Armand and Jo Anne; Penny; our children, Lisa, Lorraine, Danny, and Chris; and our grandchildren;

To my friends in Island Park who encouraged me, challenged me, and weren't afraid to disagree with me;

To the most wonderful and dedicated executive assistant anyone could ever have, Margie Dillon, who's been with me since 1969, and who deserves canonization for putting up with me all these years;

To my colleagues who have worked with me through good and bad times;

And, finally, to all of those who have allowed me to be part of their lives and they a part of mine.

I would like to give a special thanks to those who made the writing of this book possible–Kay McCauley, my dynamic agent who worked tirelessly to find just the right publisher–Hyperion; Kevin McDonough, who helped me compile this book and kept me focused on writing when so many other things competed for my attention; and my editor, Brian DeFiore, who polished my prose.

I would also like to thank the dozens of people who have called me over the last two years to remind me of stories, to jog my memory, and helped me track down the names, places, facts, and photos that make up this book, including Brian Ahearn, Mike Armstrong, Wayne Berman, Rich Bond, John "Riverboat" Campbell, Tony Cornachio, Cheryl Davis, Marian Ungar Davis, Gus DiFlorio, Jerry DiMarco, Helen Elovich, Arthur Finkelstein, Stanley Fleishman, Craig Fuller, Jim Gill, Judy Harris, Assemblyman Dov Hikind, Malcolm Hoenlein, Barbara Jones, Donna Kaufman, Congressman Peter King, Anne Mae Leonard, Neil Levin, Gary Lewi, Jack Libert, Kieran Mahoney, Ed Martin, Richie Miranda, Zenia Mucha, Rick Nasti, John O'Mara, Tom Palladino, Jack Pesso, John Sitilides, Larry Twomey, Tony "The Hat" Vislalli, Jeff Weisenfeld, John Zagame, and the list could go on and on.

FOREWORD

Al D'Amato and Bob Dole—at first glance it seems like an unlikely friendship. One was raised on his mother's pasta in the heart of America's largest city. And the other was raised on his mother's fried chicken on the plains of rural Kansas. But when New Yorkers sent Al to the United States Senate in 1980, it didn't take me long to discover that we had a great deal in common.

Both of us call them like we see them. Both of us believe in the neighborhood values that made America great—values like hard work and personal responsibility. Both of us don't give up without a fight. And both of us have never forgotten from where we came.

Anyone who knows Al D'Amato has a story to tell about him. And I'm fortunate to have fourteen years of stories about a remarkable public servant.

I remember an official trip to Italy, where Al and I were joined by several other senators. One evening, the Italian government sponsored a reception in the beautiful village of Castel d'Aino, just miles from where I was wounded in battle during World War II.

While government officials waited to greet us, Al cut through diplomatic protocol and improved Italian-American relations by going straight to the people. He escorted an elderly Italian woman into the middle of the street, and delighted the entire village by dancing with her. He took the baton and conducted the village orchestra. It was typical Al D'Amato–making the "average" citizen feel like royalty.

He does that every day in the United States Senate. I think Al is the only senator who has a pair of boxing gloves hanging on his office wall. New Yorkers love a fighter. And in Al D'Amato they have one who never gives up. I have seen him come from 26 percentage points behind with just six weeks to go until the election and retain his Senate seat. I have seen him time and again taking on the entire federal bureaucracy on behalf of one constituent. And I have also seen him talk on the Senate floor for fourteen hours straight in an effort to save 875 jobs at a factory in upstate New York. I have often said that Al is so persistent, he doesn't even take "yes" for an answer.

"Aggressively fighting for the right is the noblest sport the world affords." Those are the words of Teddy Roosevelt, and they're engraved on a plaque in Al's office. And when it comes to the issues of our day, just as when it comes to the people he represents, Al D'Amato never tires of fighting for the right.

He knew it was right to insist that America stand with the newly emerging democracies of Eastern Europe. And a *New York Post* headline framed on Al's office wall leaves no doubt where Al stood: "D'Amato vs. Gorby: 'I'll Kick Him in the Baltics.' "

He knew it was right to warn America about the dangers of Saddam Hussein, and no one saw those dangers as early and as clearly as Al D'Amato.

He knew it was right that the alleged murderers of a young Orthodox Jew be brought to trial, and he engaged in a successful one-man battle to convince a reluctant Department of Justice to seek a federal indictment.

He knew it was right for Congress not to ignore its oversight responsibilities, and, and even in the face of intense personal attacks, he led the fight to shed some light into the murky depths of Whitewater.

Boxing gloves, plaques with quotations, and framed headlines are just a small sample of what you see when you enter Al's office. What you cannot help but notice in that office are the photographs. Not photographs of Al with presidents and prime ministers, even though there are some of those.

But there are far more photographs of Al with his family—at his daughter's wedding; playing with his grandchildren; standing with his parents, Armand and "Mamma" D'Amato in front of the Statue of Liberty on Bedloe's Island. Like countless others, Armand and Mamma's parents arrived at Ellis Island dreaming of freedom, and dreaming of a better life for their families.

Al D'Amato is proof that the American dream can become a reality. He is proof that hard work, perseverance, and personal initiative do succeed. And as long as he is "aggressively fighting for the right," I am confident that he will make the American dream a reality for countless more citizens around the world.

—SENATOR BOB DOLE

INTRODUCTION

Prior to Al D'Amato's running in the Republican primary against Senator Jack Javits, I had never heard of him. I was then mayor of the City of New York. It was 1980. Bess Myerson, John Lindsay, John Santucci, and the eventual winner, Liz Holtzman, were running in the Democratic primary. I was for Bess Myerson. When she lost, I decided that Javits deserved another term, his last hurrah. He was dying of Lou Gehrig's disease.

Al D'Amato quickly became known to the New York public with the extraordinarily effective ads featuring his mother, who became affectionately known throughout the state as "Mamma" D'Amato. She did for him what my father did for me when I ran against Carmine DeSapio in 1963. My father, then a fur manufacturer, dropped a twenty-foot banner outside his loft window on the eleventh floor at 208 West 30th Street that read VOTE FOR MY SON, ED KOCH, FOR DISTRICT LEADER, [signed] LOU KOCH. It was very effective, and Mamma's comments extolling her little boy, Alfonse, were even more effective.

Al D'Amato won the Republican primary. And Javits, who was unopposed in the Liberal Party, now faced both D'Amato and Holtzman in the general election. I publicly made known my decision that I thought Javits deserved reelection and that I was going to vote for him on the Liberal line. It was clear, however, that Al, who had beaten him in the Republican primary by stressing that Javits was seventy-six and in poor health, would trounce him in the general election, too. The only question was whether he could also beat Holtzman.

Everyone recognized that Javits had lost the primary and would lose the November election because of his health. He was then in a wheelchair and with the passage of each day his condition seemed to worsen. I decided I would call the Javits campaign people and suggest they take on the health issue directly. My advice to them was a tough new slogan for Javits posters and media: "One Year with Javits Is Worth Six with D'Amato." The slogan was rejected, and the voters rejected Javits and Holtzman. D'Amato won.

Before the election, as we marched in the Steuben Day parade, Al had said to me, "After the election, may I come in and talk with you?" I said, "Sure." It was clear to me then that he was in all probability going to be the next U.S. Senator from the State of New York. After the election, he called and made an appointment to see me.

He sat down in my office in City Hall. He was a very engaging person, immediately likable, with none of the artifice or pretentiousness to which so many public officials who win against great odds succumb. They begin to believe their own act, and worse, the statements of sycophantic aides who tell them they are a natural to run on the national ticket for vice president.

The new senator and I quickly agreed to be on a first-name basis. He said that while he had won, he was very distressed that he had not done well in the Jewish community. And he didn't understand why. He wanted to correct that for the future. He wanted them to know that he was very supportive of Israel and that he thought of Jewish concerns here in the United States as reflective of the broad centrist middle class. They should like him and his views, which he thought would be reflective overall of theirs on many if not most issues.

I said to him, "Al, let me fill you in on a little secret. There are, aside from the issues that every American responds to, particularly middle-class citizens, two issues that obsess the lives and minds and hearts of most Jews. They are the security of Israel and rescuing Russian Jews, allowing them to leave the Soviet Union." I went further and said, "Al, make those your two issues, and the Jews will love you, at least as much as the Italians who love you now for natural reasons of identification." I went further, "The Jews give little credit to Jewish legislators who take on these two issues because it is expected that they will, but when a Christian legislator does it, they will vote for him forever." He said he would and he certainly did over the ensuing years.

What is particularly interesting is that when he ran for reelection against Attorney General Bob Abrams, a popular Jewish candidate, in 1992, it was the Jews–who rarely vote as a bloc and even more rarely for Republicans, certainly in New York City– who to a large extent put Al over the top. He got an amazing 42 percent of the Jewish vote. But the Upper West Side Jews, the sophisticates, the progressives, the academics, they hated him. Why? They couldn't forgive him his right to exercise his conscience and oppose abortion. While they loved the sophistication of Mario Cuomo's mind and speeches, they thought D'Amato–far more down to earth and certainly not cerebral–déclassé. For them he was their image of the southern Italian ethnic, too "limited" for their taste, a male Anna Magnani, unlike their image of the cultured northern Italian, an image they thought fit Cuomo–a duplicate of Marcello Mastroianni–who delighted them with his Jesuitical logic and Hamlet-like introspection.

But the Jewish working stiff, and particularly the Orthodox community angry at the indifference of so many Jews and non-Jews to the Crown Heights pogrom of August 1991, and the death of Yankel Rosenbaum, loved the fact that Al D'Amato had taken up that cause. And did he. He was everywhere denouncing what had occurred when a black mob ran through the streets of Crown Heights yelling, "Jew, Jew, kill the Jew," and then killing Yankel Rosenbaum, assaulting eighty Jews over a three-day period, and destroying hundreds of Jewish-owned properties.

According to a comment attributed to Governor Cuomo about a conversation he had had with Mayor David Dinkins, the mayor said he had allowed the mob to vent its rage for three days and, regrettably, it had abused that courtesy by engaging in violence. It was only stopped three days later by police ordered in by the mayor. D'Amato did not hesitate to denounce those who, like the mayor and his police commissioner, had left the Lubavitcher Hasidic community in Crown Heights in harm's way. I loved him for doing that.

When D'Amato ran for reelection in 1992, I was no longer mayor, but I still had credibility and a following in the Jewish community. I campaigned for Al. I had dinner with him on election night at an Italian restaurant in Manhattan. At the dinner was his pollster, Arthur Finkelstein, and my law partner, Jim Gill. It was early, and Al believed he was going to lose, as my partner and I did. Finkelstein announced to us about a half hour into dinner, after receiving word from his office, that exit polls showed Al two points ahead and that he'd win. I said to Finkelstein, "I would rather know the truth, even if it will be more difficult for us to finish dinner, so please don't make up comforting information." He said, "Mayor, I am telling you the truth. Al will win."

I really didn't believe him, but I said thank you. My fears increased when Finkelstein later announced that Bush was running 25 points behind Clinton statewide. Everyone, including Al, went into a funk because the top of the ticket usually runs ahead of everyone else on the line. Al turned to me and said quietly, "Ed, when the returns are in, and if they are bad, please take care of Mamma." I felt chills running down my spine because it was so loving on his part and so eloquent and reflective of his decency.

I thought at that moment of a scene that had occurred when I was campaigning for Al. I mentioned it at dinner as part of our small talk to relieve the tension. I had taken a lot of abuse from the sophisticated Jewish community that hated him and couldn't abide my being so active on his behalf. I recalled entering the building where my law office is located and a woman greeting me on the sidewalk, saying, "Mayor, I really like you, but I don't understand your support for Al D'Amato." I said, "I don't have much time. Follow me into my building," and she did. When we came through the revolving doors, I stopped and said to her, "I don't have time for a long explanation, so let me sum it up for you." I had concluded she was Jewish, so I said to her, "I'm for Al D'Amato because he is good for the Jews." She said, "Oh, I didn't know that." I knew I had gotten another vote for Al D'Amato.

On election night at the hotel, we didn't go down for Al to claim victory until close to two A.M. when 90 percent of the vote was in. It was a very tight election, swinging back and forth. As we walked into the crowd, a young man, a member of his staff, came over to him and Al put his arm around his shoulder. The young man, crying tears of joy, made clear how happy he was that Al had won. Al kissed him on the cheek and thanked him and then asked me to walk with him into the ballroom. He was crying, too. I said, "Al, you've won. Don't cry." He said, "I am crying because"—and then he mentioned the young man's name—"has AIDS and he is dying. And he's so happy for me. I will miss him." As we entered the ballroom and the crowd cheered him, I thought to myself, "Al D'Amato, you are a mensch."

—ED KOCH

POWER,
PASTA &
POLITICS

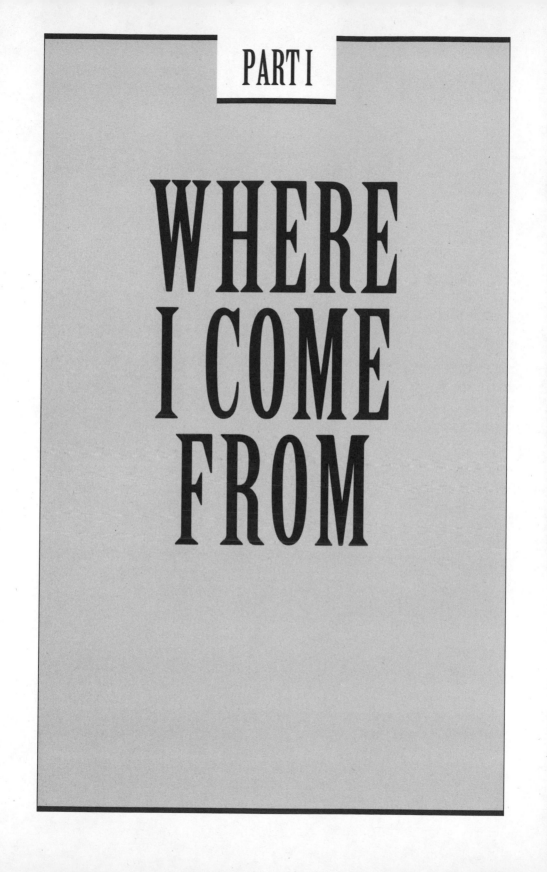

PART I

WHERE I COME FROM

CALL ME ALFONSE

I was born on August 1, 1937, the day before the Catholic feast day of St. Alfonso. My mother told me that's the reason I was baptized Alfonse. With all due love and respect to my grandpa Alfonso and my uncle Alfonse, and St. Alfonso, I hated my name and spent most of my childhood pretending it didn't exist.

When we moved to Island Park in 1945, Italians were hardly in the majority, so Italian names were a bit odd to most kids in my class at school. If my name had been Peter or Paul or Tony or even Francis, it wouldn't have made a difference, but when the teacher called my name my first day in school–"A-L-F-O-N-S-E"– the whole class erupted in laughter. It was agony. What kind of name was Alfonse? Half the fights I got into then–and I seemed to have more than my fair share–resulted from some smart aleck making fun of my name. There was a Johnny Cash song sometime back about a boy named Sue. His father gave him a girl's name so he'd have to get tough and defend himself as he grew up. When I look back at all the teasing I took and the fights I got into defending my name, myself, and my honor, maybe it was all a good preparation for my career in politics.

My parents wasted no time in giving me a nickname: Tippy. I was an excitable baby–maybe I was hyperactive. Describing me one day, my mother compared me to the neighbor's dog, a high-strung poodle called Tippy. Apparently this was so hilarious to all concerned that the name stuck, and I was Tippy from that day forward. There was a popular song when I was a year old that went, "Tippy, tippy tee, tippy, tippy tan." Someone was singing about *me* on the radio! I couldn't imagine the Andrews Sisters or the Inkspots ever crooning about an Alfonse.

I never used the name Alfonse. Teachers, priests, and coaches all called me Tippy, as well as my friends, neighbors, and everyone in the family. I had friends for years who never even knew my real name, and that was fine with me. Every once in a while when some substitute teacher read our names in class or at some formal roll call, "A-L-F-O-N-S-E" would be called out loud and the class would laugh uproariously.

Once, when I was about thirteen, walking to the store with my father, I confronted him with the question that had bothered me for years: "How could you do it to me? How could you name me Alfonse?" Having blurted this out, I was afraid he would be more than a little annoyed, and I was ready to run. To my surprise, Dad said to me, "Son, your grandfather Alfonso was a man of means, and that's how we got the down payment on the house." Now my father told me that in jest, but I've told the story, even on the political stump, for years. Mamma doesn't think it's so funny.

Since my oldest daughter, Lisa, married a wonderful man named Jerry Murphy, I've added a new twist to the story. They have three boys and a girl–Gregory, Dennis, Kevin, and Katie. I have offered to make the down payment on their house if they would name a child after me. Lisa told me, "Forget it, Dad. I love you, but there will never be an Alfonse Murphy."

My nickname, Tippy, stuck until I ran for public office. Almost all of my old friends from Island Park still call me Tippy. I may be a U.S. senator to strangers, but to my neighbors and the people I grew up with, I guess I will always be just plain Tippy. I know I'm home when I hear that name.

Early in my first Senate term I received a heartwarming letter from a little boy, Alfonse Fox. Handwritten in an earnest, child-like scrawl, Alfonse Fox's letter described a life of poverty and isolation. His daddy had died, leaving him and his mother all alone. If that wasn't hard enough, his classmates and neighbors made fun of his name. Then he asked me how I had liked having my name and how I survived, and if I had any suggestions about coping with such an unusual name. "After all," he wrote, "you grew up an Alfonse and you made it to the United States Senate."

I receive thousands of letters every year, but this one struck a chord. Here was another Alfonse. I told my press secretary Ed Martin that we had to reach out and find this kid. It wasn't enough to send him a nice letter on Senate stationery.

Alfonse Fox's letter had a return address in the San Francisco area. I called my old friend Joe Barletta, the publisher of the *San Francisco Examiner*. Joe used to be the executive VP of the *New York Daily News*. A superb newspaperman and a real human being, Joe, if anyone, could track down "little Alfonse."

I told him that all of our attempts to find the child by calling Information and combing phone books had come up empty. Maybe his mother had reverted to her maiden name. Perhaps they were so poor that they had no telephone. I suggested that he send a reporter out to find this little boy. After all, it might make a nice story to have us meet. Joe thought it was a good idea. He saw the human interest of a U.S. senator moved by a boy's letter with shared experiences.

A reporter was sent to the return address on Alfonse Fox's letter to find the young letter writer, but without success. Nobody lived there. Then one of Joe's reporters discovered that "Li'l Alfonse's" return address was a postal drop used by a freelance writer. Joe had his doubts: maybe I was being had. I had fallen for this letter hook, line, and sinker, and had visions of flying "Li'l Al" to Washington, D.C., to meet with Senator Al. After all these years, another Alfonse joke! In mock anger, I dashed off a letter to the writer in which I told Li'l Al that if I ever caught up with him, "I'll wring your little neck!"

I was not the only one to fall for this prank. The mysterious writer had sent letters to many public figures with odd-sounding first names and had used the same tear-jerking ploy. He wrote to

Caspar Weinberger about being a Caspar Fox. He shared his problem with Senator Arlen Specter. Everyone sent "Li'l Fox" a kind letter in return. Some even sent him autographed pictures of themselves. Later, he compiled the replies in a book he published himself. It even had my response.

MY
FATHER'S
WORLD

It wasn't easy. My father was born in Newark, New Jersey, on the kitchen table with a midwife in attendance. He was the second of nine brothers and sisters born to Italian immigrants who had come in their teens from Avalino, Italy, a town twenty miles north of Naples. My grandfather, Ettore D'Amato, was a jeweler who, like my grandmother, spoke only Italian. My father didn't know a word of English until the age of five, when he went to elementary school. He grew up in a household where only Italian was spoken and lived in a neighborhood that was composed primarily of Italian immigrants.

Turn-of-the-century Newark was home to dozens of new industries. Chemical firms, breweries, and factories attracted an extraordinary variety of immigrant workers, resulting in a quilt of Irish, Italian, Jewish, and Polish neighborhoods that kept pretty much to themselves. Today we might call them ghettos, but in my father's day they were the small parts of the world where you felt safe, where neighbors knew your name and probably spoke the language of your homeland. Newark had a top-notch school system that drilled all of its students, from every race and ethnic background, in the rudiments of reading and writing the English language. There was no Mickey Mouse attempt, as there is today, to kowtow to the notion of bilingualism. Thank God for my father, and for me, that his teachers in Newark weren't as "advanced" as they are today. He might otherwise have been enrolled in special "Italian-only" classes and have been subjected to linguistic segregation from the time he was five.

If English lessons were a task, learning music was a pleasure that my father enjoys to this day. It was hard enough to put food on the table to feed a family of eleven, but my grandparents did manage to come up with fifty cents a week for an old German lady to come to the house to give piano lessons to my father's younger brother, Michael. As the teacher drilled Uncle Mike, Dad would sit and watch and memorize everything, and then start to practice once the teacher left the room. It took her more than a year to catch on that she was giving two lessons for the price of one.

Soon my father could teach himself, and he quickly learned to play the violin and ten other instruments. He joined a fife and drum corp when he was eight years old, just so he could sample every instrument in the band. For a little boy growing up in a sprawling industrial city where Italians were not always considered first-class citizens, marching down the streets in his uniform gave him a powerful sense of pride and connection to the community. He often remarked with great sadness how schools today have largely abandoned marching bands and music lessons, and that maybe if more children were in bands and orchestras, there would be fewer kids in gangs and in trouble.

Like the sons and daughters of many immigrants, my father's early years were marked by sacrifice for his family. I have never met anyone who placed greater value on education than my father. Still, he and his older brother, my uncle Al, were forced to drop out of high school temporarily to work in order to help support the family. My father sold magazines in New England and sent his paycheck home every week. Even while he was trudging through the snow selling magazines door to door, he was determined to go back and finish high school. And he did.

When he finally went away to college, first at Trenton State and then Montclair State, his piano-playing skills were the only thing between him and starvation. Every weekend my father played in local taverns, pounding away at Broadway show tunes, vaudeville numbers, polkas, tarantellas, and ragtime from late afternoon until two or three in the morning.

As a college student in the thirties, my father was hardly immune to the economic and political upheaval of the time. In fact, like many students of that era, he was quite a radical. In 1935, he helped organize a student strike at Montclair State in support of the Oxford Peace pledge, which declared that the college youth of America would not go off to fight in an "imperialist war." For all of his youthful fervor, my father quickly shed such pacifist idealism when Stalin started making deals with Hitler and the bombs started falling on Pearl Harbor.

My father fell in love when he was just nineteen. Every once in a while, his mother and father would take the family to visit the cousins in Brooklyn, and it was there that my father first laid eyes on the love of his life, Antoinette Cioffari. It would take him more than two years to gather up enough courage to tell her.

By then he was twenty-one, and he and my mother began a romance that involved commuting every weekend from Newark to Brooklyn. My father would take the Hudson "Tubes" (now the PATH train) and then a trolley that took him across the Brooklyn Bridge and to Bedford Avenue. My mother would come the same way to Newark on alternate weekends. Their courtship continued for two years, and might have gone on forever had not Grandfather Alfonso put his foot down. After all this time, he was tired of waiting up while his daughter and her boyfriend from Newark stayed out until the appointed hour of midnight. He was sick of keeping this vigil and losing his sleep! He confronted my father and told him as much. Where was this endless courtship headed? "What," my grandpa affectionately but emphatically enquired, "are your intentions?"

My father nervously replied that his intentions were perfectly honorable, but that he wanted to wait until he graduated from college before proposing. And since it was the very depths of the Depression, he wanted to wait until he found a job to get married.

My impulsive, dramatic, busybody grandfather would have

none of this practicality. "You want to get married, get married *now!*" He couldn't stand staying up late any longer and would prefer to have his daughter and her new husband living with him rather than lose any more sleep. Having forced my father to propose, Grandpa even set the date. There was no stopping him. To this day, when I tell this story, my mother says, "Grandpa could never mind his own business!" I thank God he couldn't.

Thus my parents came to be married, less than a month after my father's graduation, on the Fourth of July, 1936.

Fifty years later, on the Fourth of July, 1986, Armand and Antoinette D'Amato celebrated their fiftieth anniversary on Governors Island in New York Harbor, accompanied by President and Mrs. Reagan, who were in town to salute the one hundredth anniversary of the Statue of Liberty. With millions of tourists on hand to see the fleet of "tall ships," the U.S. Navy, and a spectacular fireworks display, New York City was throwing an unprecedented party for the entire world. For me and millions of New Yorkers and Americans watching on television, it was a glorious day to remember for an entire lifetime. Too much of our personal and national memory is shaped by tragic events like the day Pearl Harbor was attacked, the afternoon Kennedy was shot, or the morning the Challenger exploded. Here was a day, like V-J Day or the American Bicentennial, that was marked by patriotism, euphoria, and good feelings. The weather was perfect, the harbor glistened with a thousands ships both big and small, and the entire city seemed to swell with pride. After a decade or more of near bankruptcy, crime, and decline, New York and America seemed to be saying, "Look out, world, we're back and we're better than ever!" Both Mayor Ed Koch and President Reagan were at the peaks of their popularity and they could be justly proud for infusing both the city and the nation with pride once again.

But I had no time for the aircraft carriers, aerial displays, fireworks, or hoopla. I was simply bursting with pride to see my mom and pop at the center of the festivities.

Like any surprise party, it wasn't easy to pull off. Foreign leaders, CEOs, and dignitaries from all over the world had arrived to salute the Statue of Liberty. I would have understood if the President had explained that he had to spend the time with France's President Mitterrand. The fact that both he and Nancy, who always had a busy agenda of her own, took time to be with us is a testimony to their decency, and the affection they had for my parents. I also believe that they realized there was something wonderfully remarkable about an Italian girl from Brooklyn and an Italian boy from Newark sharing their fiftieth anniversary with the hundredth birthday of that symbol of immigration, liberty, and opportunity.

Unfortunately, in the logistical scramble to get everyone, including the President, my staff, and the press, to Governors Island (and still keep this a secret from my unsuspecting folks), *somebody* sat on the cake. So there, amid the grandeur and the hoopla of it all, we had to celebrate with not much more than crumbs and smeared icing. If my mamma and pop noticed, they didn't say. They were surrounded by their friends, children, and grandchildren, a testament to their fifty years together. I'm sure they were thrilled that the President was there, but to my folks, a simple party at our local American Legion Hall would have been just as nice, if we all could be together. I will never forget the sight of the President making small talk with my father as my mother ate cake with Nancy Reagan and talked about how fast the years seemed to go by.

A DREAM GROWS IN LITTLE ITALY

T his was not the first time that my parents had met the President. In March 1981, Mike Deaver of the White House called to say that the President and his wife were coming to New York and that the President would like to join me and my family for a small luncheon in Little Italy. As much as I was flattered, I knew that he was not coming just to pay a social call on the D'Amatos. The President was well aware of the millions of Italian and other ethnic Americans who had crossed party lines to vote for him, and in this small way he wanted to show his gratitude and solidarity.

Naturally, I was overjoyed. I had been a U.S. senator for all of two months, and the President was coming to visit me among Italian-Americans. It was a great honor and no small political coup to bask in the glow of his presidential popularity. After all, *he* had won by a landslide. I had just squeaked in.

My euphoria soon gave way to practical concerns as the White House hounded my office with a dozen calls concerning the logistical hurdles involved in hosting the President in a city with as many special considerations as New York. First, the White House called to insist that we had to have lunch at a restaurant in Little Italy with "no connections." Easier said than done. How was I supposed to know? Did they expect me to ask? "I'd like to make a reservation for twelve, no smoking, and oh, by the way, do you have organized-crime connections?"

I contacted the intelligence unit of the New York Police Department and put them on the case. Once they started snooping around, it seemed that the whole neighborhood was aware of our impending visit, as well as our search for the right restaurant. My office was besieged with calls from restaurants in Little Italy offering to host the President. The most memorable one came from a man who said, "I have the best restaurant. If you bring the President here, he eats for free." The caller identified his restaurant as Umberto's Clam House. Umberto's was the scene of a bloody rubout in the 1970s where the colorful gangster "Crazy Joe" Gallo and a few of his associates died in a hail of gunfire. I told him, "You don't have a very good safety record." He didn't think that was funny.

"If you bring the President here, he eats for free."

Initially, I tried to talk Deaver's office out of bringing the President to Little Italy. I told him if he really wanted to see his constituents, Italian-American "Reagan Democrats," in their own neighborhood, Bay Ridge or Bensonhurst in Brooklyn would be far better. There were plenty of family-style restaurants in Brooklyn, and a Saturday in Bensonhurst would find thousands of people out shopping, providing the President with a great opportunity to meet and greet his Italian-American constituents in a district that had voted solidly for both of us.

The White House quickly nixed that notion. The Reagan people were masters of imagery and they knew that Little Italy still meant a "real" Italian neighborhood for millions of TV viewers. More importantly, getting a presidential motorcade from the Waldorf-Astoria to South Brooklyn would have shut down the Brooklyn Bridge and most of the Brooklyn-Queens Expressway, creating a traffic nightmare that may have resulted in more resentment of the presidential visit than jubilation.

In the end we settled on Angelo of Mulberry Street. The White House still called with new preconditions every day. Their last request was to make sure that no illegal aliens worked at the restaurant. I asked myself what restaurant in New York could possibly meet this condition.

The President arrived in New York on Saturday, March 14, 1981, his first trip to New York since his inauguration. His schedule was a mixed bag of politics and pleasure. He rushed from a meeting with Ed Koch, who hounded him for more federal aid, to meet with the editorial board of the *Daily News*, and finally joined my mom and my pop, Congressman Guy Molinari and his wife, and myself on the streets of Little Italy.

The thirty-degree temperature did not stop thousands of neighbors, tourists, and well-wishers from jamming Mulberry Street. The President gave a brief, completely off-the-cuff talk in front of Angelo's, praising the voters for electing Guy Molinari and me, and urging them to help him "beat inflation, reduce unemployment, and restore America's rightful place in the world." For a minute, it seemed like the 1980 campaign was still going on.

Once inside Angelo's, the President dispensed with politics and settled down to a wonderful lunch of stuffed breast of veal. Angelo's cuisine didn't hold a candle to my mamma's cooking, but I never let on. The President was in a great mood and entertained us with one story after another from his campaign and about the Hollywood stars he had worked with as an actor and as president of the Screen Actors Guild. He told the following joke, which broke up everyone at our table:

"A young guy named Tony goes to the barber before setting out on his first trip to Rome. As he cuts his hair, the barber proceeds to throw cold water all over Tony's plans. 'Oh, forget about that trip,' the barber says. 'I went there and my flight it was terrible. The hotel was dirty and the food was bad. And don't even try to see the Pope. You'll have to wait on line for hours, and then you don't get closer than a hundred yards from him. If I were you, I'd save your money and stay home.'

"A month later, Tony returns to the barber and tells him about his wonderful trip to Rome. The barber, it seems, couldn't have been more wrong. The flight was great, the hotel splendid, and the food legendary. He even got to see the Pope! And what's more, the Pope took time out to say a few words to him.

" 'Tony, you talked to the Pope?' The barber was stunned. 'What on earth did the Holy Father have to say to you?'

" 'Well, he took me aside and gave me his blessing, and then he turned to me and said, "My son, my son, where did you get that terrible haircut?" ' "

After our lunch I never had to wonder why the President would come to be known as the Great Communicator. For all of his official concerns, he never seemed anything but completely at home in Little Italy. Later that day he would charm everyone at the Broadway matinee performance of *Sugar Babies,* and then go on to the ballet, followed by dinner with Nancy at Le Cirque, the ultra-exclusive restaurant where, I later read, he was seated only two tables away from Andy Warhol and Bianca Jagger. Wherever Ronald Reagan went, whether Angelo's or Lincoln Center, it was obvious that he was completely at ease, in charge, and utterly charming.

Angelo's was miles from Le Cirque, but the President was genuinely happy to be spending the afternoon with us. My mother has never been a shrinking violet, and she made a special point to joke and banter with the President, who seemed particularly taken with her.

"Mrs. D'Amato, you must be very proud of your son Al." Reagan was no doubt familiar with the ads we had run in the 1980 election campaign showing Mamma D'Amato asking voters to back me. He was keenly aware that she had done a great job of reaching those very "Reagan Democrats" who had voted for both of us.

My mother beamed and told him of course she was proud, and then the President picked up the conversation. "We're proud of our son, too. As a matter of fact, we're in town to see Ronnie dance. This is the first time we're going to see him." Ron Junior was to dance that evening with the Joffrey Ballet at Lincoln Center. To my amazement, my mother rolled her eyes when she heard the word "dance". I kicked Mamma's foot under the table to get her to cut it out.

After my initial nervousness, we all settled down to a wonderful meal and really relax. After lunch, we introduced the President to the Italian liquor Sambuca. Often served with coffee beans, Sambuca is similar to anisette, but more potent. Reagan was in fine form; he had two Sambucas and continued to regale us with stories. We made our way up to the famous Ferrara's pastry shop right around the corner, where the President bought some cannoli for his wife, Nancy. She was spending the afternoon with friends at the Waldorf. Despite the winter temperature, it was a radiant Saturday afternoon. American and Italian flags were everywhere and the throngs of well-wishers gave the day a holiday feeling.

Insulated from the pressing hordes by some pretty grim-looking Secret Service agents, I savored the moment and the spirit of camaraderie of this small circle of friends who just happened to include my folks and the President of the United States.

Hundreds of cheering fellow Italians were a powerful reminder that I was the first Italian-American senator from New York. The presence of Ronald Reagan, the most popular president in a generation, along with my mother and father seemed like a dream. It was a dream—the American dream—and it can and does come true.

GRANDPA ALFONSO

There is no better example of the American dream come true, or of the Italian-American immigrant experience, than the story of my mother's father, Alfonso Cioffari—my grandpa, mentor, hero, and best friend. Like millions of his fellow Italians, he arrived in this country in the first decade of this century, and worked hard to thrive in a nation that gave him the opportunity not available in his native land.

But my affection for Grandpa Alfonso goes beyond family ties and ethnic pride. More than anyone else, he showed me that with the right attitude and a little guts, life could be an adventure. Alfonso was certainly no saint. Well into his eighth decade he had more mischief in him than a roomful of teenagers. He was a charmer, a rogue, and a gambler up until the moment he died—while playing poker with friends.

Like everything else about him, Grandpa's immigrant story was completely out of the ordinary. The son of a well-established professor from Rome, Alfonso was not among the teeming millions of poor who flooded New York's Ellis Island in the late nineteenth century. The Cioffaris were well established in Rome's middle class, and his father made a comfortable living both as a professor at the University of Rome and as a bureaucrat in the

Treasury Department of the Italian government. Cioffari Senior certainly had no intention of uprooting his family for the hardships of immigrant life in America.

The youngest in a family of four sons and a daughter, Alfonso was a born mischiefmaker and an indifferent student, whose lackadaisical study habits and insubordination in class got him thrown out of more than one school. The only books that interested him were dime novels and adventure stories filled with tales of cowboys, Indians, and the wild life on the American frontier. Far from Rome's well-entrenched families, habits, and customs, dreams of America beckoned Alfonso from the time he could first read. He romanticized the New World out of all proportion and reality. It filled his boyish daydreams and distracted him from his studies and responsibilities.

By the time he turned sixteen, Alfonso's father had tired of trying to talk sense into his son and decided he would teach him a lesson about his fabled America. He made arrangements for Alfonso to travel to New York alone and live with family friends there. An apprentice job was arranged for him at the Italian-language daily newspaper *Il Progresso*. He was confident that a few months of hard work on the streets of Manhattan would show his spoiled and lazy son just how good he had it in Rome.

So, in the first decade of this century, Alfonso Cioffari arrived in New York. While the job that his father arranged at the newspaper was sheer drudgery–he was the lowest gofer and messenger boy on the staff–it was luxurious compared to the lot of the millions of Southern Italians and Sicilians who had arrived in the preceding decades. Many of them were consigned to the most backbreaking labor, digging the tunnels, quarrying sandstone, and working in hazardous pits, mines, and on road gangs to build parkways, bridges, aqueducts.

Alfonso's first two weeks in New York consisted of nothing but work and sleep. His New York hosts made sure that he got home and stayed home after his twelve-hour shift. His father's plan of making his New York experience as dreary as possible seemed to be succeeding. Then one night, Alfonso met another

Italian boy his age, and they decided to defy his hosts and explore the sights of his new city.

For a pampered boy from Rome, New York was a wild and terrifying place, filled with different languages and the sounds and smells of four million people, elevated trains, a hundred sailing ships at a hundred docks, and a brand-new subway that could take him from lower Manhattan all the way to Coney Island, Brooklyn, for an Indian head nickel. Walking cobblestone streets past brownstones, honky-tonks, mansions, brothels, and tenements, Alfonso and his friend discovered a city where languages changed from one block to the next. Alfonso caught snippets of conversations in Italian, Spanish, Yiddish, Russian, Hungarian, and the brogue-inflected English of the ever present Irish. It was more exotic, dangerous, and wonderful than any dime novel could have described. It was New York—and Alfonso knew he had finally arrived where he always belonged.

His host parents met him at the door with a cold supper and a stern lecture. No one left in their care would be out walking the streets at night! He was given strict orders to come home straight from work, then sent right to bed.

A few hours later, as his kind, well-meaning hosts lay asleep, Alfonso slipped out of his bedroom window and disappeared into the night. It would be three years before his family heard from him again.

Once on his own, Alfonso used his fluency in English, Italian, and French to secure a number of restaurant jobs in what was already known as Little Italy. While he may have been a terrible student, he did heed his father's insistence that all the Cioffari boys learn to cook. Armed with this talent and sheer boyish bravado, he quickly learned to support himself.

Before long he had a wife to support as well. He met my grandmother, Josephine, working in a restaurant, and they married before he reached his eighteenth birthday. She was just sixteen. Once my uncle Louie was born, Alfonso decided it was time to finally inform his poor father of his whereabouts. Long given up for dead—or worse—Alfonso and his bride and baby were invited back to Rome for a reunion befitting the most prodigal of prodigal sons. Yet all the love in the world could not persuade Alfonso to return to Rome once he had settled in his beloved New York.

When my mother, Antoinette, was born, Alfonso quickly realized that he would need more than a cook's salary to support his growing family. Aware that a good living could be made in New York's fur business, Alfonso became a cutter of Persian lamb's wool for the lustrous black coats that were in fashion in early decades of the century. Soon he was making a good enough living and reputation to support his family in the comfort and style that his father would be proud of. The adventurous teenager was on the verge of becoming respectably middle class.

This would end with World War I. Italy entered the war on the side of the French and British in 1915, and loyal sons of Italy, both at home and in America, were called to the front. Though he would make much of his heroism in later years, Grandpa spent four largely boring years near Albania as the Italian army and its Austro-Hungarian counterpart faced each other on one of the least dramatic fronts of the war. After four years on the front, he was given a citation by the Italian government and a certificate showing he was a "Commendatore," a veteran of the Italian war effort.

With a flair for the dramatic, Grandpa returned home in 1919 without a word of warning to his wife and family. When he walked in the door, my poor grandmother let out a cry and fainted on the spot. My mother, who was only four years old at the time, wondered who this strange man was and why he had such an awful effect on her mother. She picked up a broom and began whacking him, screaming at him to leave them alone. Such was the homecoming of Alfonso Cioffari.

Between the wars, Grandpa's fur trade flourished. Coats of lamb, raccoon, mink, sable, and fox were all the rage in the Roaring Twenties, and still in enough demand to see Grandpa through the lean Depression years. As soon as my uncle Louis was old enough, he joined his father as a partner and designer. Together, they established the firm of Cioffari and Son.

My earliest memories of my grandpa are at his brownstone house on Greene Avenue in the Williamsburg section of Brooklyn. Every Sunday, all of Alfonso's children and their children would gather for a Sunday dinner that was more than a meal; it became a family ritual that continues at my parents' house in Island Park to this very day. Back then my mother, her sister Violet, Uncle Louie's wife, Lucy, and my grandmother would take over the kitchen and cook for hours while trading gossip and talk about the children, while the men were consigned to their poker game in the basement. There we were often joined by Grandpa's friends and cronies from his Masonic Lodge, the Garibaldi Lodge, as well as unofficial cousins and neighbors.

As the oldest grandchild, I was a fixture at these games–part pest, part good-luck charm, part gofer. I got them fresh drinks, emptied ashtrays, and generally hovered about as I learned the ways of men and cards–a life of bluffing, folding, smoking, bragging, and losing a game without losing your composure. No hand was ever worth more than a pile of quarters, but every game was played with such exaggerated bravado, you would think that the gold of Fort Knox stood in the balance. In a room filled with cigar smoke and good feelings, I soaked in the news of the day, tales of the fur trade, complaints about taxes, worry about Hitler and the war, talk of the Brooklyn Dodgers, and pride in a guy named DiMaggio who played in the Bronx. If I stood by a winning hand, I might get a dime or a nickel and a pat on the head. If I stood by a losing hand, I made it a point to find another hand.

When dinner was served, we emerged for a steaming banquet of pasta, peppers, roast chicken, lamb, or roast beef. Except during the war years, when rationing sometimes made meat impossible to obtain, I never remember a meal that wasn't an outstanding climax to this weekly ritual of family and Grandpa's special circle of friends. There never seemed to be fewer than a dozen people over the house for these meals. It was like having a Christmas or Thanksgiving feast every week. And Grandpa was never so busy with his food, his cards, or his conversation not to take time for me and all of the grandchildren. More than any adult I ever knew, he *listened* to children and never condescended to me because I was only seven or eight in a roomful of adults. It was just as important to talk to me about school as it was to plan the business of the week with my uncle Louis. Grandpa was filled with stories, most of them completely fabricated and fantastic, but that never mattered. It was as if he was weaving his own personal brand of fairy tale just for you, and if he happened to play the leading role, so much the better. I only knew that to be around Grandpa Alfonso was to be under his spell.

As a little boy I had no idea how special he was. What did I know? I thought everyone's grandpa had a pencil-thin mustache and a delightful French-Italian accent and a glint of mischief in his eyes. In 1949, when he was already well into his fifties, a time when many men start to slow down, Alfonso embarked on a new career. He opened a restaurant named the Brio (Italian for happiness, exuberance) in Manhattan on Forty-ninth Street on the ground floor of the Hotel Chesterfield. The Chesterfield, like so much of Manhattan of that era, no longer exists. In the language of its day, the Brio was swanky. My eyes practically popped out the first time I saw it. Grandpa had murals of beautiful, voluptuous women on the walls. With their come-hither looks, and their blouses falling off their shoulders, these women gazed down at the goings-on at the Brio, creating an atmosphere of continental ease and sophistication that was a world removed from Williamsburg, Brooklyn. Grandpa knew how to live! Practically under the shadow of Rockefeller Center, the Brio vibrated with excitement.

At the Brio, I soon discovered that prizefighters, actors, chorus girls, and Hollywood stars found Grandpa as charming as I did. Among my grandfather's most dependable customers was the mayor of New York himself, Vincent Impellitteri. Impellitteri had been elected primarily because of his defiance of the Tammany machine, which still pretty much controlled Democratic Party politics in the city at the time. I can remember the radio ads, featuring him with his wife, telling voters that Tammany had threatened him, but that he had stood up to the bosses. Impy did not tower over New York politics for very long. Truth be told, Mayor Impellitteri spent entirely too much time at the Brio, drinking more than he should have while my grandpa entertained him and kept him sheltered from the press and his political foes.

Grandpa ran the Brio all through the 1950s. It came as a rude shock to me and everyone in the family when in 1961 he announced he was leaving the management of the place to Uncle Louie and going off to Italy to spend his retirement with Grandma. As my wife, Penny, and I saw him off on the ocean liner–Grandpa always traveled in style–I was certain I was saying good-bye to my friend for the very last time.

Grandpa no doubt planned a retirement every bit as dynamic and exciting as his several careers. After having run the Brio, he was certainly not ready to settle down to playing cards and bocci ball with fellow pensioners. He was ready for *la dolce vita*, and for several months we received postcards from every resort spot from Rome to the Italian Riviera. But while Alfonso played the playboy, Grandma grew increasingly miserable. She missed her children and grandchildren, and with Penny expecting, she realized she would be separated by an ocean from her first great-grandchild. At the same time, news from New York was not so good. Uncle Louie may have been a great fur cutter, but he was a lousy restaurateur. Within nine months, the Brio was on the brink of bankruptcy. The checks Grandpa depended on for his retirement were no longer forthcoming.

To my joy and relief, Grandpa returned to sell the Brio and settle his affairs. Then he surprised everyone by launching yet another career as he turned seventy years old. Together with a friend from the restaurant business, he scraped up $15,000 to buy a hole-in-the-wall restaurant on West Fifty-ninth Street near Tenth Avenue, across the street from the CBS television studios. With little competition to speak of, Alfonso's quickly became a regular haunt for everyone who worked in the neighborhood, from the stevedores and sailors off the ocean liners and freighters docked on the West Side to the television crews from CBS. Ed Sullivan became a regular. Sailors who had been around the world would disembark and head straight for Alfonso's. Grandpa always brought home the exotic gifts and trinkets they gave him. Once he even brought back a cursing parrot who became my cousin Anthony's favorite pet.

As a young man just starting out as a lawyer, I watched in awe the incredible hours Grandpa put in without showing any signs of age or fatigue. He literally slept above the restaurant five nights a week, and still managed to come home every Saturday night to host the Sunday feast for the entire family. Some weeks he would barely break even. He told me that he envied his cook, who at least drew a salary.

It's a sad measure of how much New York has changed to remember that despite the fact that Alfonso's was not in such a terrific neighborhood, we never worried about him getting hurt or held up. Grandpa always loved running his own business, a place stamped with his name and personality. He felt that if you couldn't make it in New York, you couldn't make it anywhere. For him, it was still the city of his immigrant youth, a place bursting with opportunity. Now it's the city and state that taxes small business owners to death and drives them to the suburbs. It's a place where they're harassed by inspectors looking to flaunt their authority or looking for a payoff. A place where the storeowner gets the ticket if someone litters on the sidewalk. New York will never truly be a great city again until it gets off the backs of small business owners and lets people like my grandpa Alfonso make it here.

As the years passed, I became increasingly worried about Grandpa staying in town and driving back to Long Island at three or four in the morning. In 1964, when I was already active in local Republican politics, he asked me to do him a favor. I told him, "Sure, Grandpa, you know there's nothing I wouldn't do for you." Then he showed me the speeding ticket he had received and that he wanted me to take care of for him. I shook my head and told him it was difficult to get a speeding ticket dismissed. This made no difference to him. Leave it to Grandpa to ask me for the impossible. I think he took a secret joy in testing me. I could see in his eyes that he was thinking, "Let's see what my grandson the big hotshot lawyer can do."

My mouth dropped open when I read the particulars of the case. He was not only speeding—he was doing 60 in a 30-mile-an-hour zone! Grandpa's expression then changed from that of a proud and taunting old man to that of a sheepish relative. I told him I'd do what I could.

I knew my only hope of getting Grandpa out of this jam was to delay his hearing as long as I could and then raise the issue of identification—could the arresting officer still remember Grandpa and pick him out of a crowd with certainty? I figured that after six months or so, any cop who had given out hundreds of tickets would have difficulty remembering my grandfather.

I succeeded in putting off the trial for almost a year. As we finally arrived at the courthouse, I told him to sit in the back and blend into the crowd. It just so happened that the assistant district attorney was Leon Stern, a friend of mine. Leon asked me, "Al, how are you going to win this case? This guy's charged with doing sixty in a thirty-mile zone." I told him, "Leon, he's my grandfather and I'm going to try." Then Leon called the name of the officer who had issued the ticket and said to him as he approached, "Do you see the defendant, Alfonso Cioffari?" The officer scanned the room for no more than ten seconds and pointed straight at my grandpa. "There he is, right there." My heart sank. My brilliant year-long strategy was shot to hell.

Leon turned to me and said, "What do you want to do now?" The court was jammed, and Leon had more than a hundred cases to dispose of, so he agreed to reduce the speed to 45 miles per hour, to which Grandpa would plead guilty and pay a fine of $10.

When I called Grandpa up to the front of the court and told him he would have to change his plea to guilty, he muttered under his breath, "Why did I have to waste all this time, take a day off from work? I could have pleaded guilty without you, my big-shot grandson." He was really giving me the needle.

I still found it hard to believe that this police officer could pick Grandpa out of the jam-packed courtroom. As we left the courtroom, I saw the police officer in the hallway and I had to ask him, "Officer, how on earth did you remember my grandpa after all this time?"

The officer looked at me with a bemused smile. "Remember him?" he said. "That bird? How could I forget him?" For the first time, Grandpa hung his head a little lower as the officer explained the night in question. "I had just turned onto Long Beach Road when I heard this *whiz*. At first I thought it was another squad car. I mean, it was a blur. I had to chase this guy for two miles before he'd pull over. I put down sixty because he was a nice old gent, but he was going closer to seventy. You'd better watch out for him. When I handed him the ticket, I could see that he was feeling no pain. I followed him the rest of the way home just to see that he didn't hurt himself. And that's when he invited me in for a nightcap."

I knew all along there were some details that Grandpa had conveniently forgotten to tell me.

After this incident we prevailed on Grandpa and convinced him that he was getting just too old to be driving back from the city at three in the morning. It's hard to tell anyone that they're getting on, but for an independent old scoundrel like my grandpa, it was a full-time job just getting him to listen to you. Eventually Alfonso's was sold, but he still insisted on getting a job. If he couldn't have a restaurant, he'd go back to cutting fur. Styles and times had changed, and I was afraid he'd be crushed when he discovered that his old skills for cutting Persian lamb weren't needed anymore. I thought he was like an old vaudeville hoofer trying to get a job in Las Vegas. Boy, was I wrong. Within a week, not only did he have a job, he was given a raise when his young bosses discovered that he was the fastest and most economical cutter they could find. It meant everything to him still to be appreciated for his talent and recognized as the best. When he and Uncle Lou got together for lunch in the fur district, it was like the old days of Cioffari and Son all over again.

It seemed that Grandpa might go on forever. The years went by and he and Grandma still came to my mother's house to cook and preside over Sunday dinners. Grandma had gone blind by now from diabetes, and they had moved to a ground-floor apartment in Mineola, but she still cooked and cleaned for herself, and

Grandpa still maintained a commuting schedule that would tax a thirty-year-old.

Then Grandpa fell on the ice one winter day and shattered his leg. His age and the bitter weather made it imperative for him to be hospitalized for the next several weeks. I visited him every day, and saw the agony and frustration in his eyes, not from pain, but from the indignity of being reduced to a sick and dependent old man. I knew the spirit of the sixteen-year-old Alfonso Cioffari was still soaring within him, but now it was trapped in the body of a bedridden man. He was an absolutely incorrigible patient and drove the nurses crazy. I didn't help matters by smuggling gin martinis into his room every day. At his age, he deserved anything he asked for.

After this painful incident and incarceration, Grandpa could only walk with the aid of a cane and steel pin in his leg. Before long, like everything else he had ever done, Grandpa managed to turn

> I didn't help matters by smuggling gin martinis into his room every day.

even this infirmity into a stylish and elegant statement. Walking with his cane, and a fedora hat, dressed like a dandy from a 1930s movie, he moved through the streets of Mineola and Williston Park like a gentleman from another, more refined era. Nothing stopped him from flirting with the ladies or sticking his nose in everyone's affairs. In his own dapper way, Grandpa was strolling into a leisurely retirement.

On his daily strolls he discovered a fish store run by a couple of young Italian-Americans in Williston Park. After a few weeks of idle chatter, Grandpa just sort of moved into the store and became an unofficial fixture with both the owners and the customers. Everyone loved his stories, and before long he had a new crowd calling him the Commendatore. In exchange for this new venue, Grandpa ran errands for the boys, worked the cash register when he could, and generally did everything possible to be useful to his new young friends. From his new post, Grandpa observed the comings and goings of the neighborhood and kept me abreast of every hardship case and emergency he encountered.

He was particularly sensitive to the needs of the new Portuguese immigrants in town. He was in my office on a daily basis lobbying for his neighbors; whether it was a letter of recommendation for a youngster trying to get a job or a special language class, he was always trying to help.

There were times, as in the speeding incident, when Grandpa simply asked me to do the impossible; and he was constantly nudging me on behalf of his friends. I loved him dearly, but he was certainly no saint. There were many days when I had to chase him out of my office to get some work done. He would have used my Supervisor's office as his private social club if he could.

He was very proud of me, and made a point of bragging about his grandson the Supervisor to everyone he encountered. This once resulted in an ugly and embarrassing incident. It seems he was down at the County Clerk's office one day picking up health certificates the fish store needed for export sales. Someone overheard him referred to as "Commendatore." At the same time Grandpa was talking about his grandson, Al D'Amato, the Hempstead Town Supervisor. Listening to Grandpa, with his Italian accent, some busybody jumped to the conclusion that he was calling himself the "Godfather," as in organized crime. This tidbit found its way into the D.A.'s office.

Two investigators showed up at my grandparents' apartment in Mineola. They interrogated Grandpa while scaring Grandma out of her wits. She thought, "What did he do now?" They asked him, "Are you Alfonso Cioffari?"

He said yes.

"Do people sometimes call you 'Commendatore'?"

"Why, sure."

"You admit that?" They were incredulous at Grandpa's admission. "You admit that they call you Commendatore!"

He looked at them with a combination of pity and contempt. "Come over here and I'll show you." He calmly walked them over to his certificate from the Italian government, dated 1919.

Slightly set back but undaunted, an officer asked, "Is it true that you claim to be the Godfather of Supervisor Al D'Amato?"

Grandpa told me later that when they asked this question, he finally figured out what these two jackasses were thinking, and he replied with some disdain. "No, I'm not the Godfather, I'm his grandfather." This seemed to floor these two dimwits, who then proceeded to pose the question: "How's that possible? Your name is Cioffari. His name's D'Amato."

Grandpa calmly explained my genealogy. "You see, Al D'Amato's father is married to my daughter, Ann Cioffari. Do you understand now?"

By this time it should have dawned on these Sherlock Holmeses that they had made complete fools of themselves and they should retire from the scene. Not these two. They actually threatened to subpoena Grandpa in front of a grand jury if they found out he was lying. They departed as rudely as they had arrived, with no regard for the feelings of an old man and my sightless grandmother.

To my amazement, Grandpa did not tell me about this episode. I only found out later from my mother. I was in the midst of an election at the time, and he thought it might distract me. That's how considerate he was. This absurd case of misinterpretation might be brushed off as a comic interlude with a couple of Keystone Cops were it not indicative of a kind of anti-Italian and anti-immigrant bias that is still too prevalent. Here I was, one of the highest elected officials in the county, and my elderly grandparents with their Italian-accented English were still subject to threats and intimidation. I was outraged to realize that no matter what kind of exemplary life they led as proud Americans, my grandparents could still be accused of being possible mafiosos. This would not be the last time members of my family were subject to such outrages.

I'll never forget the day Grandpa died. It was a Sunday afternoon, and the Island Park Republican Club was having its annual cocktail party at the American Legion Hall two short blocks from my mother and father's home. The hall was jammed with over three hundred people. I was shocked to see that my dad, who seldom attended these parties, had come into the hall and was looking for me. He took me aside and told me, "Al, Grandpa's had an accident. He's in the hospital in Queens." We left and headed for my car. I was a little puzzled that Dad didn't get in the car. "Come on. Let's go." It was only then that he told me, "Al, it's too late. We can't help him." Dad didn't want to see me break down in front of all my friends, so he took me outside to explain that Grandpa had already died.

Grandpa had been at his regular Sunday poker game with his friends when he complained of indigestion. He asked for a glass of Brioski, an antacid popular with older Italians. After that, his friends said, they resumed the game. He was dealt a hand, looked at his cards, and quietly put his head on the table. He never woke up.

My dad realized how deeply pained I was over the loss of Grandpa. I could see that in his eyes. He let me know without saying a word that he knew I had lost my very best friend.

In a lifetime of encounters with presidents, prime ministers, dictators, and the pope, I have never met a man who had a better perspective on life than my grandpa. If knowing how to live to the fullest is a science, then Grandpa was surely an Einstein. I knew there were many points when he probably had a hard time making payroll for his employees for the week, but that never put a damper on him or slowed him down. Even though he helped my parents buy their first home, he never mentioned it to anyone. For Grandpa, money was just a fringe benefit for a life well lived. More than anyone, he taught me that to chase money was to waste one's life. "Seize life, even at the expense of wealth. That's the only way to live."

I hope they have gin martinis in Heaven. If they do, who knows? Maybe Grandpa's running the bar.

CHILDHOOD

I was blind as a bat as a young boy. My eyes were horribly crossed from birth and this reduced my vision to a blur. My depth perception was awful. Until I was ten, I lived in a world of shapes and shadows and noises. Had it not been for the love of my parents, family, and neighbors, I might have retreated into a shell.

Oddly enough, for all the problems my poor eyesight created, I remember being happy and always active. I didn't know how bad my eyesight was. I thought everybody saw things as I did and got used to it. I was the oldest grandchild, and there weren't any other young children on our block, so my father insisted that I go to nursery school to mix with other two-year-olds. Day care of any sort was uncommon in 1940, and my mother was concerned that this would reflect badly on her. Dad prevailed, and I got into the social mix. According to my mother, I started talking immediately and haven't shut up since.

While my first words may have been the traditional "mamma" or "dada," I have been told that as soon as I learned to verbalize, my favorite word was "why?" followed closely by "how come?" This innate curiosity, combined with my nervous temperament, made me a holy terror for my classmates, family, and anyone who would listen to me. I was a born pain in the neck, determined to get real answers to my questions, and not just be silenced by the traditional response, "Because . . ." or, "That's the way it is." I'm sure that my terrible vision added to my inquisitive nature. Unable to see leaves, trees, and sunsets like everyone else, I focused on an internal world of discovery. While I could make out the shapes, shadows, and smells of my immediate surroundings, I could never really see things in sharp focus.

As the first and only grandchild, I was the center of attention and affection for dozens of doting aunts and uncles. Coming from this warm, extended family, I found the Newark public school system to be fairly cruel and forbidding. Unable even to make out the chalkmarks on the blackboard in the front of the room, I was put in the back of the class. Here I was, six years old and labeled a hopeless case.

After almost fifty years I still hurt when I think of how I was just dumped into the "dummy" reading group. There is nothing more frustrating than being ignored. Sometimes these teachers would talk about me right in front of me and remark to each other how teaching me was a waste of time, how they felt sorry for my poor mother, and how I was a hopeless dummy. They talked as if I wasn't even there! It was really cruel. I am certain that it was unintentional, but that didn't ease the pain.

This early handicap made me more sensitive to others, whose disabilities dwarfed mine as a youngster. I remember very early on in my first year in the Senate looking up to Bob Dole, a man who overcame horrible war injuries to become one of the great leaders of our nation. In 1981, I had the audacity to challenge Dole over the issue of Industrial Development Bonds, and for a very short period, we were battling furiously on the opposite sides of a bill. It soon occurred to me that this was a mistake. I talked to Bob Dole in the Senate cloakroom and told him that I wanted to be fighting with him, not against him. Instead of blasting me as a freshman upstart, Dole smiled, and we've been friends and confidants since then.

It's impossible to meet Bob Dole and not be immediately impressed by his tenacity and courage. He was shot to pieces while fighting in Italy during World War II. He spent more than three years in hospital beds recuperating from numerous operations, and still has little use of his right arm. Like many brave Americans, including Teddy and Franklin Roosevelt, he not only triumphed over physical adversity, he emerged a better man for his years of struggle and hardship. I am certain that my early struggles with my eyesight were essential to building my character. I gained the strength and the determination never to give up.

The Newark of the early 1940s could be rough. It was hardly as dangerous as it has become, but to a half-blind kid, it was a jumble and a maze of streets that had their share of bullies. My father was away in the service during the war when I entered school, so I lived with my mother and was taken care of by any number of my aunts when she went off to work in downtown Newark at a factory that welded fuselages for bomber aircraft. With the war on, Newark's industries were working around the clock, and women were hired to replace the men shipped overseas. My mother and her girlfriends were part of the great mobilization of "Rosie the Riveters" who made it possible to create the fantastic war machine that defeated Germany and Japan. As a little boy during this period, it was impossible not to be completely swept up in the patriotic fervor. It was more than an abstraction, it was a life-and-death struggle. You *prayed* that we won so that Daddy and Uncle Al, Dan, Mike, and Albert, would come home alive. And they all did. I played on streets lined with houses with blue star decals in the windows indicating that there was a man from that house away in service. And sometimes you would come across a house with a gold star decal, which meant there was a mother or a widow inside whose son or husband would never come home.

It is easy to get dramatic or even melodramatic about the little parts we played in this tumultuous world conflict, yet the thing that is most difficult to explain is how normal and unremarkable it all seemed to me at the time. To me, little Tippy, it was the only world I had ever known. Dad was at war and Mom worked at the airplane factory and I walked to the Sumner Avenue Elementary School. This total involvement in the war was something that marked me and my whole generation. We saw our parents sacrifice uncomplainingly for this greater cause, and we were inspired by them. My mother tells a story about how, during the war, I was always asking her to have another baby so we could surprise Daddy when he came home from the war. "Let's have a baby and surprise Daddy," I asked her at least once every day. She would laugh at me and say, "That would surprise him, all right!"

While America was fighting the forces of Hitler and Mussolini, I was confronting my own private bullies. We lived only a few blocks from the Sumner Avenue School, and like most children, my walk to and from school was my first real excursion into a world outside my parents' protection. It was exciting and gave me a chance to mix it up with kids my age. We'd find times to play marbles on the way home. We'd trade them. The big clear ones were always the most prized. We played tag and hide-and-go-seek, and jammed into the tiny corner candy store together, picking out our favorite penny candy.

But this idyllic existence for a half-blind seven-year-old was not without its perils. A boy named Johnny was a year older than me and lived across the street. He was a little bigger, a lot tougher, and just plain mean. For some reason, Johnny singled me out. He'd pick on me almost every day, sometimes twice a day. He taunted me by calling me "Four-eyes." Calling me "Four-eyes" was Johnny's way of tormenting me. I would go home in tears, and my mother would repeat the age-old saying, "Sticks and stones may break your bones, but names will never hurt you. Ignore him." It's pretty hard to ignore someone who waits for you morning, noon, and after school just to make fun of you in front of the neighborhood kids.

This miserable situation could have gone on indefinitely, but Johnny went just too far. One day, he chased me down the street with a rock in his hand, shouting, "I'm going to kill you, Four-eyes. I'm going to kill you!" I honestly believed he meant it. This was the first time I felt real fear. I was only seven, but I knew that if I didn't stand up to him, I might wind up getting hurt or even killed.

I knew Johnny was a regular candy buyer at the drugstore on the ground floor of our apartment building. Not an afternoon went by when he didn't go in for some licorice, or a Mary Jane bar. So the next day I waited for him to come out. He didn't know what hit him. He was unwrapping his candy bar when I whacked him behind the knees with a stick that was bigger than both of us. I was amazed at how easily he went down. He was dumbstruck. He couldn't believe it. I poked at him a few times and shouted, "How do you like it, how do you like it?" I was terrified but triumphant. Johnny the bully had never expected little Four-eyes would actually turn around and attack him. And now that I had him down, I liked it. I screamed, "What do you say now? What do you say now?" as I continued to poke him. "Are you going to leave me alone? Do you promise, do you promise?" The kids gathered around. They thought I was crazy, and I probably was. I was victorious, overjoyed, and scared out of my wits at the same time. The bully, who was now in tears, pleaded with me to leave *him* alone. He never picked on me again.

I was only seven but I had learned a valuable lesson. If you placate a bully, he will take advantage of you forever. He gets used to your misery. He depends on it and thrives on it, and he holds you in contempt. The Duke of Wellington once said that "the Battle of Waterloo was won on the playing fields of Eton." I didn't go to Eton, but I can definitely say that I received my first lesson in foreign policy on the streets of Newark.

We moved to Island Park in 1945, when I was eight years old. I loved Newark and have many fond memories of my life there, but it was in Island Park that I really thrived. I became a person there, no longer confined to urban blocks and busy streets filled with strangers. Island Park was a small community, where people knew your name. It was slowly transforming from a summer vacation village to a year-round community. The year-round population of about two thousand was not entirely thrilled when Island Park was invaded by families like ours fleeing the congestion of the cities.

To this day, Island Park is populated by working- and middle-class families. It is exceedingly untrendy, but it's the place I call home and where I feel mighty comfortable. Its beaches are largely ignored by outsiders, who prefer Jones Beach and Long Beach. It's surrounded on three sides by the tracks of the Long Island Railroad, a mountainous landfill, and ungainly and un-glamorous oil-storage tanks. Island Park may not seem like much to a commuter or a weekend traveler on the way to the beaches, but to me it was heaven, and it remains my safe haven.

The village was filled with empty fields and lots and oppor-tunities to roam and explore. It was a magical time for me, with a whole new set of people who looked out for me and helped give me a sense of belonging. I am not saying that everyone loved me– far from it. I was a pesky little kid with glasses who, more often than not, was probably cutting through somebody's backyard. All the same, I was part of the neighborhood. I may have been a pain, but I was *their* pain, and this was important to me.

One of the reasons we had moved from Newark was my mother's concern that her blind little Tippy might walk in front of a bus or car and get killed. Out of the city, she thought I had a better chance of surviving. This, however, was not the case. One day I did walk in front of a neighbor's car. I was lucky and wound up with only a couple of bumps and bruises. But my mother fi-nally put her foot down and insisted I undergo an operation to correct my sight. My family had been reluctant to do this because some doctors had warned of a chance of permanent blindness. But after the accident, my mother insisted that we go ahead with the surgery, saying that this was no way for a boy to live.

The surgery, which was performed at the Brooklyn Ear and Eye Hospital, is a routine procedure today, but fifty years ago I spent more than two weeks in the hospital. My eyes were ban-daged for most of that time. But when the bandages were finally removed, a whole new world opened up to me.

Imagine how my mother felt when I said, "Mom, I can really see for the first time!" It was the beginning of a new life for me.

After my eyes were uncrossed, it took more than two years for my mind to catch up with my new sensations. It would be more than two years before I could really read. Then I could leave Is-land Park just by opening a book. Suddenly, rainy summer after-noons weren't so dreary. I could escape to the historical adventures in *Drums Along the Mohawk, Treasure Island,* and my favorite, *The Hunchback of Notre Dame.* I gravitated toward history and biography, and read with fascination how Teddy Roosevelt grew from a sickly little boy to become a big-game hunter and one of our most outstanding presidents. With books, I no longer had to badger a dozen teachers with a thousand whys. There were libraries filled with answers, and I was eager to read every one of them. I was learning to read about five years later than I should have, and was eager to make up for lost time.

I wish I could say that this period of my life was marked only by a surge in intellectual curiosity. After my liberation from near blindness I exploded with adolescent energy and poked my nose into everything. My mother called me Grandpa Junior, after his immense energy and inquisitive nature. I ran from my blind existence at a maddening pace, changing from little Tippy into persistent mischiefmaker.

One day during seventh grade, the sky turned black and the clouds opened up for a rainstorm of almost biblical proportions. I should have known I was in for it that day. The weather was so bad, everyone's mothers showed up with umbrellas to take us home from school. My mother was anxiously waiting for me as the school emptied. "Where's little Alfonse?" she wondered. Well, she soon found out. Earlier that afternoon I had gotten into a shoving match with Tommy Broder during gym class and was ordered to report to the principal's office after school. Seeing my drenched and humiliated mother make her way down the hall, the principal, Mr. Lynch, took her aside and told her, "Ann, I just don't know what to do with him."

I had seen my mother mad before, but never like this. As we headed home, I knew I was in for it. My only hope of avoiding the beating of a lifetime was to try to delay the inevitable until my father got home. I knew that in this situation, Dad would be a softy compared to my mom.

At first, it looked as if I was going to get off easy. My mother told me, "Get into the house and wait for me," as she disappeared into my grandmother's house across the street. I figured the worst I would get was a good yelling at and Dad would ground me for a week or two. Grandma would probably calm my mother down in the meantime. Boy, was I wrong.

About thirty minutes later, my mother came into the house with a look on her face that I had never seen before. I was concerned. My concern quickly turned to fear when I saw her unscrew the handle of the carpet sweeper. Then she said to me, "Come here!" I said, "Mamma, put down the handle." She repeated, "Come here," and I said, "Put the handle down." And she said, "Don't you tell me what to do!" Now the chase was on.

We lived in a big old house with lots of rooms that connected one to the other. Some rooms had as many as three doorways, and I bedeviled her by flying in and out from one room to another as she swung the handle at me. There was no way she was going to catch me. But every once in a while as I was zigging and zagging from room to room she would double back and get in a good swipe at me. I begged her to put down the stick, but she wasn't listening and was determined to track me down. The five- or ten-minute chase seemed to last for hours and she seemed to grow more enraged by the minute. After flying in and out of the doors, I changed my strategy. I figured if I could keep her in my sight at all times, I would be less likely to feel that stick. So I ran into the dining room, where I figured I could keep the huge table between me and her while still keeping my eye on that stick.

We whirled around about three or four times while I prayed to God for my father to come home early. And then she outsmarted me with a brilliant coup. She figured out that there was no way to catch me, so she began to slide some chairs to one side, blocking my route. She followed this by making a mad dash around the other side. Before I could jump over the barriers she had erected, I came to feel the full wrath of Mamma D'Amato as that stick came crashing down on my legs and arms. I remember shouting at her as she whacked away, "You broke my arm. I'm going to tell Dad!" That was a dumb thing to do as it just infuriated her further. "You want something to tell him about, I'll give you something to tell him about!" She proceeded to hit me till she ran out of breath.

Let me tell you, though I emerged with no broken bones, more than my pride was hurting that night, and for the next couple of days. Years later, just before I was sworn in for my first Senate term, I found myself in a similar chase scene. But this time my twelve-year-old son, Dan, who had been teasing his sister Lorraine, pushed me to the point where I was chasing him all over the house trying to get my hands on him. But suddenly, *poof,* he ran right out the front door. I followed, slipped on the ice, and broke my finger. I couldn't believe it: I thought back to when I was that age and Mamma chased me around. I *never* would have run out the door. Now here it was thirty years later, and I thought, "He just ran out the door!" I was amazed. I would never have thought of that. Times have certainly changed.

The sad thing is that if my mother were to discipline me the same way today as she did was when I was in the seventh grade, I might have complained to the school psychologist, who undoubtedly would have reported this to family court, subjecting her to charges of child abuse. The fact is that Mamma's approach to discipline was one of the best things ever to happen to me. From that day forward, I never spent a minute in Jim Lynch's office. Did I behave out of goodness? Absolutely not. Fear, and fear alone, kept me out of trouble. It's a powerful motivator to a twelve-year-old boy. This may seem an outrage to progressive parents and educators. I only know that it gave me the incentive to settle down and pay attention.

Mamma showed me that she was the boss, and she taught me with painful clarity that either I behaved or there would be real punishment. I chose the right way—I didn't want to face Mamma's wrath again any time soon.

Not all of my childhood days were spent fighting or sitting in detention. My first brush with romance came when I developed a crush on my neighbor and classmate, Geraldine McGann. It was Valentine's Day and we were in fifth grade. I was determined to buy Geraldine a box of candy and show her how I felt, so I shoveled sidewalks and driveways to earn some spare money, and bought a box of chocolates.

Geraldine was shocked beyond belief when I shoved this token of affection into her hands. She was horrified. Her embarrassment was soon accompanied by hoots of laughter from the entire class. To add to my shame and dejection, the teacher confiscated the candy and distributed it to the rest of the class. It was my first experience of unrequited love, and to this day, forty-five years later, Geraldine and I still joke about it.

Geraldine and her husband, Doc, have been my closest friends going back to my days in grammar school. We raised our kids together, and have shared triumphs and heartaches. Their home is one of my favorite sanctuaries from the world of politics.

When I graduated from the eighth grade, my mother encouraged me to apply to Chaminade, a Catholic high school run by the Marianist Brothers, who had a reputation for academic excellence and tight, almost military discipline. One look at these brothers and you knew they meant business. Getting to school every day was a daunting experience. Located in Mineola, Chaminade was thirteen miles away from my house. Forty-five years ago, local school districts did not provide you with transportation if you chose a private school. That meant I was dependent on the barely functioning private bus system, which was dependably late when it did not break down altogether. Even if it showed up on time, it took an hour. I had to take one bus to Hempstead, wait a half hour, then catch another one to Mineola. And when you arrived at school late, you were required to go to the principal's office. I was late three times before I had been in school for four or five weeks. I did my best to explain this to Brother Nath, who was the vice principal in charge of discipline.

Brother Nath was a huge, imposing man with a shock of red hair. Dressed in the spartan garb of the Marianist Order, he weighed well over two hundred pounds and was built like a fullback. The teachers in public school were nothing like this. It was Catholic boot camp. When I was about to offer my explanation that the bus had broken down, Nath told me, "If you tell me about that bus one more time, you've had it." I got the message loud and clear and was terrified by the mere thought of what the consequences of another late arrival would be.

The following day, I arrived at my bus stop a full twenty minutes early. The 6:50 bus failed to appear. As the clock ticked on and no bus was to be seen, in a total panic, I decided to hitchhike. I crossed two streets, hopped over the railroad tracks, stuck out my thumb, and the third car to pass me stopped. The driver was on his way to the Grumman plant in Bethpage, and wound up dropping me off a relatively short distance from school. I arrived a half hour earlier than usual. The next day, I decided to give up on the bus altogether. This time I caught the tenth car to pass by. I was picked up by a bunch of guys working at a sign company in Mineola, the very town where Chaminade was located, and got to school forty-five minutes early. Thus began my four-year adventure of hitchhiking every day. It enabled me to save fifty cents a day and actually get in early enough to catch up on some work.

> "Do the right thing because it's the right thing to do."

It didn't take long for me to realize that Chaminade was more than just a high school. While I am sure I would have received a fine education at Oceanside High, the local public high school, Chaminade was run by men who had taken a vow to teach young people about a life of service and the pursuit of excellence. Unlike some of my public school teachers, who treated me like I didn't exist, the brothers took a keen interest in every student. They inspired you and challenged you to do better. At Chaminade, the brothers drilled us in math, English, history, Latin, sports, and music, until we couldn't help but learn. Angelo Fernando, a lay teacher and musical director, would have us play the same piece over and over for what seemed like hours, but at the end of the day, even the most mediocre musicians had the satisfaction of having played it perfectly. Kids *can* be inspired. If you challenge them to do better, they can succeed beyond their wildest dreams.

Of all the lessons I learned at Chaminade, the one taught by our principal, Brother Darby, later Father Darby, remains the most important. "Do the right thing because it's the right thing to do," he told us time and again, "and not because someone is watching you." When I speak to young people, I often find myself reciting Brother Darby's motto and urging them to apply it in their daily life. It's a simple yet powerful message for all of us.

SYRACUSE

When it came time to choose a college, I disappointed the brothers by deciding to attend Syracuse University instead of Spring Hill, a small Catholic college in Mobile, Alabama, that they had enthusiastically suggested for me. My neighbor and future political rival Jim Fazio had gone to Syracuse, and when the Syracuse track coach Bob Grieve encouraged me to come out for the team, that made up my mind.

Like many young people away from home for the first time, one of my constant obsessions was getting good food. Having come from a family of gourmet Italian chefs, cafeteria food left a lot to be desired. I looked forward to my mother's CARE packages. These weekly treats were filled with cookies, cheese, sausages, figs, olives; everyone could smell the box as soon as they entered the hallway of my dorm room.

I lived for my mother's packages, but so too did my dormmates. Often I would get back to my room to find that my starving buddies had already devoured practically everything. I was lucky to be left with a slice of provolone cheese. The first couple of times they did this, I groused a little bit, but we were all used to playing pranks on one another. After it became a habit, I was looking for a way to even the score.

One day I discovered my means of retribution when I overheard a group of girls laughing their heads off about having baked a batch of chocolate chip cookies and left them out for visitors, who quickly gobbled them up. The girls had substituted Ex-Lax for chocolate. The results were devastating. Impressed by their audacity, I commissioned these sinister chefs to mix me up a batch of explosive delights, and brought them back to the dorm. My roommate, Bob Chevis, was delighted to play along with my scam. He yelled out to the whole hall, "Alfonse's mother sent him some chocolate chip cookies!" Like seals at feeding time, half the track team pounced on the cookies. They were grabbing fistfuls, two and three at a time. The more I yelled, "Leave some for me!" the more quickly they grabbed them.

Less than forty-five minutes passed before the first of them bolted for the bathroom. One by one, the stalls filled and the halls echoed with agonized cries of "Hurry up, I have to go!" Chevis was in hysterics and almost gave us away. We even faked several runs to the john ourselves, wailing and moaning all the way.

The track coach became concerned that his entire team had come down with the runs. He suspected that the culprit were the apples we picked from the trees where we worked out. I found it hard to control my laughter as the coach lectured us about the evils of those bad apples.

Everyone recovered within twenty-four hours, except Larry Twomey, who *never* seemed to get over the runs. It got so bad that two days later he had to drop out of a big meet against Navy and Cornell. The last we saw of him he entered the woods in third place, but we never saw him come out. This was a shame because had he run his usual race, we would have won the meet. As it was, we lost by one point.

It was a mystery to me how Larry could still be in such bad shape, until I returned to my room that night to find that only *two* of my cookies remained. There were about a half a dozen left after the night of the big stampede. No sooner had I made this discovery than Larry Twomey came into the room and asked if I had any cookies left. He had been stealing them all week!

I didn't tell Larry about the chocolate chip cookie prank until years later when I was already out of law school. He called up all of the old guys and let them in on my little trick.

About three years ago, I was paid a visit by my old track team-mate Bob Osborne. He had been the high school track coach in Vestal, New York, just outside of Binghamton. He and his wife came to my office in Washington and we had a great time talking about the old days. His wife brought me a little gift. Would you believe, a tin of chocolate chip cookies. She was a lovely woman and insisted that they were baked with real chocolate and that I must have some. I pleaded guilty to indigestion and promised her I would get to them as soon as I felt better.

I gave them to my staff, and they were delicious.

While my life at Syracuse was hardly all track and high jinks, my academic record was not exactly distinguished. I was, at best, an inconsistent student. Some semesters I would hit the dean's list, and others I would find myself on the verge of failing. As I approached my junior year, I began to wonder just what I was going to major in and what career path I would follow. I knew I was no track star, and the thought of pursuing a career in marketing or accounting left me uninspired. In a move I can only describe as impulsive, I decided to take the law boards early to see if I could skip my senior year and go directly to Syracuse's Law School. To my surprise, I pulled a pretty good score, and wound up entering law school a whole year earlier in what normally would have been my senior year.

Unfortunately, this lucky stroke only fueled my cockiness. After all, if it was so easy getting into law school, how hard would I have to work to stay there? I coasted through my first year, and my grades reflected it. I had arrogantly pushed myself to the brink of failure. In fact, I came so close to flunking out that I was forced to go to summer school to get my grades up.

The summer of 1959 started out as a horror show and ended up being the greatest time of my life. My back was to the wall. I had to maintain a near A average to survive. It was not going to be easy. But my academic woes were kid's stuff compared to the smoke and fire coming from the direction of Island Park.

When my pop got wind of my performance, he responded with the most chilling letter I have ever–and I repeat ever–received. Now, I have read CIA dossiers. I have been the subject of death threats. But that letter from my father is one that I can still recite to this day. It contained a check for $500–the cost of tuition and expenses–and a simple one-sentence bombshell: "Dear Son, lest the pen spilleth over, this is it."

Allow me to translate. While this may sound like the Bible, I knew that Dad was saying that it was the end of any tuition money. From now on, I was on my own. Even after this summer session I had two years of law school to pay for, and I didn't have a clue how I was going to do it.

After paying tuition and finding a room behind Archibald Stadium, I had a grand total of ten dollars a week to live on. I was on thin ice academically, and I was just ahead of the bill collector. It was probably the best thing my father ever did for me.

I spent the summer working my tail off to get my grades up, and looking for work. Luckily, I was befriended by one of Syracuse's great champion wrestlers, Bill White. A fellow Long Islander working on his master's degree, and a full-time janitor for the university, he recommended me to be hired as a janitor as well. Who says connections don't pay off? I was given a mop and the princely salary of $1.65 an hour. Now, I was a full-time law student as well as a forty-hour-a-week custodian. Our boss was a man named Bob Rainbow, a campus character as colorful as his last name. Half American Indian, and orphaned from childhood, he made it a point to help students in need. He knew that this job was all that stood between me and dropping out.

I survived my summer courses and went on to two more years of law school. But most of my memories of that period are of my janitorial job. Syracuse had its share of snobs: arriving as a freshman from Island Park with a name like Alfonse Marcello D'Amato made me painfully aware of that. By graduating from college in only three years and advancing right into law school, I had achieved some degree of status. Being a law student meant something then.

But nothing cuts through pretense like an overflowing toilet, especially when you're the one who's got to clean it up. Working as a janitor was every bit as important to my education as my law courses. It made me appreciate how most workers go through their lives treated like invisible people or worse, and how wrong that is. In all my years in local and national politics, I am hard-pressed to name a man with more talent or compassion than Bob Rainbow. He was an artist, a sign painter. I was going to be a lawyer and probably make many times his salary, but this never got in the way of the job we had to do and the respect we had for each other. He made it a pleasure to mop a floor. You can't ask much more of a boss.

Another great thing about being a janitor is that you sure know where you stand with people. I went out of my way to intro-duce myself as "Alfonse the Janitor." I quickly learned that if peo-ple snubbed you because you were a janitor, they weren't worth knowing in the first place. If they did accept you on those terms, they were likely to be friends for life. Luckily, that was the year I met my wife.

My friend Bill White was more than just a great athlete. He was also a lady-killer. Today, he'd be called a hunk. All I know is that coeds always flirted with him. I was lucky to be his pal, and be around to comfort some of those coeds whom Bill did not have time for.

That's what happened when I met my future wife, Penelope–Penny. Now it's not entirely flattering, but it's true–she was after Bill. They had been making idle chatter on the line at our cafete-ria when I first burst on the scene. They were talking about how the cooks had just run out of potatoes when I came up to Bill with my cafeteria tray and made my acquaintance with Penny. Lucky for me, Bill had to leave for a class and she was left alone with me. She was working on her master's in art education, beautiful, so-phisticated, and self-assured. All I could do was ask her out, and to my surprise, she accepted.

I didn't tell her right off that our "date" involved a slight de-tour. I had twenty minutes of mopping left to do at the college ROTC Center. In retrospect, I can see what a classy move this was. The sure way to a woman's heart is to share some janitorial duties. I wouldn't have been surprised if she left me wearing a mop on my head, but Penny was different. Wonderfully different. She didn't care that I was a janitor. She even helped me fix a mop I was having trouble with. We saw each other every night for the next ten evenings, and she introduced me to all of her artist friends as "Al the Janitor." We got more than a few laughs out of that.

We were married within a year. Things were different then—we thought nothing of getting married right in the middle of law school, settling down, starting a family right off the bat. This was a very different time, with different expectations. We were fifties kids, part of a generation that is not often talked about by the pundits and writers of today. We were playing in sandboxes when Pearl Harbor was bombed and just entering high school during the Korean War, but were too old to serve (or refuse to serve) in Vietnam. We fought Hitler and Tojo with our toy soldiers, collected tin cans and scrap metal for the war effort while our fathers went off to fight and our mothers worked in munitions factories. More than anyone, we absorbed the patriotic spirit of the time as only children can. As we have grown older, our generation has been dismissed as the conformist, quiet children of Eisenhower, and often stereotyped as crazed over Elvis, tail fins, and prom gowns; but we are more than that. We are the generation that raised kids, built America's most prosperous communities, and tried to build on the opportunities of the postwar period. Many of us were married and settled before the "sexual revolution." The drug use of the baby-boom generation occurred when we already had kids of our own. I had two kids before I ever heard of pot. We were too busy changing diapers to get excited by Bob Dylan's "The Times They Are A-Changin'." We were postwar, pre-drugs, and pre-Beatles, and often the media treat us like we don't exist. Caught between the GI generation and a generation defined by sex, drugs, and rock 'n' roll, we had a quieter and almost plodding dedication to getting things done.

We are a bridge generation, an ignored but vital link between the World War II era and the current reign of the so-called baby boom. We are old enough to remember the sacrifices and struggles of the war years. We grew up close enough to the Great Depression to know that the economic prosperity of the fifties and sixties was a blessing built from hard work, and not the norm. Since many of us were not raised only in the suburbs, we are witness to the urban decay of the fifties and sixties, when once proud cities literally rotted and exploded under the weight of failed liberal social experimentation and the dreadful side effects of a welfare culture.

Many of the pundits and instant experts who analyzed the 1992 election were caught up in the symbolism of George Bush, a World War II veteran, being defeated by Bill Clinton, a baby-boomer. Clinton is discussed as the first of many baby-boomer presidents, and his election is considered as dramatic a generational change as when John F. Kennedy declared that "a torch is passed to a new generation" in his 1961 inaugural address, or as when Franklin Roosevelt said his generation had a "rendezvous with destiny" in his 1933 address. As a fifties kid, all I can say is, "Wait a minute. What about us?"

I believe that one of the fundamental yet unexplored aspects of the recent Ross Perot phenomenon is that he spoke to this vast unrepresented body of voters. Perot had the respect for military experience that so many baby-boomers either lacked or felt ambivalent toward, while at the same time possessing a computer-literate, technical know-how that was simply daunting to someone like George Bush, a man who was unfamiliar with a supermarket checkout scanner. Like me, Perot came of age in the fifties, and I strongly believe that one of the reasons this complete political newcomer received 20 percent of the vote, more than half as much as the incumbent, is that he spoke to this important and largely ignored generation of voters. *Time* magazine may have passed the torch to the baby-boomers, but the voting public might just pass that torch back. You haven't heard the last of the fifties generation.

ALL POLITICS IS LOCAL— VERY LOCAL

I never went to Harvard or Yale, or the Kennedy School of Government, but I am certain that the political education I received in Island Park was a far better preparation for a political career. The dealmaking and politicking I witnessed in my own backyard equaled anything I have done in the Senate. In a little village of 2,200 permanent residents, you can really get to know every voter. While running for office in this setting may be closer to the Jeffersonian ideal of small village democracy, it can also become intensely personal and at times hurtful. After all, when you lose, it's not a question of exit polls, demographics, and strategy, it's the fact that you've been rejected by your neighbors. I've seen more bad blood shed in these village races than anything I have seen since. And I have seen some pretty rough campaigns.

Island Park was divided into two local parties, the Public and the Unity, and the battles between them were often savage. Village elections were held annually on the Tuesday following St. Patrick's Day. You could feel the tension and excitement swelling in the raw winter air as the weeks closed in on election day. Both parties were well represented at the annual Saturday night St. Patrick's Day Dance, held at the local parish hall. Hundreds of people were there, and this allowed one last chance to corner undecided voters before the big day. In such a small town, most elections could be decided by a handful of votes, so things often got pretty testy. I am sure that many times, only the fact that we were on church property prevented some real fights from breaking out. Lots of party members on both sides were church ushers and volunteer firemen, and this also tended to keep things pretty civil. After all, it's tough to get too angry at the guy passing around the collection plate at mass, or the man you depend on to save your house from the flames. I have been a volunteer fireman in Island Park since 1963. While I haven't climbed into any burning buildings in quite a few years, it's an affiliation I maintain to this day. Passing my Fire Department physical is an annual rite that I look forward to, though with a little more trepidation each passing year.

My father was an active Public Party member. As far back as I can remember, I was curious about his civic life. I must have been twelve years old before I realized that everyone's life didn't revolve around day-to-day canvassing, schmoozing, handing out buttons, rain hats, stickers, and other campaign paraphernalia. I was thirteen years old in 1951, when two of our neighbors were running against each other for Village trustee. Our next-door neighbor, Mr. Steiner, was running as a Public man, while Tom Donahue, who lived across the street and two doors down, was running on the Unity ticket. My parents were friendly with both of them, and my brother Armand and I spent a lot of time with both the Steiner and the Donahue boys, playing stickball, swimming at the beach, or catching the occasional movie in nearby Long Beach. Knowing both candidates made the election particularly exciting, and at the same time a little daunting. You knew that one friend would be delighted and the other dejected.

To add to this tension, the 1951 race between Steiner and Donahue resulted in a dead heat. What were the odds against that? The winner would be determined by lot. Names were drawn one at a time until one candidate's name was drawn five times. After a bitterly fought race, this little dramatic touch only added to the tension. And of course, against all odds, it came down to the last possible draw. Steiner's name was drawn and the Public

Party triumphed. This improbable episode taught me at the earliest age that the old saying, "Every vote counts," was surely more than a cliché.

That lesson was underscored years later when my friend Al Riehl told me that he had been working for the Unity Party during that race, and that he and a friend had given a nice old lady a ride to the voting booth. They both assumed that she was a Unity voter, but when she got out of the car, they found out that neither was really sure. She might have cast the deciding vote in that tie election! Al Riehl worried about that for years. This incident taught me the value of getting *your* people to the polls. You can spend millions on television advertising, but if your core voters are not motivated to pull the lever for you, you're going to lose. It's as simple as that.

As I got older, I realized that my father's love for local politics was based on more than just the chance it gave him to socialize or the thrill of winning a close election. The brothers at Chaminade drilled a devotion to service into me, a belief that it is your duty to serve others to make the world a better place. As I learned about the call to service, I realized I had no better example than my father, who worked long hours to found the Island Park Chamber of Commerce and successfully petitioned the Post Office to bring home delivery to our village. This was politics, but it was also a devotion to serving others and to becoming part of a cause greater than oneself. If this sounds like a confusion of religion and politics, perhaps it is. After all, John F. Kennedy once said, "God's work here on Earth must truly be our own."

I personally lament the fact that politics has come to be held in such low regard. Although many people consider politics a cynical game, I think there is nothing more ennobling than local citizens taking actions to help each other. That's politics. It's getting a stop sign put on your street corner so kids won't get run over; it's getting funding for a park, getting the streets paved and the water treated. That's politics—people going out of their way to serve other people.

In my political career I have been both praised and derided as "Senator Pothole," a man who cares more about delivering services than the practice of statesmanship. If I have become the consummate constituent-service politician, I learned to do this at my father's knee, and I hope in that way I have made him proud of me.

I had other inspirations. In addition to my father, I also watched the rise of our local assemblyman, Joseph Carlino. He was a Republican in the 1950s when most Italians were still solidly enrolled in the party of Roosevelt. I made it a point to hear him speak when he came to the Village Hall. At a time when many Italian-Americans were stereotyped as blue-collar laborers, Joe Carlino was as eloquent and persuasive as any Thomas Dewey or Nelson Rockefeller. I was thrilled to see an Italian so successful. He showed everyone that we could do it—and do it with style.

After graduating from Syracuse Law School in 1961, I returned to Island Park to study for my bar exam. During that summer I attended a fund-raiser Carlino held annually for the March of Dimes. As Speaker of the New York State Assembly, Carlino was a man to be reckoned with in state politics, and second only to Governor Nelson Rockefeller in the state Republican power structure. This was evident by the fact that Rocky himself made it a point to attend this local affair.

It was no small honor to have the governor, scion of one of the world's most wealthy and powerful families, mingle with us mere mortals. I recall the day vividly because my mother, never shy to express an opinion, bad-mouthed Rockefeller all the way to the banquet hall. "Who does he think he is, running off and leaving his wife and kids?" It was a different time. His recent divorce and his billionaire sense of noblesse oblige did not cut the mustard with Antoinette Cioffari D'Amato.

Yet when the governor encountered my mother, he turned on the charm. You no longer saw a guy with a billion dollars, you were looking into the eyes of a man genuinely interested in you rather than your vote. You had the impression that you were the only thing that mattered. He was a terrific politician, and I have seen few to rival him.

Nelson Rockefeller took my mother's hand and said, "I can't

believe a woman as young as you can have a son who's old enough to graduate from law school." You could almost feel my mother's icy dislike for Rocky melting away as our gravel-voiced governor made his way down the receiving line. I never heard her say an unkind word about him again.

Mamma was not so carried away by Rocky's pearls that she forgot her principal purpose in attending the fund-raiser. There was a job opportunity for me with the Nassau County Attorney's Office, and she asked if Joseph Carlino could put in a good word for me with the Nassau County Attorney. He agreed, and I went to work for the county as a law clerk in September 1961. Everything seemed to be working out so smoothly. Penny was teaching at the time, and I had the regal salary of $5,300 a year, so we could afford to move into our own apartment in Long Beach while awaiting the birth of our first child. It was a happy time. And barring a political earthquake I could look forward to becoming an assistant or deputy county attorney.

In 1961, Nassau County was solid Republican country. It was as predictably Republican as New Jersey's Hudson County and Illinois' Cook County were predictably Democrat. The party had lost the county executive's position only *once* since Nassau was established in 1895. The party's long domination was based on the stable population of the area, which had remained steadily WASP, Dutch, and German through the 1940s. The combination of Gatsby-like estates, wealthy suburbs, and scattered farms kept it a GOP sanctuary in the overwhelmingly Democratic metropolitan area.

The 1950s changed all that. This was the period of the great suburban migration, and Long Island (more than any other area except perhaps Southern California) came to typify this social transformation. After all, Long Island was the site of Levittown, the historic development of single-family homes begun in 1947 which provided a 60-by-100-foot lot for only $250 down, and a single-family, three-bedroom home for only $4,999. The vast majority of the new arrivals came from New York City, especially its outer boroughs. They were Irish, Italian, and Jewish, and virtually all Democrats.

Once these voters moved to Nassau, they quickly learned that it was the Republicans who had virtual control of the local political scene. The Nassau Republican Party made many inroads with these former urbanites by providing better roads, public beaches, recreation facilities, and summer jobs for their kids. Many of the new arrivals also flocked to the social organizations of the small communities, the Lions Clubs, Chambers of Commerce, and Volunteer Fire Organizations that defined small-town life. The Nassau Republican organization did a good job of making sure that it was well represented in these groups. It actively courted the new Italian-American arrivals. A Republican, Frank Gulotta, was the first Italian elected to countywide office in Nassau, and like Joe Carlino, he inspired a whole generation of young Republican Italians. His son Thomas has become a state assemblyman and is now county executive.

Dill was chosen as a puppet, and he ran like one.

The 1961 election for county executive taught me the hard way that nothing is certain in politics. When you combine complacency with incompetence, *anything* is possible.

The Democrats had a formidable candidate that year by the name of Eugene Nickerson. He had come within 25,000 votes of upsetting the Republicans in the 1960 race for the position of surrogate judge, so we knew we were up against a proven vote getter. In addition to this upstart candidate, the Democrats had a bright and energetic party chairman, Jack English, who would later become a close friend and political confidant of John and Robert Kennedy. Having come close in the surrogate judge race, Nickerson was easily persuaded by English to run for the much more important position of county executive.

We Republicans entered the year with a commanding two to one majority in registered voters in the county, but cracks were beginning to show in our powerful façade. The longtime Republican Party chairman and county executive, J. Russell Sprague, had been implicated in a scandal involving the sale and development of the Roosevelt Raceway, so for the good of the party he decided to step aside. His successor as both party chairman and county executive was a man named Holly Paterson, an old-school Republican WASP from the village of Hempstead. It was clear to most of the sixty or so local Republican leaders that Paterson was a mere figurehead and that Sprague was still calling the shots. This became even more apparent when Sprague convinced a majority of those leaders to deny Paterson the party leadership post in the summer of 1961. Enraged, Paterson decided he would be nobody's patsy and declined to run for reelection as county executive. Without an incumbent to run for him, Sprague picked a loyal party man, Surrogate Judge John Bennett, the same man who had beaten Nickerson just the year before. Everything was set for a harmonious nominating convention and a victory in November. I was secure in my job for at least the next three years.

Then the impossible occurred. Judge John Bennett said no. His father convinced him that giving up a surrogate judgeship to run for county executive as Boss Sprague's handpicked candidate was sheer folly. I am also convinced that Bennett, an honest and honorable man, was certain that Sprague would ask him to do things he might find distasteful, and decided to walk away from the whole proposition. Now Sprague was stuck again with no candidate. Not that there weren't dozens of worthy Republicans eager to take a shot at Nickerson. But after Bennett, Sprague was obsessed with finding someone completely under his control. He found that person in Bob Dill, a faceless functionary who had been appointed to the position of Collector of the Port of New York by President Eisenhower. While technically a Nassau resident, he had no knowledge of the county government. He was Sprague's man, an empty suit that he could control.

Sprague's best-laid plan backfired completely. Dill was chosen as a puppet, and he ran like one. His oratory was wooden and his grasp of the issues nonexistent. He had no idea of his constituents or even where they lived. With the race going disastrously, the party leaders huddled desperately to give Dill some advice. Joe Carlino, a brilliant speaker, suggested that Dill put more passion in his speeches. Dill took him to heart, and blasted the Democrats as "dirty, greasy pigs." Jack English immediately capitalized on this gaffe: he had party workers dress up in pig costumes and dance near the busiest highway intersections with signs saying, "I'm a Democrat, A Dirty, Greasy Pig." English's "dancing pigs" were a big hit with the media, who saw this colorful escapade as a dramatic departure from the Republicans' predictable political domination. The ridiculous insult angered and electrified local Democrats, who starting pouring money into Nickerson's campaign.

Poor Bob Dill's woes were compounded by the many Republicans who were insulted by Sprague's rude treatment of Holly Paterson. They took not so secret joy watching Sprague's patsy twist in the wind. For many Republicans, Sprague had simply outlived his era. He had run a solidly Republican county machine from the Gatsby era to the Levittown years, but he could not see that his time and his control were slipping away. As the race dwindled down to its dismal conclusion, even loyal Republicans were openly disparaging Dill. I watched Dill attempt to speak at the American Legion Post in Island Park, and I remember feeling embarrassed and thinking to myself that I wouldn't vote for this guy in a million years if my job didn't depend on it.

Election night arrived, and although the Republicans had, as usual, virtually a clean sweep of every countywide position (sheriff, county clerk, and comptroller), they lost–for only the second time since 1895–the all-important county executive seat. Nickerson's tiny 7,000-vote victory was a testament to the power of the Republican machine. But even they couldn't put the pathetic Bob Dill over on the people of Nassau County. To his credit, Gene Nickerson went on to be reelected two more times. In 1964, he was swept back into office in the LBJ landslide. In 1967, he defeated the handsome and articulate young Supervisor from the town of North Hempstead, Sol Wachtler.

Wachtler would have won that year, but his campaign was sabotaged by a rival Republican, Ralph Caso, the Presiding Supervisor of Hempstead. Caso didn't have the nerve to take on Nickerson himself, but knew that if Wachtler had won, he would have been eclipsed by the good-looking young upstart. (Wachtler went on to be elected to the state's highest court, the Court of Appeals, and was later appointed to the position of chief judge of that court by Governor Mario Cuomo. Seemingly at the peak of his career, and considered a potential governor, Wachtler was sent to prison in 1993 after losing his mental bearings and stalking his former lover, Joy Silverman.)

After Eugene Nickerson was elected, I was informed that he would be bringing his own people into the County Attorney's Office and that my job and those of most of my Republican colleagues were over. With our first baby on the way, losing my county salary seemed like a nightmare. What I didn't know was that it was the beginning of my road to the Senate.

UNITY PARTY CHAIRMAN

In 1961, my attention was not focused solely on county party politics. My home town, the village of Island Park, faced crisis and economic decline. The carefree summer village quality was fast disappearing as vacation cottages were converted to year-round homes, often with blatant disregard for housing codes and zoning regulations. Abandoned stores and vacant gas stations were beginning to crop up on Long Beach Road, the village's main thoroughfare. If these eyesores weren't bad enough, slumlords had discovered Island Park and were beginning to relocate welfare families into any and all of the vacant apartments.

These poor and unfortunate families were simply being dumped in town by the Welfare Department. Absentee landlords and shady real estate speculators were making a killing ripping off the welfare system as they squeezed whole families into tiny basement apartments, garages, and converted attics—regardless of safety, health, or zoning violations. Longtime residents were outraged as confused and isolated homeless men roamed the streets and frightened children as they drank, and sometimes even urinated, in public. A tragedy was unfolding before our eyes. Our beloved little village was becoming a seaside slum.

Nature itself seemed to be turning on Island Park, as serious flooding and backed-up storm drains afflicted the village on a regular basis. The tides had risen in recent years as a result of the thousands of acres of marshlands that were filled to make way for Long Island's rapid development in the 1950s. Island Park itself was built on filled marshlands. Whenever there was a "moon tide" accompanied by a northeasterly wind, most of the streets in the southern part of the village were flooded. High tides would also back up storm drains and flood the streets, causing severe property damage.

Between the slumlords and the moontides, Island Park was suffering—literally sinking into decay. Local leaders seemed powerless to change things. The only real solution to the flooding was to raise the streets and sidewalks in the affected southern section of the village, but this would cost money. Given the nature of Island Park politics, the party in power was reluctant to suggest expensive repairs that would call for tax increases because they were sure that the party out of power would attack them. For the same reason, it was impossible to pass the necessary local bond issues to finance the flood-control program. This was serious political gridlock.

In March 1962, the Unity Party enjoyed a three to two majority on the Village Board, and they asked the voters to approve a bond issue to finance raising the streets. The Unity Party had also introduced the idea of getting federal urban renewal funds to improve and renovate parts of the downtown area. Urban renewal would give the town the right to condemn property and then redevelop parts of town, using the federal funds. I was among the many people in the village who were very wary of this notion. By 1962, urban renewal already had a notorious reputation. While its principal aim had been slum clearance and highway development, it had become infamous for destroying the fabric of towns and urban communities. There were ten horror stories for every success. Too often, outside contractors, architects, and city planners made a quick profit, and the town was left a shambles. Many local lawyers (and politicians who were lawyers) made money on condemnations, and the sale of property, and so they were often enthusiastic. With this history, most of the people in Island Park were scared out of their minds, and with good reason.

The Public Party capitalized on these fears. In March 1962,

the flood-control bond issue was voted down and all Unity Party candidates but one were voted out of office a month later. These twin setbacks left the Unity Party leaderless and dispirited. It seemed that catch-22 was the only political law that applied in Island Park, and that we would be caught on this dismal merry-go-round until the whole town was reduced to a waterlogged slum. In the wake of this defeat, at the age of twenty-four, I became Unity Party chairman. I was young and almost completely inexperienced, but I was determined that I had to lead my party to recapture the local government and reverse the decline and deterioration taking place in Island Park.

Once in power, the Public Party began to change its tune about the wisdom of urban renewal. I found this astounding. The Public Party chairman, Jim Fazio, had been a friend of mine for years. As a Syracuse University alumnus, he had persuaded me to go to that school when the brothers at Chaminade were strongly urging me to attend Spring Hill College instead. Fazio was the Village attorney, the Democratic leader in Island Park, and a remarkably bright guy. Despite the fact that he was a Democrat and the chairman of the rival Public Party, he and I enjoyed each other's company. For that reason I was all the more stunned when he began to move forward with the urban renewal projects he had so adamantly opposed when his political party was not in control of the Village government.

When I confronted him on this, Fazio calmly assured me that he had only been against urban renewal when the Unity Party was proposing it. He didn't trust us to carry it out in the best interests of the village. Now that he and his cronies were in charge, it suddenly became a good program! While I was astounded by his logic at the time, I have seen this pattern repeated over and over at all levels of government. Fazio's change of heart was helped along by the fact that he got to expand the personal patronage payroll. To top it off, he had himself appointed as counsel to the Urban Renewal Authority.

Whatever Fazio's internal reasoning, I was outraged by his about-face, and I swore that I would do all I could to take back the Village Board and save Island Park from outside exploitation and possible destruction. I was certain that if the voters knew the truth, Jim Fazio's name would become synonymous with political greed. Campaigning against urban renewal, we won another seat on the Village Board in the next election. The following year, the death of the sitting mayor, William Langraff, gave us the opportunity to take back the board.

I asked my old friend and neighbor Al Riehl to come out of retirement to run for mayor. Al did this at great personal sacrifice: he had retired earlier from the board when his wife was dying from cancer. But he recognized that we were at a crossroads, and I convinced him that his return was for the good of the village. We turned the race into an informal referendum on urban renewal. The Public Party didn't just sit back and take it. They labeled me "Alfie D. Fear." Imagine, I was only twenty-five, and already people were calling me names and trying to divert attention from their failed policies by making me an issue. Thirty years later, Mario Cuomo and Rudy Giuliani would do the same thing. The people of Island Park didn't buy the "Fear" campaign and elected Al Riehl by a margin of almost three to one.

Our Unity Party has remained the dominant party because it has been open, welcoming both Democrats and Republicans, and actively courting former Public Party members. My father, an old Public man, was a perfect example. We also made good on our promises. Instead of introducing a grandiose federal project, we used our local power to crack down on the homes and businesses that were violating zoning laws and housing codes. This ended the doubling and tripling up of families in bungalows. We condemned some dilapidated properties and had the village buy them to provide parking facilities for business, churches, and temples. We were inventive, but on a small scale. We bought an old abandoned gas station and sold the property to the local Methodist church, which needed larger quarters. The Methodists in turn sold their old church to the emerging Greek Orthodox community. It was government on a small scale—neighbor helping neighbor—and it made the most sense for our tiny community.

My efforts to enlarge the Unity Party did not go unnoticed by the county Republican organization. I was called upon in 1965 to become the chairman of the Island Park Republican Party. The year 1964 had been a national catastrophe for the Republican Party. Lyndon Johnson trounced Barry Goldwater at the presidential level and his coattails seemed to carry into every local precinct. Nassau County, long a Republican stronghold, went solidly Democratic. When Gene Nickerson was reelected county executive in a landslide. Democrats won county positions they hadn't held for decades. Even our local assemblyman, Joe Carlino, the Speaker of the New York State Assembly and my family friend and hero, lost to a local Democratic car dealer by the name of Jerry McDougal. After beating Carlino, McDougal was immediately dubbed the "Giant-Killer."

In 1965, the "Giant-Killer" decided to run for Presiding Supervisor of the town of Hempstead. The town of Hempstead may sound like a small community, but it has a population of more than 700,000 and encompasses many smaller communities, including Island Park. I was an assistant town attorney in the town of Hempstead, a position that was clearly in jeopardy should a Democrat become Supervisor. As a new Republican leader and town employee, I had two very real incentives to work my tail off to defeat the "Giant-Killer." And we did. Our candidate, Ralph Caso, defeated McDougal by more than 25,000 votes.

With the defeat of McDougal, I saved more than my job. I was beginning to become a bit of a local political phenomenon. As Unity chairman, I had led the changes that shattered local governmental paralysis and started the revival of the village of Island Park. My Democratic friends and neighbors saw what we were doing in the Unity Party and became involved. As they did, many of them shed their other party affiliation and joined the Island Park Republican ranks as well. By 1965, I had helped move Island Park from the Democratic column to the Republican. My efforts did not go unnoticed or unrewarded by Joe Margiotta, the Republican Party chairman, the "Boss."

In 1966, I was appointed public administrator for Nassau County. As administrator, it was my job to secure the assets and property of people in the county who died without wills, and without known heirs. It gave me invaluable experience handling estate matters, and allowed me more time to participate in politics.

SAM LETTINI AND "THE MONSTER"

Without a doubt, one of the real characters in Island Park is my friend Sam Lettini. Everyone in the village calls him "Sam the Plumber," because that's his trade. I know there is another "Sam the Plumber"–a notorious gangster–but our Sam is just a plumber, a local eccentric who never flies, and seldom leaves the village. In an area village where most of us grew up together and knew each other, no party or Fourth of July picnic is complete without Sam, or a Sam story, or better yet, Sam telling one of his own unforgettable tales.

Sam is the local storyteller, the keeper of our oral history. One of my favorite stories of his is the time that he and Anthony "Nene" Russo raced into a burning building to rescue an infant as a hysterical woman shrieked, "Save my baby, save my baby!" Tony came out of the smoke-filled building clutching not a baby but a little Chihuahua dog. To add insult to injury, the dog even bit Tony's hand. I've probably heard that story thirty times, but I still love it.

In 1968, after I became public administrator, a woman with no known relatives died. She was a virtual hermit. Her neighbors called the police when they noticed that her lights had remained on for more than five nights. The house was filled with cats, and by the time the cops broke in and discovered her body, it was a grisly sight and there was a horrible stench. To make matters worse, the cats were starving and had started eating her decomposing body.

As public administrator it fell on me to secure all such properties, no matter how ghoulish or foul-smelling. And this place stunk. On top of that, the place was filled with trash, old newspapers, and the clutter and chaos of a woman who had lived her life without throwing anything out. It was also dark as a tomb. She had two 25-watt bulbs in the whole place. No horror movie had ever prepared me for this, but as public administrator I knew that it was precisely houses like this that could contain the valuable assets—bankbooks, jewelry, unsecured cash—that I was responsible for. For all we knew, she might have kept a million dollars in her mattress (in fact, I later worked on a case where we discovered tens of thousands of dollars hidden in paper bags in another messy house).

The stench was so awful, I just couldn't get past the front door. I threw a few air-freshener bombs in and opened as many windows as I could. Later that day, Sam Lettini lent me a few of the Fire Department's air packs. They're not unlike scuba gear that enables firemen to enter smoke-filled buildings. I figured if they worked in smoke-filled buildings, they would at least get me through the stench.

That evening, Sam and I put on our gear and started to search this spooky, reeking house. I took the upstairs and Sam took the downstairs. It was pitch-black up there. The air pack made a sucking noise, like that an astronaut or a scuba diver makes, and this weird, dislocated sound only increased an already creepy situation.

All of a sudden, I opened a door and saw this monstrous creature standing right in front of me. My hysterical screams were muffled by my gear as I stumbled down the stairs. Sam was pretty scared himself, so when he heard me screaming, he wasted no time running out of the house. He was coming through the kitchen and almost tripped over dead cats when he reached down to pick up a garden sickle. He didn't know what was chasing me, but he sure was ready for it. Sam and his sickle were all set for action when all of a sudden a flash of light exploded in his face and he heard a voice scream out: "What the hell are you doing in here?"

Sam found himself face to face with a very confused policeman. With his raised garden tool, Sam was lucky the cop hadn't shot him. He explained that he was with the public administrator, trying to secure the house. The cop asked who was doing all that hollering upstairs. "That's the public administrator," Sam explained.

Meanwhile, I had problems of my own. I was having the

worst time finding my way downstairs, and all the while the sound of a ringing bell was following close behind me. Someone, or some *thing*, was hot on my trail, and I was hell-bent to get out of there. I finally found my way downstairs to join Sam and the cop, who was having the hardest time believing that these two clowns in this old house were really working for the county. He immediately asked me for my ID and I had a hell of a time getting my card out of my wallet—my hands were shaking so badly.

Now *had* I really seen a monster? It turned out that in the shadowy darkness of that creepy old house, I had opened a door and looked into a full-length mirror. In the darkness I saw myself in that mask and air pack—my imagination did the rest. As I ran away, the air pack started running out of air. When that happens, a bell automatically goes off to warn its user. I was ready to jump out of my skin, so I was ready to believe anything. The officer finally let us go, but not without letting us know that he thought the county had a real live one as public administrator!

That is how the story of Sam, Alfonse, and the Monster was added to Sam Lettini's repertoire of local legends.

My First Election

Despite such adventures, after three years as public administrator I was ready for a change. I had not gone to law school so I could run around with air packs on my back looking after dead people's property for the rest of my life. I was an effective political leader, and after having run campaigns for others, I wanted the chance to run for public office. It was 1969, I was thirty-one and not getting any younger, and we were expecting our third child. If I wasn't going to advance as an elected official, it was time to devote more energy to building a private law practice.

Joe Margiotta didn't want to lose me, so he recommended that I be appointed Receiver of Taxes for the town of Hempstead. My term was a one-year interim term that would end the next year, when I would have to run and be elected in my own right. Looking back, I realize how clever Margiotta was. He was at the same time giving me a great opportunity and issuing a personal challenge. By naming me as tax collector, he forced me to prove myself as a vote-getter for one of the least popular public positions. It's almost in bad taste to run an enthusiastic campaign to become collector of taxes. "Vote for me–I'll tax you like nobody else," are not words to build a career on.

All the same, Margiotta made it clear to me that if I won resoundingly as Receiver of Taxes, I was destined for bigger and better things. It would determine for all time if I had a future in elective office.

Tax collectors have always been despised. Even the Bible talks about the sins of the "publican," the receiver of taxes of old. I had my work cut out for me, and frankly, I was a bit at a loss as to how to run my own campaign. Then opportunity knocked in the strangest way, accompanied by burning fabric and breaking glass.

The year 1970 was proving to be an unusually dramatic and emotional election year. President Nixon had succeeded in winding down the involvement of U.S. forces in Vietnam, but there were still hundreds of dead Americans coming home in flag-draped coffins every week. The President's efforts to destroy enemy sanctuaries in Cambodia in the spring had reignited the student protest movement, and in May 1970 four student protesters had been shot to death protesting at Kent State. Student radicals and many in the media portrayed these events as a virtual civil war.

Nassau County was hardly immune to the raw emotions of the time. I felt very strongly that the vast majority of Nassau residents resisted the media's favorable portrayal of the student radicals. I thought that the unsung heroes of the day were the brave boys who did their duty and risked their lives in an unpopular war half a world away.

One morning I arrived at the office of the Receiver of Taxes to find that someone had thrown a rock through my window and had torn down the American flag hanging outside our door. I felt this grotesque assault on my office and our flag was all too typical of what was going on all over the country. So I changed the tone of my campaign. No longer was I running just for Receiver of Taxes,

I was going to show the bums who desecrated the flag outside my office that the vast majority of the county's voters supported our boys in Vietnam.

My race turned into a referendum on the flag and patriotism. We saluted the flag at every rally. We included plastic flag decals with every pamphlet and bumper sticker. At a time when patriotism was considered passé, we were proud to appeal to the voters Richard Nixon had called "the Silent Majority." Some of my friends asked me, "Alfonse, are you running for Receiver of Taxes or are you running for president?" I was running the campaign of my life, and we won by a landslide–a margin of more than 70,000 votes.

Joe Margiotta was duly impressed and assured me that the soon-to-be-vacated Supervisor's position was mine. In January 1971, I took the oath of office of Receiver of Taxes, and retired twenty-three seconds later to be sworn in as Town Supervisor.

PART II

FIGHTING FOR THE FORGOTTEN MIDDLE CLASS

1980

There is a great old movie called *Double Indemnity*, starring Barbara Stanwyck, Fred MacMurray, and Edward G. Robinson. Robinson plays an insurance investigator who is certain that something fishy is going on between Stanwyck and MacMurray. He tells MacMurray that he has "a little man" inside him that tells him something's wrong. When he listens to that "little man," he knows he's right.

Call it a hunch, call it instinct, but the ability to know the right time to make the right move is essential in politics. History books are filled with great men who never had the nerve to act fast enough or decisively enough. Both Nelson Rockefeller and Mario Cuomo might have won their party's nomination for president, but they never jumped into the fight with both feet. On the other side, there are plenty of men who chose the wrong time to run with disappointing results. Al Gore ran in 1988 and sat out the primaries in 1992. That's why he's the number-two man right now.

Going into the year 1979, I knew it was time for me to take my shot. After Nelson Rockefeller died, I knew the whole political landscape had been altered. From 1958 to 1973, Governor Nelson Rockefeller was the undisputed king of Republican politics in

New York State. His vast fortune; press contacts; political, financial, and legal power had international reach. As a four-term governor, perpetual presidential hopeful, world statesman, and then vice president, Rockefeller towered over every other party leader. With a name that was popularly identified with extreme personal wealth and power, he sometimes exhibited a sense of paternalism that rubbed conservative Republicans the wrong way. And his attempt to deny Barry Goldwater the 1964 nomination earned him the loud denunciation of conservatives.

Rockefeller's ties to international business and wealth provided him with a view of politics that at times kept him cut off from the average middle-class working voters who were my supporters in Nassau County. To many, Rocky was a Republican version of FDR—another genteel millionaire who "knew best" what was right for the people. In 1993, Senator Jay Rockefeller of West Virginia told me that Uncle Nelson had been ready to appoint him to the U.S. Senate in 1968 after Bobby Kennedy's death. In 1984, Jay spent $17 million of Great-Grandpa's money to be elected senator from West Virginia. He spent more money per vote than in any election before or since—including Michael Huffington's unsuccessful 1994 Senate bid, which cost more than $20 million.

Jay still seems to share many of his uncle Nelson's attitudes about the government knowing what is right for the people. When Bill and Hillary Clinton's health care plans seemed to be going down the tubes in 1994, Jay Rockefeller was quoted as saying, "The American people are going to get health care whether they like it or not." This is precisely the kind of attitude the American voters rejected overwhelmingly in 1994, telling politicians like Jay Rockefeller, "Enough is enough"—enough of government and politicians telling us what is good for us.

As governor, Nelson Rockefeller was steadfast in his support for New York's senior senator, the liberal Republican Jacob Javits. Like many in my party, I wanted a more reliable Republican in the U.S. Senate. Once there had been talk of a primary fight, but Rocky effectively crushed that by threatening not to run if Javits were challenged. Rockefeller's money and influence meant too much to the party, so no serious rival ever arose. By 1979, Jacob

Javits had become one of Jimmy Carter's most enthusiastic supporters. In fact, Javits voted for Jimmy Carter's positions far more often than most Democrats. He had championed Carter's giveaway of the Panama Canal when popular Republicans like Ronald Reagan were making it a litmus test of conservatism.

With the death of Nelson Rockefeller in January 1979, the world of Republican politics in New York State changed forever. With a 1980 Republican primary approaching and no Nelson Rockefeller to defend him, there were certainly going to be challengers to Javits's renomination. I was determined to be one of them.

As Presiding Supervisor of Hempstead, I thought I had both the experience and the political base to make a serious challenge. Not too many others shared that point of view. To the media, Long Island was a machine-politics backwater that had long been taken for

> He told me to "knock it off, and concentrate on being reelected Presiding Supervisor."

granted by the state Republican Party. Nassau County regularly sent a dozen state assemblymen to Albany, and two and sometimes three representatives to Congress. It was also home to more than a million people, many of them a new kind of Republican voter. While the stereotypes of the New York State Republican were of Wall Streeters, Silk Stocking blue bloods, and upstate rural WASPS, Long Island in fact was home to Italians, Poles, Irish, Jews, Greeks, and others who had abandoned the Democratic Party when they left the confines of the city. Add to these the registered Democrats fed up with welfare, taxes, and the social experimentation of a drifting, post-McGovern Democratic Party, and the seeds were sown for the phenomena of the Reagan revolution and the Reagan Democrat that electrified the country in 1980. I was ready to tap this current and ride this wave.

To get on the ballot for the Republican nomination, I needed to secure the support of at least 25 percent of the Republican state committeemen. To have a prayer of doing this, I would have to have the solid backing of my own county. And to do that, I would need the support of the county chairman, Joe Margiotta. When I approached him with my idea in July 1979, he was less than enthusiastic. To put it bluntly, he thought I was insane, and if you look at things from his point of view, maybe he was right.

To Margiotta, I should have been concentrating on my upcoming reelection bid for Presiding Supervisor of Hempstead. We both knew it was hardly in doubt. The only question was the margin of victory. Joe Margiotta felt I should be happy, grateful, and above all, *patient.* He did not see the wisdom in taking on a four-term senator. Margiotta and county chairmen before him had spent many years wooing the Jewish voters from their habit of voting for Democrats. He had no intention of seeing that effort spoiled by my rash decision to tangle with Javits. He also reminded me that he had invested a lot of political capital in my career. He told me to "knock it off, and concentrate on being reelected Presiding Supervisor."

I left that meeting mighty downhearted. I knew that it would take more than one conversation to change Margiotta's mind. I also knew that no matter what he thought of my chances, the fact remained that Rocky was no longer around to protect Javits. *Somebody* was going to challenge him. I didn't know who it would be, but there was no doubt in my mind that if I could figure out that Javits could be beaten, so would others.

A couple of weeks later I received a phone call from former Congressman Bruce Caputo. Bruce had been the Republican candidate for lieutenant governor in 1978 when he and Perry Dureya had squandered a 40-point lead against Hugh Carey. We were not particularly close, and I wondered just what he was up to. My suspicions increased when Caputo came on in a friendly manner and asked me how my campaign for Presiding Supervisor was going and what he could do to help. I was looking at a certain landslide, so why did I need help from someone with his track record? The polite thing for me to do would have been to simply give him the address of my fund-raiser and ask him for a donation. I wasn't in a polite mood.

"Bruce," I snapped, "just what are you up to? What's your angle in offering out to help me when I obviously don't need help? Are you running for office?"

Caputo left out a sigh of relief. He was as glad as I was to dispense with phony pleasantries, and bluntly told me that he was mounting a challenge to Javits. A bomb went off inside my head. If Caputo was the first to challenge, he would seize the momentum and become the focal point of opposition to Javits. He was seizing the moment while I was campaigning in Hempstead. It was time for me to move—with or without Margiotta's approval.

In the blink of an eye I made the most important decision of my political life. I simply told Caputo I couldn't back his challenge to Javits because I was going to mount my own. In hindsight it was probably a dumb thing to just blurt out, but I couldn't help myself. Every instinct told me that it was now or never.

After the momentary euphoria of surprising the hell out of Bruce Caputo, I was faced with the fact that the news of my challenge was now out of the bag. It wouldn't take long for this to get back to Joe Margiotta, who wasn't fond of these kinds of surprises. And if he wasn't behind me, who would be? No other party leaders in the state would risk alienating the "Boss" by backing me.

Meanwhile, I waited for the right opportunity to tell Margiotta I was serious about running. I said, "Look, if you don't support me, Caputo is going to run against Javits, whether you like it or not." He finally agreed to look at it once my race for Presiding Supervisor was over. In November 1979, I was reelected with a solid 57 percent of the vote. While I was running in Hempstead, Bruce Caputo was working full-time trying to position himself as Javits's only serious challenger.

Margiotta knew how disappointed I had been in 1978 when I wanted to run for state Attorney General. He had been sympathetic, but told me that it was not my time. He threw his support to Ralph Marino, the state senator from Oyster Bay. As it turned out, neither of us got the Republican nomination, which went to a Rockefeller man, Michael Roth, who was defeated. Ironically, had I run that year, my Democratic opponent would have been Bronx Borough President Robert Abrams. I guess it was not our fate to tangle until 1992. In all humility, I know I would have beaten him. The South Bronx was burning, crime was rampant, and Abrams was never challenged on his lack of leadership. My campaign would have been: "Bob Abrams wants to do for the people of New York what he's done for the Bronx." But I never got the chance.

While I had played the good soldier in 1978, this time I knew I had to confront Joe Margiotta. My friend Marty Bernstein, a successful entrepreneur and town councilman from Oceanside, knew how to push my buttons. He knew how upset I was about getting passed over and told me that if I missed the boat this time, I would regret it for the rest of my life. With his needling wit, he helped me see that this was a once-in-a-lifetime chance. "You're not going to run," he taunted me. "You're just going to complain. Twenty years from now you're still going to regret this, and blame yourself for not running. If you want to run, *run!* If you want, I'll help you raise the money."

With friends like Marty behind me, I gathered the courage to face the "Boss" once again. In the privacy of Margiotta's office I could tell that my efforts were beginning to pay off. I was no longer being brushed off. For the first time, Joe was beginning to talk like he believed that Javits was beatable in 1980. He was not yet convinced that *I* was the man to do it, but I could see that I was getting through. But before he would reconsider, he wanted to consult his own pollster, Arthur Finkelstein, about my chances in a statewide primary.

Arthur Finkelstein is one of the most brilliant and unusual characters I have ever met. Finkelstein seemed to take pride in his casual attire. Rarely in a tie, he would often take his shoes off in the middle of a meeting and pace up and down the room dictating speeches or political strategy. While I could immediately see that he was brilliant, I was not that sure, upon first meeting him, that I was going to like him, or he me. He looked me right in the eye and told me, "Between you and Bruce Caputo, Caputo's the stronger candidate. He's better-looking, he's a better dresser, he doesn't have a Brooklyn accent like you, and you have no experience running outside of Nassau County, and besides, you're very headstrong. You will be a very difficult candidate." To say the least, Finkelstein's brutally frank assessment was not a confidence builder.

And Finkelstein's poll numbers were no kinder. They showed that Javits would beat me by 67 to 4 percent. And to add insult to injury, Finkelstein explained that my measly 4 percent was probably too high. As a pollster, he knew that at least 3 percent of my support came from people who thought that I was someone else. My real base of support was closer to 1 percent!

But I knew that such figures were meaningless at this stage. What the poll revealed about voters' impressions of Jacob Javits was far more important. It showed that despite Javits's liberal voting record, he was considered a conservative by more than 50 percent of the registered Republicans polled. Even more telling was the fact that despite his advanced age, those polled thought he was about fifty-five years old. When voters were informed that he was seventy-six years old, running for a six-year term, many turned against him. And when informed of his close cooperation with the Carter administration and his support of the Panama Canal Treaty, they were even less likely to support him.

But just because Javits might be vulnerable did not mean that Margiotta would suddenly back me. After all, there might be a dozen possible challengers with more than 4 percent against Javits. He shrewdly hedged his bet. Margiotta would not provide a public blessing and endorsement, but he would do nothing to discourage me. This "non-endorsement" would be perceived as a silent nod by insiders, particularly the Nassau party delegation, but at the same time it would protect Margiotta from any damage should I fail. But if I prevailed in this thousand to one shot, I would be in his debt, and he would look like a political genius.

I understood perfectly that Margiotta was not primarily concerned with my fate, but worried what others would think of his political judgment in supporting me. Were we, he wondered, on a fool's errand?

One of the first people he turned to, after consulting with Arthur, was former President Richard Nixon. We went to his Manhattan apartment, not for public endorsement but private advice. Many politicians still secretly sought Nixon's advice and political benediction despite his unofficial exile. As I sat there with Margiotta, I marveled at the fact that these two foxes were conferring on my fate. Nixon was enjoying himself. He may have been a world statesman, but he was a reservoir of knowledge on local as well as national politics, and took real joy in showing his expertise.

Nixon understood the dynamics of the New York party and was certain that Javits would be vulnerable in an open primary. He respected Javits's intelligence and shared some of Margiotta's reservations about alienating Jewish voters, but ultimately agreed with me that the party that had elected him four times beginning in 1956 no longer existed. He said, "Al, you have a chance, a very good chance. It won't be easy and the press will tear into you for taking on an institution, but it is certainly doable."

Nixon was among the first to congratulate me on my election victories in 1980 and again in 1992, when he sent me a wonderful note, stating: "You surprised them, but I know you could do it." He was very supportive during some of my tougher times and even sent me a note after *60 Minutes* raked me over the coals. It said, "Don't let the bastards get you down."

I always admired Nixon's brains, his scrappiness, and tenacity. I, more than most, can appreciate his lifelong love-hate affair with the media. I think that much of the press's coverage of his death and his funeral was fair and respectful, almost as if they were going out of their way to make up for fifty years of animosity. Even Nixon's greatest detractors had to admit that his grasp of foreign affairs was second to none.

Having secured the private blessings of Nixon and Margiotta, I now had to shore up my most critical base of support—my own family. Our meeting had taken place the day before Thanksgiving, so I couldn't wait to rush home and share my enthusiasm with Penny, my kids, Mom and Dad, and my brother Armand. I can still see their faces when I made my announcement. My mother was delighted. My kids were immediately concerned that they would have to move to Washington. My father pretended he did not hear what I said. "You're going to run for what?" he asked me in a tone of disbelief that bordered on contempt. I said, "I am going to run for the U.S. Senate." To which he responded, "Son, you should run to see a psychiatrist."

I said, "Dad, I'm trailing 67 to 4, I can't go down much." He quickly responded in his baritone voice, "You'd be surprised." He was troubled all through supper, and it put a damper on my spirits. He was really upset, so much so that after dinner, when my brother Armand, he, and I usually had our rowdy game of pinochle, he refused. Pinochle was an institution in our house, and when the three of us got together, we rarely missed an opportunity to play. Instead, he put on his coat and told me he had to go out for a walk. "And when I come back," he told me, "I don't want to hear any more of this nonsense about you running for the Senate."

Later, when we had a chance to be alone and talk, I told him how I really thought I could win. I tried to persuade him of Javits's weaknesses and of my strategies. He didn't argue with me. He told me, "I know you can win, and that's what bothers me. Have you thought about what this situation will mean to your children, your marriage? You have a great job. People love you. You have it good. Are you sure you want to do this?"

I assured my father that I knew what I was undertaking and that it was the chance of a lifetime. And looking back, I realize in my eagerness to show how confident I was, I didn't fully appreciate just how proud he was and how worried he was for me. He could see, much better than I could ever conceive or predict, just how much turmoil and turbulence a statewide race and a national office would wreak on my family life. At the same time, I was heartened that he did not think I was crazy or quixotic to run. He knew I could win, and that's what scared him.

From that day, I had no time to look back. Caputo had been out sewing up Republican support and angling for the Conservative Party nomination. It had been clear to me all along that the Conservatives were the key to a challenge against Javits. They were the core of dissident Republicans who had long seethed under Rockefeller and Javits. A spirited and successful insurgency would energize the Conservative Party as well as its candidate. Ten years earlier, they had succeeded in electing James

Buckley to the U.S. Senate, defeating liberal Republican Senator Charles Goodell and the liberal Westchester Congressman Richard Ottinger. They knew lightning could strike again.

Caputo was eagerly courting Brooklyn Republican leader George Clark, who had long been vocal in his displeasure with Javits. Caputo made the most of his experience as a former congressman and a statewide candidate in 1978 for lieutenant governor. Meanwhile, most voters knew little of the Hempstead Presiding Supervisor.

Arthur Finkelstein had been a key player in James Buckley's victory in 1970, and was also a close confidant of New York State Conservative Party chairman and party founder Dan Mahoney. He was invaluable in demonstrating that I was the kind of candidate that ideologically driven conservatives could support.

Calling Jacob Javits to inform him of my challenge was not an easy phone call to make. There is no polite or pleasant way to say to someone, "Hello, I am going to spend months trying to defeat you and take away your job." He was as gracious as could be, told me that he had always encouraged young people, and assured me that my time would come. I told him I was forty-two years old and I was certain that my time had come, that it was the right thing for me to do at this stage of my career. I assured him that I was not entering the race to embarrass him, but to make a difference for the party, the state, and the nation.

My next call was to Congressman Jack Kemp, the former Buffalo Bill's quarterback and favorite of conservative Republicans. The Conservative Party nomination was his for the asking. There was also no doubt that he could easily get at least 25 percent of the state committee's delegates to mount a Republican challenge. I told him, "Jack, if you run, I'll be happy to support you in the primary." I went on to say that if he did not, I would formally announce my candidacy in January 1980. I told him, "You've certainly earned the right to enter the race, and I will support you if you do." Coming from different corners of the state and from very different backgrounds, Jack Kemp and I did not have the closest relationship in 1979. I wasn't sure exactly what he made of my phone call. It probably seemed kind of strange for me to call him out of the blue. I wouldn't be at all surprised if he viewed my whole effort with some amazement or even disdain.

My campaign began officially in January 1980, when Marty Bernstein sent a fund-raising letter to his close friends and associates that brought in more than $50,000. I cannot overestimate my depth of gratitude to Marty and these early donors who gave of their time and money at a time when I was nothing but the longest long shot imaginable. On January 6, more than two thousand friends and supporters joined me at the Waldorf-Astoria Hotel in New York City to announce my candidacy. Many of these people had never been involved in anything larger than a countywide race. Most rarely ventured outside of Nassau County. But here they were in the fabled Waldorf lifting their glasses to a local boy.

To my surprise and annoyance, my announcement got exactly three lines in the New York City newspapers. This was my first introduction to the objectivity of the New York press. On the Democratic side, Bess Myerson had about twenty-five people at her announcement and received TV coverage as well as pictures and stories in all the New York dailies. She was virtually certified as the front-runner. Liz Holtzman received similar treatment. I may have had thousands at my side, but to the media, and the liberal establishment, I was strictly a hick pol from Long Island with no chance to win.

After my warm Waldorf send-off, which included kind remarks by Margiotta and the support of Suffolk chairman Tony Prudente, I embarked on a tour of upstate New York that provided an inauspicious beginning to my long campaign. In January, Buffalo can be a cold and forbidding place. Winds whip in off Lake Erie and it is not uncommon for daily snowfalls to be measured in feet rather than inches. It was not the coziest place to launch an insurgent campaign. My tour would take me through New York's snow belt from Buffalo to Syracuse and then Albany. Buffalo Airport closed when the winter winds reached 80 mph, so we were forced to land at Niagara Airport.

I will never forget sitting in my hotel reading of winds so bad that a driver who had been out changing a tire on his car had been blown off a bridge to his death. I could hear the metal garbage-can covers clanking in the alleyways below my hotel window and the almost frightening sound of the whistling wind, and thought to myself that my father was right, that I was insane to enter this race. There is nothing like the bleak, white cruelty of a Buffalo blizzard to accent the negative. I was seriously thinking how I could pull the plug on the campaign with minimum expense and embarrassment. What on earth was I doing here?

After this dark night of doubt, our press conference the next day was hardly a pick-me-up. Attendance was sparse, to say the least. Press reception was little better than it had been in Manhattan. And our next stop, Rochester, was worse. In fact, I would have preferred no Rochester press coverage at all. Instead, we got to look at a picture in the paper of me addressing an empty room with a caption reading: "Candidate and no one there to greet him." At least I had friends in Syracuse. Among my classmates who gave a semblance of turnout were Tucker Leone from Auburn and my old friend from the track team Larry Twomey. Yet even they tempered their enthusiasm with remarks like: "You're *really* running for the U.S. Senate?"

Albany rounded out our campaign's disastrous maiden voyage, and I returned to Long Island chastened, to say the least. Margiotta played it beautifully. He kept his hands off and watched as my campaign spun its wheels. The last thing on earth he wanted to do was get solidly behind a stillborn insurgency.

Then, as it would several times that year, lightning struck. Fate arrived in the person of the old Manhattan Republican warhorse Vince Albano. Albano was the Republican chairman of New York County, and a longtime supporter and ally of Javits. In a story that appeared on the front page of the *New York Times,* he personally attacked Joe Margiotta for having the nerve to support someone like Alfonse D'Amato against a man as distinguished and deserving as Jacob Javits. And he didn't just attack *me.* He went straight for Margiotta, calling him the "Don Rickles of the Republican Party." Thank God for Vince Albano. It was like waving a red flag in front of a bull.

It was just my luck that neither Vince Albano nor the *Times* understood the subtle nuances of Margiotta's non-endorsement of my candidacy. By insulting him, Albano had forced Margiotta to show his hand. Had they wanted to destroy me, they would have done best to simply ignore me (as most of the state party seemed to be doing at that point!); instead, they enraged Margiotta and got him solidly in my corner. Within twenty-four hours Margiotta had assembled the Nassau County Republican Executive Committee and formally endorsed me. With this one move, I was strengthened on two strategic fronts. Having the support of the party's two most powerful Republican counties, Suffolk and now Nassau, I was in a great position for getting the necessary 25 percent of the delegates. Now I could turn my full attention to securing the Conservative Party nomination.

Founded by Dan Mahoney and his brother-in-law Kieran O'Doherty, the Conservative Party was dedicated to steering the Republican Party away

> "I think there's a guy here who could beat Javits."

from its "me too" philosophy. To many Conservatives, the Republican Party of New York State had created many of the candidates who were almost carbon copies of welfare state Democrats. To them, the party that created Willkie, Dewey, Rockefeller, Javits, and New York State Attorney General Louis Lefkowitz was nothing to get excited about. They were worse than Democrats; they were wolves in sheep's clothing. Having tasted blood in 1970 when they ran a true believer, Jim Buckley, the Conservatives were certain they could win again in 1980, a year when the national electorate was so dissatisfied with the mess Jimmy Carter and the liberals had made of the economy, the military, and foreign policy.

Since I was virtually unknown to most of the Conservative Party members, I spent the next few weeks going out of my way to meet with virtually every Conservative leader in the state. More often than not, this involved informal meetings in restaurants or taverns where we would drink and tell stories until midnight to assure all concerned that I was a regular guy who could be trusted. We were all feeling each other out, and I was not at all sure that I was succeeding.

One Sunday morning in February 1980 I appeared on a WCBS-TV *Newsmaker* program. I was sure that no one but my wife and kids would be tuning in. After all, everybody else was probably at church or sleeping late. I was getting grilled pretty good by the reporters, who were blatantly dismissing me and my effort. Who was I, a town supervisor, to challenge Jacob Javits? But I gave as good as I got and fired back that Javits had lost touch with his people and his party and voted more like a Jimmy Carter Democrat than a Republican. Republicans from Queens, Buffalo, and Albany deserved a candidate who expressed their philosophy and represented the interests of working middle-class people, not the editorial-page writers of the *New York Times*. It might have been a forgettable appearance on a low-rated show—except for the fact that Kieran O'Doherty just happened to be watching in his Queens living room. He called Dan Mahoney and told him to turn on Channel 2. "I think there's a guy here who could beat Javits."

Later that week, at Arthur Finkelstein's suggestion, my wife and I met with Serphin Maltese, executive director of the New York Conservative Party, and his wife, Connie, and Dan Mahoney and his wife, Kathleen, for dinner at Dan's favorite Italian restaurant. This was probably one of the most crucial political meetings of my life, and to my pleasure, we never spoke a word about the election or any of our past exploits. As the evening wore on and our wives seemed to be hitting it off as well as we were, Dan took me aside and told me how he had dreaded coming to meet this eager local politician. He was afraid I was going to bore him to death with war stories. Instead, we told jokes and I played the piano till three o'clock in the morning. We wound up closing the place.

I think I did a good job of convincing Mahoney and Maltese that I was prepared to fight to the finish against Javits and the liberal establishment. We all agreed that this was a year of decision and opportunity and that it was time to take dramatic action. They were eager to nominate their candidate early enough to have an impact on the Republican race. Whoever won the Conservative nomination would be in a great position to corral all of the anti-Javits dissidents and take the Republican nomination. It was clear to all of us that our interests converged. Once I had assured them that I had the support of the Nassau and Suffolk GOP, they eventually supported me.

I entered the Conservative convention with the backing of the party founders and leaders and more than enough delegate support. Bruce Caputo did not even win the support of Conservatives from his home town of White Plains. When Westchester Conservative leaders John McGlorn and Carmelita Greco threw their support my way, other Conservatives in Caputo's home county rallied to me. They knew that Caputo was not really a Conservative and would not make the best candidate against Javits.

Despite this lack of support, Bruce Caputo and his people used every possible parliamentary maneuver to block my nomination. They could not win, but they were determined to make us wait out their stalling tactics. They polled every delegate's vote individually and challenged every procedure. The convention lasted more than eight hours and deteriorated from grueling to nasty to vicious. A rumor was unleashed that I was linked to organized crime. I'm sorry to say, I've gotten more used to this kind of smear, but this first time it was pretty hard to take. Fortunately for me, the decent men and women of the Conservative Party were not swayed by the rumormongering and ethnic innuendo. I emerged at the end of the day with their nomination, a pivotal turning point in my battle to unseat Javits.

I will never forgive Bruce Caputo for his underhanded tactics, and for never distancing himself from these allegations. A former congressman who had made quite a name for himself in the Koreagate scandals of the late 1970s, Caputo made the common mistake of believing his own press clippings and the stories in the *Times* which said he was the man to beat. Despite the drubbing he and Dureya received in 1978, Caputo felt he was the golden boy of the party. Caputo was so desperate to win the Catholic vote in his district, he reportedly attended mass several times each Sunday and even received communion. Now, every good Catholic must know that this is forbidden, but Caputo had an excuse. *He wasn't even Catholic;* he was Dutch Reformed.

In 1982, Caputo announced his intention of running for the Republican nomination against Daniel "Pat" Moynihan for the U.S. Senate. While conducting research on a potential rival, Senator Moynihan's administrative assistant, Tim Russert (who went on to work for Governor Cuomo and now hosts *Meet the Press*), unearthed a secret that destroyed Caputo's career: Caputo had passed himself off as a lieutenant during the Vietnam War. When Russert searched for his military records, he found that Caputo had received a deferment and actually worked as a civilian in the Defense Department. He had fabricated his record. Russert leaked the news to the press and Bruce Caputo's political career was over. A joke quickly made its way through political circles: "Who's buried in the Tomb of the Unknown Soldier? Bruce Caputo."

After securing the Conservative nomination, qualifying to run in the Republican primary was the next hurdle. With the entire Long Island delegation behind me, I entered the Republican State Committee meeting on June 6 with almost 20 percent of the delegates—just under half of the number needed. I knew that Brooklyn and Queens were not happy with Javits. If I could get their support and some upstate delegates, I had it made. In the end I received all of these delegates and more, and got over 35 percent. I was no longer the nobody with 4 percent of the vote. The race with Javits was on in earnest.

The 1980 campaign brought together a unique group of people. Perhaps it was the romance of a challenger's campaign, of taking on the establishment of your own party, but there was a spirit of adventure to that campaign that brought out the best in the strangest assortment of workers. One of the truly memorable workers in that campaign was Don Turchiarelli, who worked for the Buffalo Sanitation Department. He fought for me like a pit bull. As a precinct committeeman, Turchiarelli was my only supporter from the Buffalo Republican establishment. I still don't know why he attached himself to my effort with such passion. It was probably our shared Italian roots. I suspect his resentment of Victor Farley, the Buffalo Republican chairman, had something to do with it.

Farley was clearly Javits's point man in Buffalo and western New York, and he went after me with a personal vindictiveness that was almost irrational. At the Republican Convention, he continued to pile personal assaults on me even after it was clear that I had accumulated more than enough delegates to secure a place on the primary ballot. I approached him and personally asked him to tone it down. "Victor," I explained, "I'm on the ballot. Let's lighten it up and let the voters decide." I really don't know what motivated Farley's enmity. Perhaps he wanted to make points with Javits, and thought that if he took it out of my hide, he might secure a federal judgeship one day. For whatever reason, he worked against me like a man possessed.

My good friend Steve Leider also joined my Buffalo operation. A young lawyer from the neighboring community of Oceanside, Leider had taken off from his job as an assistant town attorney with the town of Hempstead to run my upstate campaign. His wife was expecting their first child at the time, so it was a great sacrifice for him to relocate to Buffalo. In addition, Jane O'Banion of the Conservative Party and a couple of people from the Right-to-Life Party volunteered. The entire operation was run out of Turchiarelli's attic, where he had installed six phone lines. He gave the campaign 110 percent.

Sadly, after we won the primary, Turchiarelli became disaffected. He felt betrayed that after we defeated Javits in the primary, Farley and his people agreed to help us in the general campaign. After all, we were all Republicans. Turchiarelli never forgave me for accepting their help and walked away at the hour of our greatest triumph. He backed me when I was a nobody, a thousand to one shot. I still think of his effort with great fondness and appreciation.

Farley was not the only Javits operative to treat me with less than kid gloves. In fact, one of the great myths of the 1980 campaign was that I was the tough ogre taking on the refined and civilized Jake Javits. Nonsense. His people played hardball politics all the way. At times it got quite nasty.

Early in my primary campaign I marched in the St. Patrick's Day Parade in the town of Pearl River in Rockland County, about twenty-five miles north of New York City. It's the biggest St. Patrick's Day Parade, with the exception of New York City, and attracts pipe bands and school bands from all over the state. The Town Supervisor was Joe Colello, a man I'd never met, but we did have mutual friends in the Sons of Italy organization and we were both town supervisors. He was impressed that I would march in the Rockland parade. In twenty-four years, Javits had never even acknowledged Joe Colello's existence. He certainly never made any personal appearances or cemented the ties of political friendship.

Colello made it a point to accompany me to every local gathering of the Hibernians, Knights of Columbus, Sons of Italy, or wherever there were twenty or more people. I would say hello, and Colello would announce, "I want you to meet Al D'Amato. He's going to be our next senator." He walked with me all day, despite the fact that he had injured his foot earlier that week and was in considerable pain. (In fact, he later learned that he had broken his big toe, which blew up like a balloon by the end of the day.) He limped the whole day, but I knew he was making a statement by being seen with his fellow Italian-American from Island Park. He stood by me when no one knew me and my campaign was going nowhere.

By June, the Javits forces realized I was someone to be reckoned with, and they behaved in a heavy-handed manner that turned most Republican voters off. At the Rockland County nominating convention, I was sure that I could have mustered a majority of the vote, and the Javits people knew it too. The last thing they wanted was to be embarrassed by having the county delegation support me over a sitting senator. They dragged out the voting on every local and county nomination, and only then did they turn to the U.S. Senate. At that point they insisted that the county convention be polled to see if a quorum was still present. The

Javits people were instructed not to answer "present." As the hour was growing late, many delegates had already left, and the convention was adjourned without taking any vote on the Senate nomination. It was a slick bit of parliamentary gamesmanship. The mastermind of this operation was Judd Somers. We have since become friends, but that day his cohorts had the audacity to warn me "never to step foot in Rockland County again." My old boyhood friend Richie Miranda had to escort me out of the hall. We barely made it out of there without a fistfight. I told them, "You guys are wacky. This isn't Nazi Germany. This is the United States of America!"

After rising above the level of "Alfonse who?," my next problem was obvious. Primaries cost money. After twenty-four years in the Senate, Javits had incredible resources at his disposal. Raising funds for my first statewide race was tough. We were happy to raise money at Legion Halls and Knights of Columbus Halls for $10 or $20 a head. One of the first fund-raisers held for me was sponsored by my friend Bill Powers from the upstate town of Rensselaer. It was held in a small bar and grill in Albany called Mike's Place. The owner, Paul Scaringe, whose cousin was the Albany County Republican leader, donated the basement. I think the largest contribution was $100. Most attendees gave $25 and $50, and I was grateful to them all. We raised $2,200. With a wife and two young boys to support, Bill Powers worked on the Republican staff of the New York State Assembly. Once the Republican leadership learned that Bill was supporting me, they fired him.

Throughout the campaign we held picnics upstate and parlor parties and spent every single day beating the bushes for donations. By the end of June, we were deep in debt and trailing Javits by 40 points. The thought of losing and still owing hundreds of thousands of dollars was very scary. I confided in my friend and fund-raiser Marty Bernstein that the campaign owed more than $500,000. Marty asked, "Alfonse, do you have the money to pay it back if you lose?" I told him, "What, are you nuts? Of course not." To which he responded, "Then what's the problem? If you can't pay back the five hundred thousand, then what's the difference?

Borrow more!" That may have been an easy solution for Marty, but I wasn't very sanguine about it.

If our fund-raising attempts were grassroots at best, our early TV commercials were just this side of amateur hour. We couldn't afford actors and a studio, so we filmed my neighbors from Island Park in our local headquarters. The critics laughed at our efforts, but the voters seemed to respond. One ad in particular was critical to our success. Back in January 1980, the *Daily News* ran an editorial stating that Jacob Javits was seventy-six years old and in ailing health. Why was he running for another six-year term? It showed a picture of him that could only be called macabre. It went on to state that my fledgling candidacy might offer a silver lining by providing Javits with a challenge and by reminding him that he had grown out of step with New York and its needs. The *News* editorial reflected my feeling that Javits, with all of his experience and intellectual abilities, had forgotten the day-to-day needs of the middle-class families of New York.

Well, we couldn't say it better. So we didn't. We ran an ad quoting liberally from the *News* editorial. The reaction from the media was immediate. We were slammed all over the state for having the nerve to ask a legitimate question about the senator's fitness for another six-year term. The *Daily News* was particularly angry. They hadn't run that piece to help me—they never expected me to survive! They were laying the groundwork for consumer advocate (and former Miss America) Bess Myerson. Aiding Alfonse D'Amato was the last thing on their mind. They even threatened to sue us if we didn't pull the ad.

Once we ran that commercial, it was a brand-new race. It reinforced the message which we slammed home again and again that Javits was too old, too elitist, and too out of touch with the working-class people of this state. Even the media reaction to the ad probably helped us. After all, here were the big shots and know-it-alls of the press ganging up on me when I tried to raise a legitimate issue. To the *Times,* the question of Javits's age was a question of "bad taste." To the voters, however, it was one of common sense.

The Javits side did not exactly roll over. While we succeeded in reaching the entire state with our television ads, the Javits people ran their campaign the old-fashioned way, spending hundreds of thousands of dollars on telephone banks to call prospective voters. That may have worked in Thomas Dewey's day, but it was already antiquated by 1980. In addition, much of Javits's telephone effort completely backfired. In Buffalo, GOP boss Farley instructed his telephone-bank operators to call tens of thousands of Republican voters and ask them, in a mocking tone of voice, what they thought about an Alfonse "Tomato" or "DaMatteo" running against Senator Javits. If their response was favorable, they would not be called back on primary day and reminded to vote. If the response was negative, they would be targeted for a reminder call the day of the vote.

This tactic blew up on them in a number of ways. In the first place, there were still many voters who were unaware of my campaign and who would have dutifully pulled the lever for Javits had they remained uninformed. Farley was unwittingly helping to publicize my campaign.

In addition, this obvious ethnic attack rubbed a lot of voters the wrong way, particularly in a region as ethnically diverse as Buffalo. Farley's people targeted Irish and Polish voters with his "Al Tomato" phone calls. We heard from hundreds of irate voters who received these calls. What Farley didn't take into account was that many Irish and Poles were married to Italians, and he was calling them up and insulting their mothers, wives, cousins, etc. It was another clear example of the arrogant, outmoded thinking that characterized the whole Javits campaign. The ethnic voters who would turn out in such record numbers for me and for Ronald Reagan in November were not in the mood to be insulted. Farley ran the Javits campaign in Erie County and the state from Rochester west. We beat Javits soundly in that entire region, with the exception of Erie County, which Javits carried by only 500 votes out of approximately 35,000.

The Javits camp grew increasingly desperate as the September primary approached. I was repeatedly grilled about coming of political age in the Nassau County machine. They attempted to blame me for the old and now discredited practice that called for county employees to contribute 1 percent of their salary to the Republican Party. During the last weekend before the primary the Javits people dug up a letter which revealed that in 1972 I had contributed $75 from our local Republican club on behalf of a Hempstead sanitation worker who wanted a raise. They gave this letter to the *Daily News* on the Sunday before the primary. The *News* proclaimed: "D'Amato Tied to Multi-Million Dollar Kickback Scheme." This poor guy wanted a raise but couldn't afford to make a contribution, so our local club made one on his behalf. The Javits campaign people were counting on this letter to blow up my campaign. While it certainly rattled me, coming as it did just days before the primary, people were more understanding of the realities of life and paid little attention to what was obviously a political attack.

On the Democratic side, a four-way race involving former Mayor John Lindsay, Queens D.A. John Santucci, Bess Myerson, and Elizabeth Holtzman was coming down to a two-woman battle. Myerson had the money, the media, and practically every elected Democrat on her side. Myerson, who had been practically inseparable from Ed Koch during his 1977 race for Gracie Mansion, outspent Holtzman at least four to one.

As it turned out, we beat Javits with more than 57 percent of the vote. We rolled up huge margins on Long Island and easily made up for Javits's small margin in New York City. What had seemed like an impossible dream during my January trip to Buffalo had now come true. We not only won on September 9, 1980, but won decisively.

Our troubles had only begun.

In the Democratic primary, Holtzman defeated Myerson in what the media characterized as one of the great upsets. In truth, we saw it coming. We knew that just as Republican primary voters would favor my conservative candidacy, the Democratic primary would tilt to the most liberal candidate. A moderate candidate like Santucci may have had a good chance in the general election, but in a primary, where ideologically driven voters turn out, he didn't have a prayer. In New York, we understood that a McGovern Democrat like Holtzman really had the home field advantage. The media did not understand this, and naturally gravitated to Bess Myerson, one of their own. When Holtzman won the primary, the media suddenly rushed to create the impression that she was a giant-killer when in fact she had done exactly what we had expected. Now that the revered Javits was beaten, the media wasted no time in showing their support for Holtzman. While we were both insurgents, the press spun our stories in very different ways. To them, Holtzman had scored a stunning upset. D'Amato had won dirty by beating up an old man.

We had seven weeks to go, and all the momentum seemed to be on Holtzman's side. In fact, only a week after the euphoria of the primary victory, Arthur Finkelstein was already telling me that we were in dire straits. He warned me that if we didn't stop Holtzman from gaining another 2 points and going over 50 percent, we could kiss the race good-bye.

Our problems were compounded by the bad blood caused by the GOP primary. Senator Javits was still on the Liberal Party ticket, and his supporters did not want to stay on the Republican line to vote for the upstart who had dethroned him. Our internal polls showed that Holtzman held a commanding lead. Just one week after the primary, she led with 48 percent of the vote to my 27 percent, with 20 percent for Javits. The Javits camp then attempted to get the National Republican Senatorial Committee (which I now chair) to give the money allocated to the New York Senate race to Javits instead of me. Conservatives went into an uproar and the Javits people quickly backed down, offering as a "compromise" to "share" half of the money with us. The liberal establishment was still arrogantly trying to shove me aside, even though Javits had lost. They couldn't comprehend that the people had rejected their philosophy.

Jim Cannon, who was then Senator Howard Baker's chief of staff, met with Joe Margiotta and me on Long Island. Cannon was an old Rockefeller protégé who suggested that we split the money with Javits. We vehemently told him that we would not sit still while a defeated candidate running on the Liberal line pushed me aside. I made my case to a select group of donors, who each gave $10,000 to the National Republican Senatorial Committee. I explained that with Javits on the Liberal line cutting into Holtzman's vote, I could win this election. I must have made a persuasive case because at least a dozen donors told me that they would stop contributing unless the committee gave me all of the money. They liked my enthusiasm and were not particularly fond of Javits.

Holtzman aided our cause just by being herself. It did not take long for voters to recognize that Liz the giant-killer was an ultraliberal sourpuss, of the variety that even Democratic voters had grown sick and tired of. Holtzman helped our campaign because she was not only a humorless liberal, she was an *arrogantly* humorless liberal. It did not take a political genius to see that she would have been helped if Javits left the Liberal line and allowed her to run one on one against me. But did she ask Javits to step down? No, she was too smug for that. After all, she was the anointed one, the media's darling, the inevitable winner.

Holtzman had become a liberal heroine in 1972 when, at thirty-two, she unseated Congressman Emanuel Celler, the powerful chairman of the House Judiciary Committee, in a Democratic primary. Celler had served in the House for fifty years, and he, like Javits, had lost touch with his Brooklyn constituents. Two years later, Holtzman was showcased as a member of the House Judiciary Committee chaired by Representative Peter Rodino of New Jersey, when they voted to bring three counts of impeachment against President Nixon. Having beaten Celler in 1972, she was now out to replace Javits. I thought it was ironic how the press criticized me for taking on Javits's age when it was Holtzman who seemed to have made a career of running against elderly men.

During the campaign, Peter Rodino appeared in an ad supporting Holtzman. My aunt Gilda, who lived in New Jersey in Rodino's Essex County district, wrote him a scathing letter telling him how upset she was. Gilda was a Democratic committee member and ardent Rodino supporter. She felt very strongly that Rodino, one of the first Italian-Americans in Congress, should have known better than to support Holtzman. When I first met

Rodino in 1981, he seemed a bit sheepish. He asked me if I had an Aunt Gilda. I had been unaware of her letter, so Rodino explained how she had blasted him for supporting Holtzman; and he told me how badly he felt about it. I told him to forget it, but walked away thinking, "That must have been some letter."

Holtzman sanctimoniously behaved as if she was beyond reproach. She thought nothing of destroying people to get a headline. Her specialty was smearing Italian-Americans by insinuating ties to organized crime. She did this to me in 1980, and she did it again to Geraldine Ferraro in 1992.

In the 1980 campaign, Holtzman was championed by the *Village Voice* which took every opportunity to savage me and my family. Week after week, the *Voice* threw every vicious charge imaginable at me. This would have been bad enough, but they took particular glee in savaging my family. My father, who had a master's degree from NYU and had scored first on his civil service examination for his job with the county commerce department, was brutally mischaracterized as an unqualified political hack. The *Voice*'s twin vipers, Jack Newfield and Wayne Barrett, piled it high every week with absolutely no regard for the truth.

On election night, November 4, 1980, I discovered that my father was not among us. He had been hospitalized. I never knew because Mamma had sworn everyone to secrecy so as not to upset me. The ugly lies had driven a good and decent man to the brink of a nervous breakdown. Smears, lies, and innuendo had forced a fine man to the hospital.

The *Voice* is a perfect symbol of how traditional liberalism can be perverted when taken over by the lunatic fringe of the ultraleft and the politically correct thought police. Once the paper of Ed Koch's trusted friend and adviser Dan Wolf, the *Voice* has become so out of touch that former readers like Koch now hold it in contempt.

Liz Holtzman, who blew a more than 20-point lead in 1980, learned nothing from her defeat. She continued to employ the same tactics of slander and deceit whenever she thought it would benefit her. Up until her final folly–the Fleet Bank loans that de-

stroyed her career—the liberal media has been an active partici-
pant in her reprehensible habit of destroying people's reputations.

Holtzman had an uncanny facility for preaching about other
people's ethics, but she never felt bound by the same standards
she demanded of others.

Despite Holtzman's talent for alienating New Yorkers, we
were still far down in the polls and going nowhere fast. The
media was portraying me as a mean reactionary. They dubbed
me "the Jesse Helms of Long Island." We needed something dramatic to change my image, or this race was over. And we needed
it fast.

What we came up with remains the political masterstroke of
my career. It was a Saturday evening when I called up my mom
and asked her what she was doing. She told me she had just
baked an apple pie for Sunday dinner. I told her I was coming
over with a couple of friends tomorrow morning to get her reac-
tions about my campaign. The next morning, cameras converged
on my parents' Island Park home, and we shot the first of what
would turn out to be some of the most effective political commercials in history. My mother was filmed carrying grocery bags on
her way home. She was thinking out loud about how tough it was
for the middle class to make it. Just before she entered the house,
she turned to the TV cameras and said, "Vote for my son, Al. He'll
be a good senator." It was short, simple, and brilliant. I was no
longer the evil ogre from Long Island. I was somebody's son—a
human being once again. To millions of voters, Mamma D'Amato
could have been their mother. Here was a kind and decent
woman who looked right into your eyes. She wasn't a slick politician or fancy actress. She was one of them.

The middle class was trampled during the 1970s. Inflation
robbed our savings. Crime took away our neighborhoods. Two-
bit countries were kicking America around by taking hostages
and threatening us with terror. The middle class was looking for
someone to turn to in 1980, and they found that person in Ronald
Reagan—and in Mamma D'Amato and her son Alfonse.

We knew we had a winner when the first Mamma commercial hit the airwaves. Mamma went on a statewide campaign swing. She got a parade and police escort in Buffalo, and love and affection all over the state. We printed up thousands of copies of a little cookbook entitled *Mamma D'Amato's Inflation-Fighting Recipes,* and we distributed them all over the state. The Republican National Committee had assigned a smart and sophisticated aide to work on our campaign named Cheryl Davis. I knew Cheryl was a little wary about joining the upstart D'Amato team. I am sure she never expected to escort the candidate's sixty-six-year-old mother all over the state.

As it turned out, this sharp Californian political pro could hardly keep up with Mamma's one-woman campaign. Mamma thought nothing of plunging into any neighborhood from Syracuse to Brooklyn. In Manhattan, she even went after voters in OTB parlors, something that political pros would never have dreamed of. In

> "Relax honey," Mamma replied. "This is the Village. Get used to it."

one encounter in Greenwich Village, Mamma and Cheryl stumbled into a neighborhood bar. When her eyes adjusted to the light, Cheryl nearly had a heart attack. She thought she was going to get sacked from the campaign for stopping to get a drink with the candidate's mother in a bar filled with drag queens. When she nervously suggested that they move on, she realized how much she had underestimated my mother. "Relax honey," Mamma replied. "This is the Village. Get used to it."

The Mamma commercials drove the Democrats and the critics wild. All of our commercials did. One of our most criticized spots was our most effective. It was a short spot of me in Little Italy surrounded by hundreds of New Yorkers. No words, just the music of the tarantella. It was moving, beautiful, and brief. The critics blasted it as the worst commercial of the year. What they couldn't measure from their Madison Avenue offices was the pride that hundreds of thousands of Italians, Poles, Ukrainians, Jews, and others saw with this simple bit of ethnic pride. It was clear to us from that ad and the reaction to it that we were speaking to the voters.

After a while, Mamma D'Amato's effect on the campaign was so dramatic that the Democrats could not ignore it. After they attacked me and ridiculed me for running such embarrassingly corny commercials, Liz Holtzman dragged her father into the act and took him everywhere. Even Jimmy Breslin, no friend of mine, had to admit that while he would never vote for Al D'Amato, he would certainly vote for his mother.

My victory in 1980 would never have occurred without the enthusiastic outpouring of support by Italian-American voters throughout New York. Our time had arrived. It was clearly important for many Italian voters that I was going to be the first Italian-American to hold statewide office.

Without the support of the thousands of members of the Sons of Italy organization, I could not have won. Many of these local chapters had been organized or encouraged by my old friend Judge Angelo Roncallo, whom I had known since we worked together in the Nassau County Attorney's Office back in 1961. A former Long Island congressman, Angelo had helped organize and invigorate dozens of Sons of Italy chapters throughout the state, particularly on Long Island during the sixties and seventies. These local organizations helped to maintain ethnic pride while fighting anti-Italian bigotry. As the Sons of Italy grew in size and influence, many non–Italian-American politicians were eager to become honorary members.

In the summer of 1980, I had attended the annual statewide meeting of the Sons of Italy at the Concord Resort Hotel in Kiamesha Lake, New York, in the center of what used to be the famous Borscht Belt. I was a member of the Rocky Marciano Lodge from my neighboring community of Oceanside. Many members of my lodge were wearing "D'Amato for Senate" buttons. We set up a hospitality suite and invited the officers of all of the other lodges to drop by. As word spread that a fellow member was a candidate for the U.S. Senate, the convention took on the atmosphere of a revival meeting. State chairman Peter Zuzzolo, who would later become national president of the Order of Sons of Italy, declared that "it was about time that New York had an Italian-American in the Senate." His speech was met with thunderous applause. Then a surprising and delightful thing occurred.

Josephine Gambino, a member of the Liberal Party and an appointee of Governor Hugh Carey, rose and challenged the conventioneers to put their money where their mouths were: "It's time we did more than talk about supporting Al D'Amato. . . . I'm giving a hundred dollars to kick off the campaign. What are the rest of you going to do?" They literally passed around a hat and collected more than $8,000 in spontaneous contributions. To Governor Carey's credit, he did not punish Josephine. She remains a dear friend of mine, who continues her activities on behalf of the Sons of Italy and recently retired as State Commissioner of Civil Service.

Josephine Gambino was clearly not the only non-Republican to support our campaign. While many crossed party lines to support a fellow Italian-American, others voted for me out of disdain for Holtzman's extremely liberal, antidefense record. One such Democrat was Buffalo's mayor, Jim Griffin. A former state senator, he became a good friend of my brother Armand when they were both in the state assembly. As a conservative Democrat, Jim had no use for Holtzman and let it be known that if local Democratic workers wanted to desert her, he would certainly not mind. His stance brought about a wholesale desertion of ethnic and blue-collar voters to my campaign. This was certainly helped by the presence of Ronald Reagan on the ticket. Jane O'Banion of the Conservative Party hooked me up with local Democratic activists Andy Sedita and Pete Elia. Andy ran an organization called the Niagara Association, which put me in touch with Democrats of every ethnic stripe and helped me almost carry Buffalo in 1980. In fact, I carried Erie County by 63,000 votes.

In the end, Liz Holtzman had the image problem. If she had smiled, even once, she might have won. But a revolution was taking place in middle-class and working-class neighborhoods in New York and all over the country. Lifelong Democrats, union households, and blue-collar workers who had been Democrats since FDR were rejecting their party in droves. By the millions, they joined against Carter and Holtzman, and voted for Ronald Reagan and me.

Do I owe my election to Ronald Reagan? You better believe it. Do I owe my election to Mamma D'Amato? Of course I do. But all of us were riding the tides of history. We had all tapped into the frustrations of the middle class. We would speak for them, fight for them. A virtual earthquake had shattered the existing political order. When the rubble fell and the dust cleared, I was still standing. Alfonse Marcello D'Amato had become New York's first Italian-American senator.

MY
"IRISH FLING"

Less than a month after the election, I first ventured into foreign affairs with a trip to Northern Ireland. It may have seemed odd for a D'Amato to be traveling to Ireland, but during the 1980 election I had assured Irish-Americans of my concern for the ongoing suffering and oppression in the six northern counties. I promised to go to Ireland after the election. I knew that I did not have all the answers, but I felt that as a senator-elect I had an obligation to learn more about this tragedy.

I left for Ireland on December 7, 1980, with two friends and colleagues, Denis Dillon, the Nassau County District Attorney, and Peter King, a Hempstead town councilman who is now in the House of Representatives. The *New York Times* dismissed our efforts as "D'Amato's Irish Fling."

While I was new to foreign affairs, I soon realized that our State Department's policies and pro-British slant had exacerbated the violent standoff. This became more evident as I prepared for my trip. Prior to my departure, I received a briefing from the British Embassy and our State Department. To my surprise, the State Department was more critical of the mistreated Catholics in the North than even the British Embassy.

I arrived in Ireland at a dramatic time. Seven members of the

Irish Republican Army (IRA) had been on a hunger strike for more than a month, protesting their status as "common criminals." With the hunger strikers now near death, British troops were on full alert. Prime Minister Margaret Thatcher was also arriving in Dublin to meet with Irish Prime Minister Charles Haughey. This was the first time in this century that a British prime minister had ever visited the Irish capital. Security forces in Dublin were on full alert. For my first foreign trip, I had chosen a virtual war zone.

Our Irish itinerary was compressed into only two days so that I could carry on to visit victims of a recent earthquake in Southern Italy. At the airport in Dublin, we met with Sean MacBride, the Nobel Peace Prize recipient, who had previously served as chief of staff for the IRA in the 1930s, and as Irish foreign minister in the 1940s. As a teenager, he saw his father executed by the British for his participation in the Easter Uprising of 1916. He told me how much it meant for a U.S. senator to come and show concern. After speaking with MacBride, I held my first foreign news conference, in which I spent most of my time assuring reporters that I was traveling on my own accord and wasn't a special emissary for President-Elect Reagan.

Belfast was a mass of dreary buildings covered with graffiti and political slogans—"Victory to the Hunger Strikers" in the Catholic neighborhoods and "No Surrender" in the Protestant, loyalist areas. British troops and armored cars were everywhere. We would be staying at the Europa Hotel, infamous for being the most frequently bombed hotel in Europe. After complaining to Denis and Pete for their choice of accommodations, I discovered that in Belfast, we didn't really have a choice. We each got our own room, and mine was spacious, and filled with light. For a brief moment, I basked in the perks of power. Then I realized the flip side of so many windows: I was a sitting duck in Europe's most dangerous hotel.

After washing up, we met with local citizens who told us horror stories of being driven from their homes because they were of the "wrong" religion. I spoke with priests who counseled the families of the IRA hunger strikers and listened to a middle-aged woman who had been blinded by plastic bullets when a British soldier shot her for playing Irish nationalist music on her phonograph. Most moving was the mother of hunger striker Sean McKenna. In his thirty-eighth day without food, he had just gone blind. His doctors gave him only a few more days to survive. This tragedy was compounded by the fact that Mrs. McKenna's husband had been tortured to death by the British Army in the 1970s. McKenna Senior was one of the IRA members who came to be known as Ireland's "hooded men." British torture experts put hoods on their heads for days until they lost all track of time. Then they were subjected to ultrasound waves to further disorient and torture them. Finally, still shrouded in hoods, they were taken aboard a helicopter. After a short ride, they were thrown from the chopper. Only when they hit the ground did they realize that they were just ten feet or so in the air. The effect was devastating. For this modern twist on medieval torture, the British would eventually be found guilty in the European Court of Human Rights. The hooded men, however, were broken by the ordeal, and Sean McKenna's father had died soon after his experience.

As an American, I was an outsider to the civil war tearing Northern Ireland apart. At the same time, I had to wonder what would drive men to starve themselves to death. The IRA prisoners wanted the right not to be treated as common criminals. Since they had been convicted in "special courts" and denied many basic civil rights, including trial by jury, they saw themselves as prisoners of war. They demanded the right not to wear prison uniforms or do prison work like convicted burglars and rapists. The British refused. They knew the propaganda power that POW status would confer. Listening to Mrs. McKenna's story, I could feel the passion of her son's efforts, but I could not help but feel that this was just another deadly variation on a centuries-old theme of hatred, retribution, and death. I could not see the purpose in allowing young men to starve over the issues of work clothes and yard duties. But I was an American, not an Irishman. I was not part of the drama, or so I thought.

No sooner had I finished my poignant meeting with Mrs.

McKenna than I faced my first Belfast press conference and the full fury of British reporters. Objectivity was not the relevant word here. Almost all of them accused me of meddling in their affairs and of stirring up trouble. I did my best to assure them that I was not taking sides and would avoid saying anything inflammatory. Then I discovered that in Ireland, even when you think you are being impartial, you must be wary of your very choice of words.

One of the reporters lambasted me for releasing a "pro-IRA" press release to announce my visit. When I told him I had no idea what he was talking about, he referred to our desire to find out more about the conditions in Long Kesh Prison. Unbeknownst to me, Long Kesh was the name of the old prison that the Irish had burned down in 1976. The British had since rebuilt it and re-named it The Maze. The Catholic side still used the original name, in deliberate defiance of the British. In the eyes of the British press, my vocabulary made me an IRA supporter.

It was already after nine in the evening when we left the drafty confines of the Europa Hotel to witness a march for the hunger strikers in the New Lodge Road section of Belfast. The State Department had assured me that there was very little rank-and-file support for the strikers. As soon as we came to New Lodge Road, I saw teeming crowds and clear evidence of the State Department's bias. Thousands of marchers, bearing candles and torches and led by drums and fifes, marched past thousands more people shouting their support from sidewalks, stoops, and windows. There was both celebration and danger in the air. I couldn't help but notice the nervous presence of the British soldiers in our midst. Despite their very evident machine guns, these troops were just kids—scared, skinny teenagers with pimples who obviously wanted to be anywhere but Belfast.

We were taken to a spot where a flatbed truck was parked to provide a speaker's platform. As I looked around, I saw dozens of flags and a blinking light hanging from a window in an H pattern. I asked what that meant, and got another lesson in the power of semantics in the Belfast struggle. The new cell blocks in the prison that the British called The Maze and the Catholics called

Long Kesh were shaped like an "H," so the prison was now also called "H-Block" by the Catholic partisans.

Coming only weeks after a bruising campaign, I was just getting used to the idea of being a senator and only beginning to appreciate the meaning of the office. When word spread that a U.S. senator had joined the marchers, people began to tug at my sleeves and to tell me with tears in their eyes not to forget their cause when I returned to America. So many of these folks looked like my neighbors from Island Park. But these people—caught in this centuries-old tragedy—were cut off from a largely indifferent world. Even in America, filled with millions of sons and daughters of Ireland, they had been largely ignored. I got on the truck and told them I would not forget their plight. The roar of approval from the crowd overwhelmed me. It wasn't my eloquence but the fact that I cared that mattered.

It was after 11:00 P.M. when we got back to the Europa. We had all gone more than thirty-six hours without decent sleep, but I was inspired and driven by nervous energy. It had been a heady day and I guess I didn't want it to end. While the pubs close at eleven in Belfast, our manager kept the Europa's bar open so that Pete, Denis, and I could sit back and talk. We were joined by three members of the moderate Catholic party—the Social Democratic and Labor Party (SDLP). Denis excused himself and went off for some well-earned sleep. Pete and I continued our conversation with three bright, articulate guests. One was a doctor, Joe Hendron, and the others were a lawyer and a dentist whose names I cannot recall. For a moment, I felt almost relaxed, outside of the danger zone.

Sometime after midnight, I noticed that we were being watched by three men. They weren't hard to spot since they were speaking rather aggressively to our waitress and happened to be the only other people in the bar. The dead giveaway for even an amateur detective like me was the fact that they were all wearing sunglasses and trench coats and acting like characters out of a B movie. After a few minutes, our waitress came over and announced that they would like to meet with the senator. When I asked who they were, Joe Hendron told me that they were from the Ulster Volunteer Force. "They're loyalist paramilitaries," he whispered. "They've assassinated Catholics. They're a bad lot."

I sent Peter King over to tell them, as graciously as possible, that I couldn't see them. "But be nice about it," I remember saying.

From what I could gather from across the room, Pete was getting nowhere. He did most of the talking, and gesturing, while they were cool and deadly quiet, with their hands in their pockets. It wasn't long before they turned away and left.

Pete returned to our table with an uneasy look on his face and told us that they knew all about my visit to the march. They claimed that I had an obligation to meet with them. Pete tried to explain that I wasn't going to meet with any paramilitary group, Protestant or Catholic. But they were cold to any explanation and said that my attending the Catholic rally and refusing to meet them was disrespectful to the Unionist side.

Then Pete dropped the bomb. "When they left, they told me to tell Senator D'Amato that *we know what we have to do and we're going to do it.*" At this, Joe Hendron got up to make a sudden phone call. "What's going on?" I asked.

"He's making arrangements to get us out of here."

I'll never know who Joe called, or what actions were taken, but we were assured that the hotel would be secured and that we would be safe for the night. We were escorted out of the bar and waited for what seemed like hours for the ancient, creaky elevator to descend to the main floor so we could head up to our rooms. I watched the dim lights announce each passing floor and waited for bombs to go off. I couldn't get over the thought of me, Alfonse, the Italian kid from Island Park, getting blown up in Belfast.

When we got to our floor, I looked up and down the hall and saw no one. Pete turned toward his room and wished me good night. "Not so fast," I said. "You've got to be crazy if you think I'm sleeping alone in that room tonight." Pete thought I was nuts, but I followed him to his room, took his suitcase, and carried it into mine. "You're moving in with me. If they come after us, they're going to have to take on the two of us."

I quickly locked the door, pulled the chain across it, and

leaned a chair against the doorknob like I had seen them do in a dozen movies. Pulling rank, I told Pete he had to take the bed by the window. As we finally crawled into bed–it had now been more than forty hours since we had been in one–the last thing I remember telling Pete was that he better not sneak out of the room and leave me alone.

The next thing I remember there was a loud bang at the door. Daylight was streaming through the curtains, and the clock said 6:45. I pulled rank again and told Pete to answer the door. Pete's remarks are unprintable, but he did go to the door.

You can imagine the look on Denis Dillon's face when he saw Pete and me in our pajamas in the same hotel room. He had gone to bed before the Ulster loyalists had arrived and knew nothing of their threats. The more we tried to explain why we were there together, the more Denis laughed. Soon we were all doubled over with laughter.

The next week, the British and IRA prisoners reached a compromise to end the hunger strike. The seven strikers all survived, even Sean McKenna, who had slipped into a coma. He recovered some of his eyesight, but his health never fully returned. Two months later, the compromise collapsed, and a new strike began. It was led by Bobby Sands. It didn't end until ten prisoners died.

More than thirteen years later, on the eve of St. Patrick's Day, 1994, Congressman Peter King was standing outside of a Washington hotel trying to hail a cab to take him home. He heard his name being called by a man with a heavy Belfast accent. When he turned around, he saw Joe Hendron, the doctor from that frightful night at the Europa Hotel. Like Peter King, Joe Hendron's political star had risen since our first meeting. In April 1992, he defeated Gerry Adams and was elected to the British Parliament representing West Belfast. After greeting each other like old friends, Pete and Joe immediately began reminiscing about the events in Belfast. Joe Hendron said, "Senator D'Amato almost had a very brief Senate career."

Pete and Joe discovered that they were both invited to Speaker Tom Foley's annual St. Patrick's Day lunch in the Capitol. The guests of honor were President Bill Clinton and Irish

Prime Minister Albert Reynolds. It was a lively affair, complete with bagpipes, a choir from Ireland, corned beef and cabbage. At one point, Pete noticed that Speaker Foley had brought the President over to sit with Joe Hendron. Pete walked to where the President was speaking with his Irish guest, and said, "Mr. President, you have no idea how much trouble this man has caused you." Clinton gave Pete a puzzled look and turned to Joe Hendron, who told him, "It's true. It's true." Pete then told the President the story of our near escape from the Unionist assassins in Belfast. "In other words," Pete concluded, "if this man hadn't helped save Al D'Amato's life thirteen years ago, you might not be having so many problems today." After waiting a second, the President turned to Hendron and said, "Good for you. You did the right thing." But Pete wasn't entirely sure he meant it.

FRESHMAN
YEAR

After two come-from-behind victories and the most exhilarating year of my life, I felt a bit let down when I entered the Senate in January 1981. My first year in Washington would prove to be both a challenging and a painful period. After all, I was away from my wife, children, and home town four days a week. While my children were filled with pride that their daddy was now a senator, my sons, Christopher and Danny, were only ten and twelve, and it was not easy for them to have me away so much.

I spent most of 1981 and much of my first term with the haunting feeling that maybe I was an "accidental senator" who only won because Jacob Javits refused to leave the race. The media never tired of reminding me and everyone else of this conventional wisdom. But CBS's exit polls showed that Javits actually had pulled slightly more votes from me than from Holtzman. This fact never gained much popular currency, so my victory was still considered a fluke by many. The pundits also ignored the conservative wave that swept Ronald Reagan into the White House and brought a GOP Senate majority. To the liberals, I was an aberration, a one-termer they would have to endure for six years.

As a Town Supervisor entering the Senate, I was also making

a leap in responsibility. My focus changed from local to state and national issues. Washington could be a pretty rough town. D.C.'s gossip mills, press corps, and cocktail cliques had the best of some pretty tough operators. After all, Jimmy Carter and his Georgia crowd had just been eaten alive by Washington insiders. Would they feast on an Italian from Island Park? I think that after fourteen years, I've given a lot of them indigestion. Ask Sam Donaldson.

I was also going to be sharing an apartment for the first time since my marriage in 1960. It's not easy to live with roommates when you're forty-three. While much is said about the powers and perks of office, many members of Congress share housing costs. After all, almost all of us have families to support back in our home districts. Few in Congress can afford to maintain two homes. I shared quarters with Guy Molinari, who had just been elected to the House from Staten Island. He had just defeated John M. Murphy, who had been implicated in the infamous Abscam scandal. My other roommate was Assemblyman Dominick DiCarlo from Brooklyn, who had been appointed assistant secretary of state in charge of developing the United States' international policy for fighting drug trafficking. We three Italian-Americans from New York lived in the Buchanan House in Crystal City, about ten minutes from the Capitol. Dominick was our unofficial chef when we could find the time to eat at home.

BUILDING A STAFF

When I entered the Senate, one of my best assets was a fantastic staff, headed by my friend and administrative assistant John Zagame. A former assemblyman from Oswego in northern New York State, John lost a close primary race for the GOP nomination for Congress in 1980. He had joined our campaign back in September, and quickly became indispensable. His research on Liz Holtzman was so detailed that I could prove in our first debate that she had not voted for even one defense appropriations bill.

After the election, I put John in charge of the search for my administrative assistant. He came up with name after name, but none of them impressed me as much as John did, so I finally prevailed on him to take the job. It was one of the best appointments I ever made. John hired many of the support staff from retiring Senator Dick Schweicker, who had been named as President Reagan's Secretary of Health and Human Services. Many of my detractors painted me as a machine tool and expected my office to be filled with political hacks. But we did the exact opposite. Michael Hathaway, my legislative assistant for defense and intelligence matters, came in off the street. He impressed me with his brains, military record, and intensity. But we looked at more than two thousand résumés before we found him. We made it policy to hire eager, bright young people who reflected the unorthodox style and mission that I brought to the Senate. My office manager, Claudia Breggia, hunted us down with a passion. Formerly employed by Rhode Island Senator Clayborn Pell, she peppered my office with dozens of résumés and letters. She went so far as to track down John Zagame at his New York Assembly office to seek an interview. I am delighted to say her tenacity paid off, and she has proven herself to be one of the most effective and dedicated office managers in the Senate. Her ability to get things done is legendary.

We had a unique opportunity back in 1981, and we missed it.

Zagame knew that I succeeded on Long Island by responding to every voter's letter, request, and phone call. As a former assemblyman, Zagame knew how important it was to heed constituents. But I had gone from serving 700,000 to more than 17 million. I knew immediately that as much as we tried, we would never succeed with the antiquated office that we inherited from Javits. You can't serve the needs of 17 million people using electric typewriters and boxes of file cards.

Fortunately, John saw that 1981 was the dawn of the computer age, and he selected the newest in office automation technology to organize our records and correspondence. John's savvy use of technology symbolized our fresh approach.

But all the gadgets and systems in the world cannot make you a good senator. Just as we had defeated Javits by using television, our use of the latest technology enabled us to be one of the most responsive offices on Capitol Hill. We handled as many as 100,000 constituent requests in a year. That reputation for constituent service was the key to the success of my first term.

How We Failed to Freeze the Deficit

Sixteen new Republican senators were elected in 1980. The establishment derisively dubbed us the "sweet sixteen" (even staffers and clerks used this term). Because we were swept into office with the Reagan landslide, the pundits thought that the "sweet sixteen" would simply vote in lockstep. This was a gross simplification. We had our own constituencies to serve. Within a year, I had a serious tangle with the Reagan administration on mass transit, and my friend and colleague Arlen Specter openly challenged the White House on cutting Social Security. In retrospect, I should have voted with Arlen. That vote—to cut disability benefits with the idea of cutting the deficit—was one of my biggest mistakes. It did nothing to cut the deficit and only frightened senior citizens.

The year 1981 was a hectic and dynamic year in Washington. Ronald Reagan pushed through the budget and tax cuts that eventually put the economy in the position to boom by the mid-eighties. It wasn't easy, and it wasn't accomplished without a lot of hard work and politicking, but Ronald Reagan had been elected with a tremendous mandate. Many of us owed our seats to him.

Looking back, one of my great regrets is that we failed to get the budget deficit under control. God knows we had the chance. Given Reagan's popularity and ability to build coalitions between Republicans and conservative Democrats, we could have capped spending, controlled entitlements and avoided the deficit mess we are in right now, fourteen years and $4 trillion later. We had a unique opportunity back in 1981, and we missed it. How that happened is a maddening political tale.

Democratic Senator Fritz Hollings of South Carolina had proposed a spending freeze. Fritz is a distinguished southerner, six feet two inches, with a great head of white hair. He looks like everyone's idea of a senator and is well liked by his colleagues. Many on the Hill felt that Hollings's freeze was the right approach. It could have passed. Then Jim Baker, the White House chief of staff, killed it.

One Friday evening, the President was flying to New York and I was fortunate enough to hitch a ride on Air Force One. James A. Baker III was known as a savvy political operator. He ran George Bush's presidential campaign in 1980 and joined the Reagan team when Bush became the vice presidential candidate. Ironically, the former campaign manager was now more important to the President than George Bush, who was in that peculiar political limbo known as the vice presidency. To paraphrase a popular commercial, "When Jim Baker spoke, people listened."

I did my share of listening on that flight, and I was appalled by what I heard. Jim Baker was bragging about how he was going to kill the Hollings freeze. And what shocked me even more was that he never even discussed the fiscal merits of the freeze. He cared only about the politics. Baker saw Hollings as a potential rival to Reagan in 1984. That was enough for Baker to kill it.

Baker's logic was both shortsighted and absurd. Fritz Hollings was certainly no threat to Ronald Reagan! Anyone could see that Reagan would become the most popular president since Roosevelt. He had remarkable powers of persuasion and a mandate from the voters. Such power is given once in a generation. Roosevelt had it during the Depression. Johnson had it briefly before the Vietnam War. For Reagan not to use that power to support an intelligent measure to freeze spending was a grave mistake. In 1984, Hollings did not get very far past the cold of New Hampshire, losing the nomination to another Fritz, Mondale, who lost every state but Minnesota to Ronald Reagan.

This was not the last time I would witness the dubious political "genius" of Jim Baker.

My First (and Last) Fight with Bob Dole

According to conventional wisdom, a rookie senator is supposed to lay low, learn the ropes, and not make waves. Of course if I had followed conventional wisdom, I would probably be Town Supervisor in Long Island today. I was barely into my first year when I crossed both the administration and Senate Finance Committee Chairman Bob Dole in order to save Industrial Development Bonds (IDBs). Treasury Department bureaucrats and numbers crunchers wanted to eliminate these bonds to raise revenue. But IDBs allowed businesses to borrow money at 3 to 4 percent below the going rate. In Hempstead, we had used these bonds to attract and keep businesses. During the recession-plagued seventies and early eighties, when the interest rates flirted with 20 percent, IDBs were often the only thing between survival and bankruptcy for many local firms. We estimated that during my tenure as Hempstead Supervisor, we used IDBs to retain or attract five thousand to six thousand jobs. In 1981, the United States was hemorrhaging jobs to Japan and Europe. Workers were scared that the "Reagan recession" might become a real depression. The last thing government needed to do was eliminate this source of business investment.

The Treasury Department only saw IDBs as one more source of investment the government could not tax. The bureaucrats could never look beyond the immediate revenue and see that these bonds created jobs for thousands of people who in turn paid federal and state income taxes. To me, this was a good example of "supply side" economics. Opponents of IDBs also claimed that the bonds had funded less-than-worthy projects. They repeatedly trotted out the example of a local government that used IDBs to fund an adult bookshop. I can't tell you how many times I heard this story. Others felt that big businesses used the bonds when they didn't really deserve the extra break.

Despite these reservations, many of my colleagues believed that these bonds were of great help to the small businesses that create most of the jobs in this country. That is why I took unusual measures and created an unlikely coalition to fight my own party and the Reagan administration on this issue.

The bill to eliminate the tax-free status of the IDBs originated in Bob Dole's Senate Finance Committee. As much as I wanted to fight for IDBs, I was not *on* the Senate Finance Committee. As a member of the Senate Appropriations Committee, though, I thought up a tricky parliamentary maneuver to stop Treasury's proposal in its tracks. I offered an amendment barring Treasury from spending money to publish or promulgate rules relating to IDBs.

Senator Dole was not too pleased with my amendment. He sent a letter to the Appropriations Committee saying that he opposed any legislation that intruded on the Finance Committee's turf. His point was crystal clear. A freshman senator had no business defying the administration—or, even worse, meddling with his committee's jurisdiction. I was way out of line.

But I persisted. When I offered my amendment, Appropriations Chairman Mark Hatfield of Oregon read Senator Dole's letter and explained that he too opposed my amendment. Hatfield asked that I wait until the bill came to the floor to offer my legislation. Meanwhile I had been feverishly lobbying all the members of our committee. Although the Appropriations Committee had twenty-two members, seven to ten of them often had conflicts and couldn't be present. I obtained proxies from about a dozen members in favor of my amendment. The ranking Democrat, Senator John Stennis of Mississippi, strongly supported retaining the bonds. John remembered how much IDBs had meant to the poor, rural South during the Depression. Well into his eighties, John agreed with this upstart Republican that what had worked during the Depression should not be frittered away in the midst of the 1981 recession. I could see that my work had paid off.

When the committee voted, all those present but Hatfield voted with me. With the proxies added, the final tally was 19–1. Naturally, I was beaming. I had pulled a shrewd parliamentary move to defend bonds that meant a lot to New York. Dole certainly hadn't expected a fellow Republican, much less a member of the "sweet sixteen," to "roll" him.

I was delighted, and somewhat arrogantly thought, "This

Senate business isn't so hard, after all." I quickly discovered that Bob Dole was not one to cross. Treasury was also not too happy with me. I spent the next few months negotiating with Dole and Treasury to limit IDBs to sensible projects and to save the tax exemption for IDBs through September 1987.

I was helped greatly by both Senator Stennis and Senator Ted Stevens, the Republican "pepper pot" from Alaska. It was a tough fight, and the folks from Treasury were so angered by my temerity that they took every opportunity to ridicule me as "Senator Tomato." But we saved the bonds, and that's what the people of New York sent me to Washington to do–to fight for them and not roll over like a puppy dog.

From my first days in the Senate, I have tried to be the voice of the working men and women who elected me. I have stuck to the commonsense values learned on the streets of Newark, Brooklyn, and Island Park.

STANDING UP FOR ISRAEL

As much as I agreed with Ronald Reagan, particularly on foreign policy, sometimes I simply could not vote with the President. In 1981, the President asked the Senate to approve the sale of AWACS (Airborne Warning and Control System) jets to Saudi Arabia. The debate was emotional and intense. Defense contractors wanted to keep the oil-rich Saudis as steady customers. The Saudis made it clear that if Congress did not approve the AWACS sale, they would view America as unreliable and turn to the French and British for their military hardware. Billions of dollars were at stake.

The Israelis feared having to spend billions to overcome Saudi Arabia's vastly improved surveillance capabilities. Beyond dollars, there was the matter of principle. Why was the United States, Israel's best friend, selling its most sophisticated hardware to Saudi Arabia–a nation that had never recognized Israel, that funded the Palestine Liberation Organization (PLO), and that was still technically at war with Israel?

Nowhere was the debate more emotionally charged than in New York. This was an early test for me. Would I support Ronald Reagan, the man whose coattails helped get me elected?

Early on, I made clear my opposition to introducing more high-tech weapon systems into the Middle East. AWACS would not stabilize the region or enhance Saudi security. Saudi Arabia did not need AWACS to protect itself from Iran. AWACS were not a deterrent and would not help the Saudis defend themselves if Iran attacked. These sophisticated systems also could pass, either inadvertently or intentionally, into the hands of Israel's more actively hostile neighbors.

I was convinced that the AWACS sale was just another boondoggle for some contractors to make billions of dollars, and could destabilize a volatile region. This was not just some theory. From the Nixon administration through the Carter years, we sold tens of billions of dollars of military equipment to the Shah of Iran to keep him in power and to counter a possible Soviet threat to the Middle East. Despite this sophisticated hardware, the Shah fell to a fundamentalist revolution. All of the Shah's missiles, jets, and radar were no match for the Ayatollah Khomeini's revolutionaries. And now the West faced a militant Islamic state armed to the teeth with weaponry obtained from the United States and its allies. The same thing could happen in Saudi Arabia.

With emotions running high over the AWACS, the White House knew that the vote would be close. Even after I told Reagan's aides that I was going to vote against the sale, President Reagan invited me to visit him alone in his personal living quarters. This kind of one-on-one meeting was extremely rare. The President asked me to reconsider my position on the AWACS sale. He stressed how important this vote was for him. It was one of the first tests of his foreign policy and a loss would damage his prestige at home and abroad. The issue, he argued, went far beyond Israel and Saudi Arabia. The Kremlin would be looking at this vote.

It's not easy to say no to Ronald Reagan. They didn't call him the Great Communicator for nothing. Reagan had the uncanny ability to persuade you of the correctness of his position. He used all of his beguiling Irish wit and every ounce of Hollywood charm to get me to see things his way.

But I still told him no. New Yorkers would never forgive me if I reversed a vote on something so critical. Never easily dissuaded, Reagan switched strategy. Without missing a beat, he turned to me and said that he understood I couldn't go back on my word. "Maybe," he suggested with a sly wink, "you could miss the vote." I countered that missing the vote would be worse than switching sides. I would be a hypocrite and alienate everyone. But I can still remember his charming smile and powers of persuasion. I voted, and I voted no to the AWACS sale.

That same year, I took a stand in the Senate for Israel that I will never forget. In 1981, the Israelis learned that Iraq, using French technology, had built a nuclear reactor capable of producing weapons-grade plutonium. Suddenly the world faced the prospect that Saddam Hussein could process nuclear weapons. In September 1980, he had already demonstrated his thirst for power by launching the Iran-Iraq War. Now Hussein could hold the world hostage.

While other countries worried and waited, Israel acted. On June 7, 1981, in a surprise strike, Israeli jets put Iraq's reactor out of business. The Israelis knew that if Iraq acquired nuclear weapons, they would be the first target–either of outright attack or nuclear blackmail.

Diplomatic reaction to Israel's raid was fast and furious. The United Nations and European states condemned Israel. American politicians also worried about Israel's bold stroke. Virtually alone, I praised Israel on the Senate floor. Saddam had threatened to destroy their nation. The Israelis saw a bully and they cut him down to size. I was impressed, and I said so.

After my remarks, my friend and colleague Senator Warren Rudman of New Hampshire approached me. Warren would be known as the "conscience of the Senate" by the time he retired in 1992. He attributed my remarks to the large Jewish vote in New York. He asked, "Alfonse, would you have taken the same position if there were four hundred thousand Iraqis in New York?" He was teasing me, but also raising a legitimate question. I responded that since my days on the streets of Newark I knew a bully when I saw one and that Israel had done what was right. Also, only 4 percent of Jewish voters had supported me the previous November.

To fully appreciate Israel's wisdom in taking out Iraq's reactors, you have only to look at what happened nine years later. When Saddam Hussein challenged the world with his brazen seizure of Kuwait, the first thing he did was threaten Israel with imminent destruction. In fact, as soon as U.N. forces, led by the United States, attacked his positions, Hussein launched Scud attacks on Tel Aviv. Imagine the destruction if he had possessed nuclear weapons to go with his missile delivery systems. Even a limited nuclear exchange between Israel and Iraq might have plunged the world into nuclear war. Israel was right to take out the Iraqi reactor in 1981. I said so then, and I'm proud that I did.

AN AMICABLE SEPARATION

My first year in the Senate passed in a blur. As Christmas 1981 approached, Penny and I planned a Sunday afternoon Christmas party at the Island Park American Legion Hall for all of our Island Park friends. I was eager to be with my family in a room filled with friendly faces. But it was just my luck that the Senate was in session on December 13, 1981. In my fourteen years here, the Senate has had only a handful of Sunday sessions, and this had to be one. Since I couldn't be there, we set up speakers at the Legion Hall so I could telephone and express my thanks to everyone.

Later that night, forty or fifty of our friends migrated from the Legion Hall to Tom and Marilyn Brennan's house, just doors away from our own. During a break in the action on the Senate floor, I called Penny to ask her how it was going and to see how the affair at the Legion Hall went. I could tell from her voice that she was in no mood for small talk. After twenty years of marriage, I didn't need a telegram to know Penny was mad. This was supposed to be a Christmas party with our friends. And now it was a shambles, with Penny left holding the fort. I could tell from her voice that it was more than just the party, more than just this one disappointment. It was much, much more. I heard it when she said, "It's over."

I asked her, "What's over?," but I knew exactly what she was talking about. I didn't need her to tell me, "You know exactly what I'm talking about," but she told me anyway. She told me she wanted a divorce. She told me that she wasn't going to do this anymore. "This" meant sharing the life of someone who spent almost seven days a week in Washington, meeting with constituents, or raising money for campaigns. It was just too much. The spoiled Christmas party was the last straw.

It was the most devastating phone call of my life.

Penny and I soon reached an amicable separation. Penny remains the same brilliant woman I married. Though she received her master's and spent many years teaching art, she also followed her natural affinity for math and went back to school to receive several degrees in math and computer science. She is now an associate professor of math at Nassau Community College.

I am proud that Penny and I have never allowed our differences to get in the way of our love for our kids. In fact, Penny once paid Lorraine's tuition at Lehigh University without even telling me. I found out only when I received a notice from the bursar's office informing me that Lorraine's account had a $7,500 credit. How could this be? I called Penny, and she said, "I saw the tuition bill on the table and thought you might be a little short of cash, so I paid it. After all, Lorraine is my daughter too." She went on to say, "I knew you'd pay me back when you got the chance."

After thirteen years of being legally separated, Penny and I recently divorced. We still maintain a close friendship and share holidays and special occasions together with our four children and six grandchildren.

THE
PAPAL
ASSASSINATION
PLOT

I was barely into my freshman term when the world was shocked by the attempted assassination of Pope John Paul II in St. Peter's Square, Rome, on May 13, 1981. During a year that saw increased East-West tensions, the assassination of Anwar Sadat, and the attempt on President Reagan's life, the shooting of the Pope stood out as an assault on all that was sacred. In the nearly two thousand years of the Roman Catholic Church, the 1978 election of the first Polish Pope had been a dramatic, if not cataclysmic event. For millions of Eastern Europeans under totalitarian Soviet rule, the ascension of one of their own to the papacy must have seemed like divine intervention.

Pope John Paul wasted no time. His 1979 visit to his native Poland produced an outpouring of both Catholic and nationalist fervor that Brezhnev's puppets in Warsaw could not control. Speaking before 6 million delirious Poles, the Pope condemned communism with unprecedented bluntness: "No country should ever develop at the cost of enslavement, conquest, outrage, exploitation, and death." Months after His Holiness's triumphant reception in Communist Poland, the Solidarity labor movement erupted in the Gdansk shipyards. By the fall of 1980, the Polish regime seemed on the verge of toppling. Inspired by the Pope, and led by a charismatic electrician named Lech Walesa, millions of Poles were thumbing their noses at Communists from Warsaw to Moscow. It was the first major crack in the Iron Curtain.

I first saw the Pope in December 1980. After traveling to Northern Ireland, I went on to see the damage from the devastating earthquake in Southern Italy. I was amazed by the cold indifference of some Italian officials toward Southern Italians. I had always known of this regional prejudice but had never seen it demonstrated with such callous disregard. After I mentioned to Italian Senate President Amintore Fanfani that people were freezing, he callously observed that Southern Italian people just didn't know any better. I coolly responded that my mother and father were from the South–that ended our conversation.

I then had a chance to meet the Pope and share my concern for Southern Italians. When our conversation switched to the Solidarity movement, the Pope turned and said, "Yes, but that was an earthquake of a different kind. That was a man-made earthquake." He was quite proud of the upheaval that his countrymen were bringing about.

I saw him less than a year later, and he was a different man. The effects of the assassination attempt were obvious. He looked as if he had aged ten years. I had returned to Italy with my father and John Zagame, with relief money for the earthquake victims. We traveled down to Avalino, the village my father's family came from. It was a proud and moving moment for us. My father got a real kick out of the fact that most Italians thought that *he* was the senator. They called him "Il Senatore." I'd be the first to admit that my father certainly looked more like a senator than I did.

"Il Senatore" and I later had the rare privilege of visiting His Holiness at his summer castle in Gandolfo. The Pope was recuperating from his gunshot wounds. It was an amazing sight. As we sat in his room, he would go to his window and greet the thousands of pilgrims who had come to wish him well, speaking to each delegation of nuns, children, and faithful in their native language. He was obviously in pain, but had lost none of his radiant charisma. That afternoon remains one of the most moving of my life.

On this second trip to Italy, I encountered Monsignor Hilary Franco, a remarkable priest who would profoundly affect my life for the next several years. A former New Yorker from Staten Island, he had worked in the 1950s for Bishop Fulton Sheen on his world-renowned television show. In 1981, Monsignor Franco worked in the Vatican's liaison office for the Americas. He was high in the Vatican Curia. At one point I asked him what seemed a natural question, "Don't you want to be a bishop?" He replied without missing a beat, "Why would I want to be a bishop? I help make bishops."

But the monsignor had not come to talk about his career. He told me that the highest authorities of the Vatican believed the KGB was behind the assassination attempt on the Pope. I was taken aback by his certainty. In the United States, after the initial shock, the papal plot was largely dismissed as the work of a madman. Franco painted quite a different picture. He made the case that the Bulgarian secret service was behind the assassin Mehmet Ali Agca. How else could Agca have escaped from a Turkish jail into Bulgaria, stayed at Sofia's finest hotels, and moved freely between Bulgaria and Italy? In 1980, Bulgaria was one of the most Stalinist of the Eastern bloc countries. Nobody traveled freely without the state's approval. Agca's travel and hotel expenses would have amounted to tens of thousands of dollars. Where, Franco asked, did this supposed lone assassin get this money?

Franco explained that the Bulgarian secret service was simply an extension of the KGB. The Soviet's relationship with Bulgaria was always much closer than that with the rest of Eastern Europe. While the Poles, Germans, and Czechs saw the Russians as invaders, the Bulgarians revered the Russians as their liberators from the Turks. A statue of Peter the Great in Sofia symbolized the bond between Bulgarians and Russians. Nothing went on in Sofia without Moscow's approval.

To Franco and others in the Curia, the Soviets tried to kill the Pope because he would be with his people if the Russians ever invaded Poland. Franco cited a letter that the Pope had sent to Brezhnev saying as much. Facing a showdown with the spiritual leader of the world's Catholics, the Soviets decided to take him out.

Franco's theory was both fantastic and frightening. I asked how he knew about the letter to Brezhnev from the Pope. That's when he floored me. "Senator, I know because I delivered the letter to Brezhnev." I wondered why this theory did not have any currency back home. I found that Franco's KGB theory had many adherents in Rome. In fact, the Italians were surprised not by the KGB's alleged involvement, but rather by Washington's blatant policy of indifference.

When I returned to Washington, I told the CIA about Franco's revelation. Its reaction was both surprising and alarming. The CIA claimed never to have heard this story before and showed no interest in following up on it.

I had been an active member of the Commission on Security and Cooperation in Europe—the Helsinki Commission—which monitors human rights violations in Eastern Europe. During early 1982, the commission held hearings on the attempt on the Pope's life and made little headway.

Five months after my disappointing meeting with the CIA, I was amazed to watch an NBC *White Paper* on the papal assassination plot. Marvin Kalb talked to a darkly lit figure about Soviet involvement in the plot. Despite the poor light I could tell that it was Monsignor Franco speaking. Why had the CIA claimed ignorance of a theory now being broadcast on network TV?

In 1983, I assembled a staff for yet another trip to Italy. This time our sole purpose was to gather information on this incredible case. We were discouraged by both the CIA and the State Department. I had been talking with Angelo Codevilla, an aide to Senator Malcolm Wallop on the Senate Intelligence Committee, about the papal plot. Codevilla was fluent in Italian and extremely well informed. At the last minute, for reasons never satisfactorily explained, CIA Director Bill Casey convinced Chairman Barry Goldwater that Codevilla's participation in my trip would be a bad idea.

I went anyway, accompanied by my aides Mike Hathaway and John Zagame. We organized our own meetings with the Italian investigators, the Vatican, and our contacts in Rome. We also met with Judith Harris, who had assisted Claire Sterling, the brilliant reporter would later publish *The Time of the Assassins,* a study of the papal plot. In Rome, I again learned that the CIA had deemed the papal shooting a "low priority." No investigators were assigned to it. Before leaving Rome, I met with the CIA's chief of mission to discuss my conversations with Franco and others. Unlike the Italians, he treated the Vatican's theory with complete contempt. In fact, he barely looked up to acknowledge my presence and rudely polished his briefcase as I spoke. He treated me like an annoyance, and completely dismissed the opinions of the Italians I had met, saying only, "We've been trying to teach those birds how to be spies for years."

The CIA's Rome office so adamantly denied any KGB involvement in the papal plot that its position came to be known as the "cult of disbelief." Claire Sterling takes a much harsher view, saying that the CIA office resorted to "sleazy artifice and deliberate distortion" and maintained a position that hardly diverged from the Bulgarian government's press releases.

Why was the CIA so willing to frustrate our friends and allies in Italy?

Why was the CIA so willing to frustrate our friends and allies in Italy and to placate Bulgaria?

Upon returning from Italy, I could not disguise my frustration. "From the CIA's attitude," I said, "you'd think that Agca went to St. Peter's Square to shoot pigeons. We don't want U.S. intelligence to interfere with the Italian investigation, but they should try to ascertain the facts. We have a right to know." I was determined to inform President Reagan and the American people.

Within a week, I met with the President's national security adviser, William Clark, at the White House. I bluntly criticized the agency and minced no words in speculating on the reason for its inaction. By now I had learned that the CIA feared that if it made noise about the KGB and the Pope, the Soviets would retaliate by disclosing a major CIA blunder in Poland.

The CIA had recruited an Italian labor leader, Luigi Scricciolo, to funnel covert funds to Solidarity members in Poland. To its surprise, Scricciolo was a Bulgarian spy. He had provided the names and locations of the CIA's Solidarity contacts to the Soviets. The Scricciolo saga was a double disaster: not only had we betrayed our contacts, but the KGB was handed proof of Solidarity's receipt of CIA money. Now the Soviets could discredit Solidarity as an American pawn. Perhaps this terrible gaffe, I told Clark, was why the CIA ignored the papal plot.

Less than forty-eight hours after briefing Clark, some strange things began to happen. Jack Anderson's office called to inquire about a rather innocuous story he was thinking of running. They claimed that my daughter Lisa had used Senate facilities while in Washington to print six hundred copies of her term paper. I couldn't believe my ears. Why would Anderson's office call about such an outrageous story? I spoke to Lisa, who did not know what I was talking about. "Daddy, what would I do with six hundred copies?"

When I called Anderson's staffer back, he questioned me in a way that indicated he had obtained a moment-by-moment itinerary of Lisa's activities. It was eerie to think that Lisa was under such close surveillance. I was rattled when I got off the phone.

Within twenty-four hours, I was called by a reporter for *Time* magazine who said that a story was scheduled to appear in a European magazine accusing me of being an operative for the American Mafia. The article claimed that I had traveled to Italy not to investigate the papal assassination but to retrieve $12 million that the American Mafia had allegedly given to the Italian army to ransom U.S. General James Lee Dozier, whom the Red Brigades were holding hostage at the time. The European magazine was a known conduit for stories planted by the CIA.

At this point, I arranged to meet with CIA Director Bill Casey through his counsel, Stanley Sporkin, now a federal judge. Given the strange things that were happening, I did not want a public battle with the CIA director. Casey and I buried the hatchet. After I promised not to criticize the CIA, Casey confirmed my suspicions about Agca's Bulgarian connections. He told me that Agca had described "with specificity" the living quarters of the head of Bulgarian Airlines in Sofia, thereby link-ing him with Bulgarian intelligence. The next week, President Reagan ordered a thorough investigation of the Pope's assassi-nation.

PROUD TO BE SENATOR POTHOLE

In 1981, with a Republican in the White House and a Republican Senate majority, I was New York's link to federal aid. Over the years the federal government had shortchanged New York. We sent billions to the federal Treasury while other states got the lion's share of projects. In the 1960s, Lyndon Johnson made sure that Houston received billions in NASA appropriations. Other senators used their clout to bring military bases to the Sunbelt. Even liberal Massachusetts–thanks to the combined clout of House Speaker "Tip" O'Neill and Ted Kennedy–received more than its fair share of defense dollars. On the other hand, New York saw the Brooklyn Navy Yard and other military facilities disappear and, with them, thousands of jobs. While New York's senators made grand pronouncements on foreign affairs and public policy, other states beat us when it came to getting federal bacon. I set out to reverse that trend.

My desire to fight for New York sometimes ran counter to the Reagan administration's desire to cut spending. One of my early battles was to oppose a proposal by my friend Secretary of Transportation Drew Lewis to cut federal subsidies for mass transit. Our state would have lost more than $250 million a year, and commuters on the subways, buses, and the commuter rail lines

Long Island Railroad and Metro North would have had to pay much higher fares. I would not go blindly along with the administration on this.

For me, transportation is not a liberal-conservative issue. It is a people issue, one that can't be measured in dollars and cents. Mass transit is the very heartbeat of New York. My mother and father had courted on the trolleys, subways, and the Hudson Tubes. My mother and grandmother dragged me around Brooklyn on the el train on shopping sprees. Long Island would be a tough place to live without the LIRR.

In December 1982, the Reagan administration sought to impose a nickel a gallon tax on gasoline. This was controversial for a tax cutter like Reagan. The bill's passage was hardly assured. As a member of the Transportation Subcommittee of the Appropriations Committee, I made it clear to Chairman Richard (Dick) Lugar that I would support the five-cent tax increase only if one cent was set aside for mass transit. As Indiana's senior senator, Lugar did not care that much about mass transit. My administrative assistant, John Zagame, was tenacious in the negotiations with Lugar's bright young assistant Mitch Daniels. Just when it looked as if all would be lost, I allied with other northeastern senators, including Arlen Specter and John Heinz of Pennsylvania. We convinced Majority Leader Howard Baker that we would kill the whole tax if we did not get a share for mass transit. In the event, the one-cent set-aside has brought approximately $1.5 billion to New York. During this fight, I met Dick Ravitch, the chairman of the Metropolitan Transit Authority (MTA), one of the unsung heroes of New York's turnaround in the 1980s.

New York's liberals were suddenly in the uncomfortable position of watching a Reagan Republican deliver for our state. It was around this time that I was first dubbed "Senator Pothole." Though some in the highbrow media used this nickname to ridicule me, I was proud to fight for the people of Buffalo, the Bronx– and Island Park.

Many in the Reagan administration were shocked at my independence and were constantly sniping at me. While I supported the administration's goals of cutting taxes and scaling back government, some of their schemes would have devastated New York. In 1985, I opposed eliminating deductions for state and local taxes and interest on mortgage payments. Millions of New Yorkers itemized their taxes and got to deduct such taxes and mortgage interest from their taxable income. Without those deductions, they would be getting socked, and the economy of every town, village, and household in the state would suffer.

Reagan had just won reelection by a landslide, and now it seemed that one of the most extreme supply-side theories was being jammed down the nation's throat. On June 7, 1985, Pat Buchanan, the President's communications director, said that the high-tax states had a "neo-socialistic" approach to government. Buchanan apparently wanted to punish states like New York. I joined Democrats Koch, Cuomo, and Moynihan in loud opposition to the plan to eliminate deductions on state and local taxes. Senator Moynihan and I offered a "sense of the Senate resolution" criticizing the proposal. With television cameras rolling, Bronx Democratic Congressman Mario Biaggi and I staged our own "Boston Tea Party" to protest this $4 billion "double taxation" on New York taxpayers. We lobbed boxes of tea into New York Harbor and blasted the proposal. (We later had the tea picked up so we wouldn't be charged with polluting the East River.) We were accused of grandstanding, but our bipartisan efforts prevented the ruinous tax "simplification" plan from being enacted.

A CALL FROM THE WHITE HOUSE

One of the great triumphs of the Reagan administration was its commitment to increase our military readiness in the face of the Soviet threat. As our defense budget grew, I tried to make sure that New York got its fair share. We worked with Navy Secretary John Lehman to bring the Homeport for the battleship *Iowa* to Staten Island. With Homeport, we not only created more than five thousand new jobs but provided a base for the navy at *one tenth* the cost of a new facility. We persuaded Secretary Lehman to use existing New York port facilities and private sector housing for navy personnel. By combining New York resources and smarts, we brought the navy back to our harbor.

My House colleague and roommate Congressman Guy Molinari of Staten Island played an important part in Homeport's success. When the final details were still being worked out, I organized a lunch at Angelo's restaurant in Little Italy, where we had had such a wonderful time with my folks and President Reagan. There were about fifteen of us. It was a reunion of sorts—we had all served in either the Reagan campaign or the administration. It included my old roommate Dominick DiCarlo (now a federal judge), U.S. Attorney Rudy Giuliani, former Assemblyman Al DellaBovi, and Ambassador Charles Gargano. After an hour went by and Guy Molinari was still not there, the owner told me there was a phone call from Navy Secretary Lehman.

I wondered why on earth Lehman was calling me here. And where was Molinari? I barely had a chance to get to the phone when the everybody started screaming, "It's Molinari, it's Molinari!" I asked my press secretary Zenia Mucha who was calling. Zenia is as tough as she is smart. She's used to handling everyone from the White House down to the savviest New York reporter. When Zenia assured me that it was Lehman, I left the room to take the call. A rather officious young woman's voice told me that Secretary Lehman was coming on the line.

Lehman and I had enjoyed a good working relationship, but this time I barely had a chance to say hello before he started chewing me out for leaking an announcement about New York getting the Homeport. "I'm deeply disappointed to hear from the New York media that the Homeport will be announced," he growled. "You knew this news was supposed to come from the navy." I was completely baffled, since I had made no such announcement. "Well, where could the leak have come from?" he demanded. "Who else have you told?" I assured Lehman that the only one I had discussed it with was Congressman Molinari. "You should be calling Molinari, not me."

All at once, the stern voice on the other end of the line broke out in laughter. "You gave me up. Just like that!" It *was* Molinari.

He had pretended to be Lehman to see if he could fool me. After a good laugh, he explained that he couldn't make lunch and sent his regards to the rest of the gang.

Well, didn't I feel like a jerk when I got back to the table. After I told them what had happened, they all enjoyed a good laugh at my expense. No more than ten minutes later, the restaurant owner told me he had a call from the White House. President Reagan was supposedly trying to reach me. Molinari was going too far. The room exploded with, "It's Molinari, it's Molinari!" It was one thing to pull my leg, but impersonating the President was too much. Once again, a young secretary's voice assured me that the President would be on the line. I wasn't going to fall for this again.

When a voice came on the line and said, "Senator," I bellowed back into the phone, "Yes, Molinari, now why don't you stop this bull!" There was silence on the other end.

"Senator Al? Is this Senator Al D'Amato." The voice was unmistakable, and it was not Guy Molinari's. I realized with a sinking feeling how ridiculous I must have seemed to the President of the United States. I had half a mind to say, "Oh, you want *Senator* D'Amato. Hold on just a minute, I'll get him." I swallowed hard and said, "Mr. President, I didn't know it was you." To which he replied with his usual charm, "Well, I didn't think you did."

Needless to say, the President wasn't making a social call. The fact that he had tracked me down to Angelo's was a clear indication that it was pretty serious. He wanted my vote for the MX missile. He needed this new weapon system as a bargaining chip in our negotiations with the Soviets. I was inclined to support the President. But I should have taken this opportunity to make the case that New York was being overrun with drugs. Unfortunately, I was so embarrassed by my Molinari remarks that I quickly responded, "I'm with you, Mr. President." I returned to the table with a great story, but still kick myself for not asking for more funds to fight the scourge of drugs in New York.

I later had a chance to make my case, this time to White House Chief of Staff Jim Baker, who wanted to make sure that I would support the President on a close vote for funding of chemical weapons. Again, I was naturally inclined to support the President. I knew that we needed to maintain a strong negotiating position with the Soviets. Time has more than proven Reagan right. The arms race is over, the Soviet Empire has collapsed, and all of us, particularly the people of the former Soviet Union, are better off for Reagan's vision, guts, and determination.

When I met with Baker, I told him I would be happy to vote for chemical weapons if the administration would help New York stop the flow of drugs pouring into the state.

Jim Baker looked at me as if I said something distasteful. Perhaps he wasn't used to my style. Well, he'd have to get used to it. I wasn't asking for some political pork project. I was blunt, maybe too blunt for Jim Baker. "Look," I told him. "While you're calling me for help on this issue that has national and international consequences, there are issues that are vital to the life and survival of my people. And if this is the only time I can get you to pay attention, *by God, I'm going to do it*." To make a long story short, the President got my vote, and New York got the extra funding it needed.

LANDSLIDE

By 1986, I had even begun to win over some of my critics. Norman Ornstein of the American Enterprise Institute called me a pothole senator or an alderman senator, "an Everyman fighting for the working Joes." Even some Democrats like Ed Koch were outspoken on my behalf. "D'Amato's a terrier," Koch said. "Senator Javits was an institution. You couldn't talk to him like you [can to D'Amato]. . . . In one case, it's like talking to your father. In the other, it's like talking to your brother. You couldn't ask Jack Javits to be as attentive to all those items when he had a certain position in the Senate. It was more the grand view, as opposed to building the house." On another occasion Koch called me "a miracle worker . . . one of us. He's a true man of the people. Anyone who runs against him is going to have the fight of their lives on their hands. . . . I would find it very, very hard to work against Al D'Amato. Generally, he has come home with the bacon."

Before the Democratic primary in 1986, local Teamsters'

Union president Barry Feinstein, a power in the Democratic Party, endorsed me for reelection: "We believe nobody can do it better than D'Amato." Even Sandra Feldman, president of the United Federation of Teachers, had kind words, saying, "For someone we disagree with on a lot of things, D'Amato has been very responsive. There are countless little things you need a senator for, and he's been terrific. The mere fact that we could *conceivably* endorse D'Amato, that we *might* do it, is incredible."

I received praise from the African-American community, including Democratic Congressman Edolphus Towns of Brooklyn. "I'm not down here a week," Towns told the *Daily News,* "when I get a call that Senator D'Amato wants to have lunch with me. I thought it was a joke. We have nothing in common and I thought he was antiblack. So he sat me down at a nice lunch and said, 'I know we have different politics, but I want to work with you. If you have a problem, give me a call.' And he was as good as his word. He has helped. Let me tell you, it changed my mind about him. I was shocked."

In 1986, even Governor Mario Cuomo said, "He's delivered a lot of things for me." He would work for my opponent, however, because I was a Reagan Republican. But, Cuomo added, "If Reagan listens to D'Amato . . . we'll be all right."

Prominent Democrats ducked the 1986 race. My old nemesis, Liz Holtzman, was then the Brooklyn District Attorney and salivating to run against me. She had never conceded defeat to me in 1980 and felt she deserved to be in the Senate. If Geraldine Ferraro had not run for vice president in 1984, she would have been my 1986 opponent. After my 1980 election, Ferraro had wasted no time in letting it be known that she was ready to challenge me in 1986. She repeatedly took potshots at me. She believed—erroneously—that I had leaked stories alleging her husband was connected to organized crime.

I've noticed that the media delights in building someone up and then tearing them down. That's precisely what happened to Geraldine Ferraro when she ran for vice president. The press all but canonized her before she received the nomination and then went out of their way to destroy her. I had absolutely nothing to do with the stories that plagued her campaign. The emotional trauma that she and her family endured was surely a major factor in her decision not to challenge me two years later.

For a while, Harry Belafonte, the actor and calypso singer, toyed with the idea of running. I doubt he was really serious, but shortly after he made his interest known, the newspapers revealed that he had a number of unpaid parking tickets. Belafonte must have decided that this kind of scrutiny was not for him and called it a day.

Only Mark Green, who had worked for Ralph Nader, wanted to challenge me. Green was a second- or third-tier candidate. He was best known for his unsuccessful run in 1980 against Congressman Bill Green. Republicans then were concerned that some voters might pull the lever for the "wrong" Green. But even that was not enough in the liberal "Silk Stocking" district to help Mark Green, and Bill Green won by more than 20,000 votes. Bill remained Manhattan's only Republican congressman until he lost in 1992.

Things were looking pretty good for my reelection efforts. The big guns had decided to pass, and we had raised more than $3 million before the campaign had even started. Quite unexpectedly, a relatively unknown but extremely wealthy Democrat by the name of John Dyson announced his intention to run. Dyson had been Governor Carey's commissioner of Commerce, who had created quite a stir when he appeared before a State Senate hearing wearing a mask and depicting himself as the Lone Ranger. The senators were furious at what they saw as a disrespectful stunt and called for his scalp.

A conservative Democrat, Dyson would have a tough time winning the Democratic primary. Dyson would have you believe that he earned his money the old-fashioned way—hard work. But it came the easy way: Daddy—his father had an estimated $1 billion. Cuomo lined up enough support for Dyson to steamroll the Democratic nominating convention. Dyson was the antithesis of everything the Democrats stood for. He promised to spend whatever it took to win the seat and spend he did.

Mark Green fought tenaciously to win 25 percent of the convention delegates, so he could enter the Democratic primary. Without money or name recognition, the pundits gave Green no chance against Dyson and the Democratic establishment. Governor Cuomo also delivered the Liberal Party endorsement to the conservative Dyson. Here was Mario, supposedly my friend and admirer, making it possible for Dyson to run. More bizarrely, Cuomo had no use for Dyson. The two had clashed bitterly when Cuomo was lieutenant governor under Carey. Can you imagine the liberals who adamantly opposed the death penalty and nuclear power for New York endorsing Dyson? He championed capital punishment and mockingly claimed that the nuclear power plant at Shoreham, Long Island, was "safer than smoking a cigarette." Even for Dyson, this was a stupid statement. The Liberal Party had sold out its principles for years. Securing their endorsement now came down to the size of a candidate's wallet and promises of patronage jobs.

I was later told that after Mario had engineered the Democrat and Liberal endorsements, he called Dyson into his office and told him, in effect, "Don't call me again. I never liked you. I still don't." This proves the old axiom, "Politics makes strange bedfellows."

Over the years, Mario Cuomo and I enjoyed a good working relationship. Some claimed we even had a nonaggression pact. Our relationship benefitted New York, particularly with a Republican in the White House. But Mario was not content with just being a powerful governor. He had to be the nine-hundred-pound gorilla. When we both ran for reelection in 1986, he was obsessed with the need to win with a bigger margin than me and thus had to find a candidate with deep pockets, even if he had nothing but disdain for him.

I was not too pleased by Mario's activities. It's one thing to endorse your party's nominee, but quite another to line up support for your friend's opponent. His efforts for Dyson bothered me. While I never raised the subject with Cuomo directly, I mentioned it to several of his key aides, who were rather sheepish in their replies.

Dyson did not scare me. Even with his father's millions, he

lacked any real gray matter and was no real threat. If it weren't for his father's money, no one would have talked to him. The fact that Mark Green, without money behind him, managed to win 25 percent of the delegates, spelled trouble for Dyson. He went on to spend more than $6 million, mostly his own money and the most ever spent in a New York Senate primary. Even though he was outspent six to one, Mark Green still managed to trash Dyson with close to 60 percent of the vote. Despite early polls that showed him far behind, we always suspected that Green would triumph with liberal primary voters, who were far more likely to go to the polls. Dyson carried upstate precincts by a slim margin, while Green buried him in New York City.

With Green's victory, I no longer had to worry about a candidate who would spend a million a week on TV. Mainstream Democrats were not enthusiastic about Green. Buffalo's Democratic Mayor Jim Griffin came through again, saying, "Al D'Amato's always been there when Buffalo needed help." Former Democratic Congressman Lester Wolff of Long Island endorsed me, citing my efforts to stop the illegal flow of drugs across our borders. Congressman Sam Stratton praised my support for a strong military. My old friend Assemblyman Harvey Weisenberg, a former teacher, endorsed me because of my efforts to stop kids from using drugs. Because Harvey was himself running for reelection, his endorsement showed all too rare political courage.

Green's campaign deteriorated to character assassination. He falsely accused me of links to organized crime. His "evidence," pathetic as it was, rested solely on the fact that I testified as a character witness for Phil Basile, a local nightclub owner. I knew Basile, his wife, and his children for years. His wife, Arlene, volunteered on my 1980 campaign and our victory celebration was held at Phil's nightclub in Island Park. Basile was charged with submitting a false document to the federal government. He explained that he had allowed a local character, Henry Hill, to sell T-shirts of rock groups and entertainers at his club. One day, Hill came to Phil and begged him to provide proof of employment to Hill's parole officer. Phil provided him with proof of employment. He tearfully told me that he was not aware that this was a crime and that he had done it solely to help a pathetic and desperate person.

I realized that the media would criticize me if I testified even as a character witness for Phil. But I knew Phil to be a hardworking and truthful family man. And I knew he felt abandoned, so after testifying, I gave him a hug. That wasn't my smartest political move, but that's what I did. I never imagined anyone would try to connect me to organized crime because I was a character witness for a neighbor. Since then, profiles of me regularly include this story told in the most unflattering manner. I chose loyalty to a friend over political expedience.

Green also attacked me for being Senator Pothole. His tone was elitist and disdainful. "When it comes to the big issues," Green said in *New York* magazine, "D'Amato is a tourist in Washington. He does the nitty-gritty work, but I'd appoint five D'Amatos to do that kind of stuff. Do the people, when they're considering a U.S. senator, really care about the transportation grant D'Amato got for Rochester? I'm not so sure."

Connecticut's Lowell Weicker, one of the most liberal members of the Senate, took on Green's elitist view and came to my defense. "I was very close to Jack Javits. I was sour on D'Amato from the beginning. . . . But since then I've come to admire D'Amato greatly. He's been an incredible pick and shovel man for New York—and he hasn't had his head swelled by the Senate, which I thought could have happened very easily. He's stayed the same, and even though we violently disagree on a lot of things, especially social issues, he's been absolutely crucial on stuff like mass transit. He's proven that an assemblyman in the Senate is exactly what New York—and a lot of other states—needs."

Every time Green attacked me for my pothole politics, he lost more votes. In blasting me for supporting Wall Street interests, he completely ignored the fact that securities are to New York what cars are to Detroit and oil is to Texas. In the end, we buried Mark Green and his negative campaign by 650,000 votes. Even the *New York Times* said, "If Democrats are unhappy with D'Amato, they've kept it well hidden."

FRIENDS AND OTHER COLLEAGUES ON THE SENATE FLOOR

P undits say that the Senate is filled with one hundred presidents in waiting, but that's not really true. I have no desire to be president, and probably fewer than twenty of my colleagues really do. The Senate consists of one hundred different personalities who clash and compromise to conduct the nation's business.

THE TWO TEDS

One of my first friends there was Alaska's Senator Ted Stevens. Although there aren't two senators with such vastly different constituencies, I've learned a lot from Ted. He fought tenaciously to maintain air service to remote Alaskan villagers who otherwise would have been cut off more than a thousand miles from nowhere. He's the ultimate advocate for his state, even if that means ruffling feathers. Sometimes, in the "go along and get along" atmosphere of the Senate, some forget who sent them there. Ted Stevens never has. He never gives up.

While Ted Stevens is one of my close friends, that's not the case with the Senate's more famous Ted, Ted Kennedy of Massachusetts. I know we have very different politics, but ideology hasn't kept me from working with other liberals, including Chris

Dodd of Connecticut and Pat Leahy of Vermont. Delaware's Senator Joseph Biden and I are very close, and our boys roomed together at both Georgetown and Syracuse Law. We have never let politics interfere with our friendship.

Ted Kennedy is another matter. He is an extreme, disingenuous partisan. In 1987, his characterizations of Supreme Court nominee Robert Bork were unfair. Bork was a distinguished jurist, and he certainly did not want, as Kennedy claimed on the day of Bork's nomination, to force blacks to sit at segregated lunch counters or to allow rogue police to break down citizen's doors. While Bork's more responsible critics like Senator Biden debated constitutional law, Senator Kennedy's vicious personal attacks were not good for the Senate, the Supreme Court, or the country.

Senator Kennedy often does not live by the same rules that he imposes on the rest of us. In 1990, he attacked Kenneth Ryskamp, a Bush nominee for a circuit court judgeship, for belonging to a discriminatory country club. He warned that "persons who hope to serve in the Justice Department should not participate in discriminatory clubs. A resignation on the eve of the nomination is not enough to erase a professional career participation in bias." None of this mattered when one of Senator Kennedy's friends wanted to be assistant attorney general. In 1993, he conveniently forgot his own "rule" when Eleanor Dean Acheson resigned from a prestigious Boston country club—with no African-American members—just a month before her nomination. Kennedy's dual standards never cease to amaze me.

MY COLLEAGUES FROM NEW JERSEY

I admired "Dollar Bill" Bradley when he wore number 24 for the champion New York Knicks. He was a terrific competitor and New Yorkers still have a great deal of affection for him, and I'm glad I never had to run against him in New York. Bill's been a hardworking senator, but his biggest legislation has been a bust. He was one of the captains of the famous 1986 tax reform bill. This law had a disastrous effect on New York's real estate industry. It deep-sixed IRAs and added billions of dollars in cost to the savings and loan debacle. I never should have voted for this bill. I had my reservations, but the Senate has a pack mentality. I went along with the crowd and I regret it to this day.

I was not happy when Bill came into New York to campaign against me in 1992. He drew a lot of media attention playing basketball with Bob Abrams. This attempt to "humanize" Abrams made him look silly next to the great ex-Knick. He looked as ridiculous as the infamous ad with Michael Dukakis in the tank. Abrams didn't belong with Bill Bradley on the black top or in the Senate. Thanks, Bill.

I am particularly disappointed in Dollar Bill's colleague from New Jersey, Frank Lautenberg. I served with him on the Appropriations Committee from 1986 to 1994. We traveled together to Lockerbie, Scotland, to investigate the 1988 Pan Am tragedy that took so many American lives, including thirty-two students from my alma mater, Syracuse University. Frank Lautenberg also campaigned for Bob Abrams, but I write that off to politics. Cheap shots are something different.

> **Kennedy's dual standards never cease to amaze me.**

In 1994, Lautenberg appeared on the tabloid show *Inside Edition* to lambast his fellow senators for going to Utah. Former Senator Jake Garn holds an annual fund-raiser for Children's Hospital in Salt Lake City. More than ten years before, Garn's daughter desperately needed a kidney transplant and Children's Hospital performed the operation. Garn was the kidney donor. In appreciation, he sponsors an annual ski event. Over the years, the event has raised more than one million dollars.

In 1994, Lautenberg told Garn, "I can't go this year, because I'm running for reelection, but I'll be with you next year." Imagine the nerve when that same senator, who had attended the three previous years, went on TV to trash his fellow senators for going on a "junket." Lautenberg's grandstanding left a bitter taste in the mouths of many of our colleagues, Democrats included. I hope Frank got a lot of good publicity from his *Inside Edition* story, because it has certainly cost him a lot of goodwill. Shame on you, Frank.

Senator Garn's event also highlighted my own miserable skiing. Just before my last run, I told a reporter from *Inside Edition* that I didn't like to ski but I did it for Garn and Children's Hospital. Twenty minutes later I crashed and broke my shoulder in three places. Strangely, this mishap occurred no more than two weeks after Hollywood heartthrob Alec Baldwin told *Esquire* that he hoped I would hit a tree while skiing. I hope Baldwin doesn't put any more hexes on me.

Later in 1994, my singing caught public attention. In August, in protest over President Clinton's pork-laden crime bill, I serenaded the Senate with my own version of "Old McDonald":

> President Clinton had a bill,
> E-I-E-I-O,
> And in this bill he had some pork. . . .

After weeks of partisan wrangling over health care and crime, with the Senate in session weeks into its normal summer recess, I thought my little song would provide some much needed humor. Frank Lautenberg didn't see it that way and took the floor right after me. He had a temper tantrum, accusing me of smelling like "the stuff you find around the barnyard." Talk about thin-skinned. Afterward, I did promise my mother not to sing again on the Senate floor. Even my friend Senator Kay Bailey Hutchison of Texas told me, "Alfonse, I'm going to vote for you for chairman of the National Republican Senatorial Committee, but no more songs."

PETE DOMENICI

If you polled the chamber and asked who was the most liked and respected Senator, I'm sure that New Mexico's Pete Domenici would rank high on everyone's list. He has consistently supported cutting the size of your bloated federal government. No one has more knowledge of the budget than Pete. In fact, when President Clinton addressed the Republican members of the Senate shortly after taking office, he had nothing but praise for Pete's work as chairman of the Budget Committee during the early 1980s.

As an Italian-American senator from a state with a substantial number of Italian-American voters, I marvel how Pete wins with such tremendous margins in overwhelmingly Democratic New Mexico, where Italian-Americans constitute less than 1 percent of the electorate.

Both of Pete's parents were born in Italy. As a youngster, he actually saw the immigration authorities arrest his mother because she did not have her papers in perfect order. Even though his father was a naturalized citizen and a well-known business leader, these jackasses dragged Pete's mom out of the house in front of her eight-year-old son. Eventually the misunderstanding was corrected, but this incident gave Pete a special sensitivity to the hardships of immigrants. I suspect many of his Mexican-American constituents recognize this fact. Few senators possess Pete's guts, vision, compassion, and decency. I'm proud to be a friend of the senior Italian-American in the Senate.

PAUL LAXALT

Paul Laxalt of Nevada never got the public recognition he deserved. A longtime friend and confidant of President Reagan, Paul never once used that close relationship for personal or political advantage. He repeatedly refused his colleagues' requests that he solicit the President's support for their pet legislation. In a city where contacts are everything, where it's often who you know and not what you know, Paul Laxalt's wisdom and restraint reflected remarkable tact and grace.

I'll never forget that Laxalt personally assured me after the 1980 primary that he would fight to get the National Republican Senatorial Committee to fund my campaign instead of siphoning off funds for Javits as some party elders had wanted. He helped put me in the Senate.

ENTER LOWELL WEICKER

It's hard to imagine a friendship more surprising than mine with Lowell Weicker, the former senator and governor from Connecticut. Perhaps no Republican has been a greater anathema to conservatives than Weicker.

I first met Weicker through my friend and fellow Long Islander Mickey Chasanof. In 1980, Mickey took a great deal of grief from his friends when he backed my attempt to unseat Senator Javits. Weicker called Mickey and asked him to contribute to Javits. He was shocked when Mickey told him, "Lowell, I've always supported your requests, but not this time. I'm helping Al D'Amato." Weicker went off on a tirade and told him I was some kind of ultra-reactionary kook who would be shellacked in the primary. Mickey held firm and bet Weicker $10 that I would win. He never collected on the bet, but instead insisted that Weicker join Mickey and I for a Sunday breakfast right after my election.

As we sat down to breakfast, I was impressed by Weicker's imposing physical presence. He is a big bear of a man. I don't see eye to eye with him on most social issues–from busing to the death penalty–but I admire his willingness to stick to positions, no matter how unpopular. President Clinton could certainly use that trait.

In 1986, the Reagan administration sought to freeze cost-of-living adjustments for Social Security. I was dead set against it. When President Reagan called me over to the White House to twist my arm, I told him, "Mr. President, I was your campaign manager in New York State [in 1984] and we won. One of your commitments was that you were not going to touch Social Security. Yet here you are proposing to freeze it." He argued that he wasn't cutting it, but I countered that a freeze was as good as a cut to the poor. Then, the President took me into his confidence and told me he didn't really like the cuts either. I said, "If you don't like it, why are you pushing it? He told me, 'It's Packwood's idea.' " Reagan didn't like my opposition, but said, "I respect your position."

Reagan's class didn't stop the Senate leadership from hound-ing me down to the last minute before the vote. As things got tense, I hid in Lowell Weicker's office. I knew no one would ever look for me there. Lowell got a big charge out of hiding me.

The Republican leadership finally prevailed. To secure the fiftieth vote, they wheeled in Senator Pete Wilson from his hospital bed, where he had been recovering from surgery. Vice President Bush cast the tie-breaking vote. Senate Republicans patted each other on the back for their great courage. "What were we celebrating?" I asked myself. I feared this vote would end the Republican Senate majority, and that's what happened in November 1986. Even worse, after making Republican senators walk the plank, the administration dropped its support for the freeze and it was never even considered by the House. I'm still shocked by the naïveté of my Republican colleagues for celebrating a victory that would be their undoing in the next election.

The media doesn't help by reducing every major vote into a life-or-death referendum on the President. Democrats who saw Bill Clinton pass his huge 1993 tax hike with Al Gore's tie-breaking vote immediately celebrated. They "saved" Clinton's presidency. But this "victory" proved even more costly. In November 1994, voters reminded Clinton that they remembered that he had promised a middle-class tax cut. This broken promise propelled a Republican landslide that saw us win control of both the House and the Senate. The people had justifiably said, "It's time for real change, not just broken promises."

MY "FIGHT" WITH HOWARD METZENBAUM

There comes a time when you have to take a stand. For years, I had watched Senator Howard Metzenbaum of Ohio hold up legislation on the Senate floor. He single-handedly blocked hundreds of provisions from becoming law because he decided that they weren't good or because he didn't have sufficient time to study them. It didn't matter to him if ninety-nine other senators agreed. Howard was nicknamed "the gatekeeper," and he enjoyed the fact that any senator trying to make a last-minute change or add an amendment to a bill literally had to get his permission. It didn't matter if Howard knew nothing of the issue and the senator seeking an amendment had worked months or even years on a bill. Howard was a dictator. Senators who had been Howard's colleagues for years or who had even more seniority had to plead with him.

I never said anything about this nonsense until the 1993 deficit reduction bill came up for approval. The real estate industry in New York was in desperate shape. I was offering an amendment to right a wrong we had enacted in 1986. This amendment would not cost taxpayers one penny and had the support of everyone in the Senate but Howard.

"The gatekeeper's" staff told my staff that Senator Metzenbaum objected to the provision. Senator Moynihan, chairman of the Senate Finance Committee, supported this measure. His staff tried to convince Metzenbaum's staff and were confident that they had satisfied all of Metzenbaum's "concerns." But Metzenbaum persisted.

The Democratic and Republican leadership asked me not to go forward because Metzenbaum threatened to hold up the entire bill with a filibuster. To say that I was annoyed is an understatement. I was livid. Howard had offered absolutely no reasonable explanation for his opposition. Every question he raised had been answered. He was just opposed in principle to helping the real estate industry. His obstruction left me furious and speechless, but not for long.

With only seconds to go before a final vote on the bill, who do you think tried to win unanimous consent to pass an amendment? "The gatekeeper" himself. If I had blinked, I would have missed it. His amendment, about "orphan" drugs, had been cleared with the leadership of both parties. It was clear sailing. I've often heard my mother use the expression "What's good for the goose is good for the gander." I was determined to use Metzenbaum's tactics against him. I had no idea what his provision was about. I was mad, and I frankly didn't care if all ninety-nine of my colleagues signed off. When the clerk asked whether there were any objections to Metzenbaum's amendment, I said, "I object." I was immediately surrounded by my colleagues asking me why and telling me it was a good amendment. I responded that Metzenbaum had all day to consider my amendment but had capriciously killed it. The clerk called out a second time and I objected more than once. I had had it. It was time to give Metzenbaum a dose of his own medicine.

Metzenbaum finally asked me what was wrong with his amendment. I didn't beat around the bush, and I think this sort of took him by surprise. I told him my amendment was pretty good too, but "you refused to allow its consideration." I told him that "if you'll reconsider my amendment, I'll reconsider yours." It was as simple as that. I was blunt. But given the circumstances, I was reasonable. Metzenbaum was furious, bellowed at me, "Drop dead," and stalked off in a huff.

The next week, the *New York Times* wrote about this incident in an article titled "Backstabbing in the Senate." Metzenbaum's staff fed this story to the *Times* and created the impression that I was less than forthcoming in my actions. In fact, what shocked Metzenbaum and the others about my behavior was how upfront I was. If other senators wanted to acquiesce to Metzenbaum's self-appointed role as "gatekeeper," that was their business. I just wasn't going to play that game anymore. To Metzenbaum's credit, the next day he apologized to me for his "drop dead" remark. I told him I'd heard worse.

FILIBUSTERS

Of all the parliamentary weapons at a senator's disposal, the filibuster is the most extreme and dramatic. A filibuster allows a single senator to hold up business—no votes can be taken, no bills introduced—as long as the senator holds the floor. Sometimes, the minority can use the filibuster, or just the threat of one, to kill a bill or to force the majority to shape it more to the minority's liking. When one or just a few senators filibuster, it is often to make a point, to demonstrate that they will not go quietly along when something they care strongly about is threatened.

There have been two occasion when I felt compelled to filibuster. In October 1986, I filibustered to stop the Senate from cutting funding for construction of the T-46 trainer jet, which was to be built on Long Island. The T-46 was a good and needed plane. I had a report from the independent General Accounting Office (GAO) to back me up. My colleagues were annoyed, if not angry, but I was determined to make the point that it was unfair to cut funding for the T-46. The GAO report supported the plane, but the old-boy network was killing it. It angered me that this kind of politics got in the way of doing the right thing. The air force had strongly urged the development of a new plane, testifying that "the old one cost too much to maintain" and that it was "throwing money down a hole" to continue to repair them. The chairman of the Armed Services Committee, Senator Barry Goldwater, wanted to stop the T-46. I was told that the reason Goldwater so vehemently opposed the plane was that an old friend of his, a former general who had been working at the plane's manufacturer, Republic Fairchild, was dumped after it won the contract. In the end, I got fewer than a dozen votes. Republic Fairchild closed its plant on Long Island, and New York lost thousands of jobs and hundreds of millions of dollars. The filibuster taught me an important lesson. Even though the facts, especially the GAO report, were on my side, it didn't matter. Not every battle is won on the merits. Barry had lots of friends, and an upstart New Yorker wasn't about to roll the chairman of the Armed Services Committee no matter how right I might have been.

SMITH-CORONA AND THE BETRAYAL OF AMERICAN BUSINESS

Six years later, in October 1992, I faced a similar situation. The Smith-Corona Company, located in the little town of Cortland, New York, was the last American maker of typewriters. It was on the ropes and ready to relocate its factory to Mexico. Smith-Corona's management didn't want to desert New York, but they were being unfairly underpriced by Brother, a large Japanese firm.

The Brother/Smith-Corona story sadly illustrated how our government has permitted the destruction of a significant portion of America's manufacturing base. Congress simply has not had the guts to protect our companies from unfair foreign competition.

Smith-Corona was getting killed by Brother because Brother was dumping its typewriters in the American market. This isn't hyperbole, it's fact. It was proven on eight different occasions by the U.S. Commerce Department. Brother could afford to sell its products in the United States at unfairly low prices because in Japan, where it had no competition, it sold its products at much higher prices. In effect, Brother used its Japanese monopoly to subsidize its destruction of competition in the United States. Once Brother obtained a monopoly here, it would raise prices for American consumers. Even though Smith-Corona had dramatically increased its efficiency, Brother's unfair competition was driving it out of business.

But, you may ask, if the Commerce Department had proven that Brother had been dumping on eight occasions, why was nothing done? Good question. Brother *circumvented* the law by manufacturing its parts and components in one place and assembling the machines in another. If the Commerce Department found that Brother was guilty of dumping a machine assembled in Singapore with parts manufactured in Malaysia, Brother would simply import machines manufactured and assembled in other countries. It was a vast shell game, and it lost America business.

The CEO of Smith-Corona promised me that if Congress outlawed circumvention of the antidumping laws, he would keep the company's plant in Cortland. Otherwise, he would be forced to relocate to Mexico. Senator Moynihan and I included the necessary amendment in the 1992 tax bill. Our amendment then had to be reconciled with the House's version of the bill. Somehow, during that conference committee meeting, our circumvention provision was dropped. *Who did it?* Both Senators Moynihan and Dole had blessed this amendment. It took serious clout to remove it. Who killed it? Was it Finance Committee Chairman Lloyd Bentsen of Texas? House Ways and Means Chairman Dan Rostenkowski? No one would say.

Brother has its American headquarters in New Jersey and Senator Bradley of New Jersey, a member of the Senate Finance Committee, worked behind the scenes to eliminate the circumvention provision. It turned out that IBM had a business relationship with Brother and had used all of its lobbying clout to kill the provision. The Japanese also pay more than $300 million a year for their lobbyists in Washington, and they now were getting their money's worth. The noble ideal of free trade becomes a joke when you have one side buying the other's government and rigging the rules.

Brother had established a "phantom" plant in Tennessee Congressman Don Sundquist's district, where no real manufacturing took place. It was merely an assembly plant where components made all over Asia were put together. Brother used this plant to circumvent our antidumping laws. Brother put great pressure on Sundquist. If the circumvention provision went through, Brother would close its Tennessee plant. It's amazing how the Japanese have pitted us against each other. Here, a congressman who faced the loss of jobs in his district was used to destroy thousands of New York jobs. I later learned that the day *before* the circumvention provision was officially dropped, Sundquist was proudly announcing that he had "saved" the Brother plant.

I can understand Sundquist fighting for jobs in his district. But the consequence of his success was that our laws continue to be circumvented and high-paying American manufacturing jobs lost. Smith-Corona wasn't the first instance of this economic larceny, and it certainly won't be the last. I was determined to bring the whole story to light.

When I found out the circumvention provision was removed, I was mad beyond belief. At ten o'clock that night, I took to the Senate floor and started to speak my mind. I didn't know how long I would talk. Two hours. Three hours. In the end, I didn't stop speaking for fifteen hours and fifteen minutes. While I wanted the world to know of the betrayal of Smith-Corona, I was also biding time. I figured if I could hold up Senate business, I might get Senate Majority Leader George Mitchell to include my provision in the conference report and to ask the House to accept it at the last minute.

Filibusters are about filling time. As anyone who has spoken in public knows, talking for a minute can be an eternity. To begin with, I read the names of hundreds of people at Smith-Corona who would lose their jobs. I read each employee's job record, and talked about their home towns, their seniority, and the difficulty they would have finding comparable jobs. I serenaded the Senate with my best version of "South of the Border–Down Mexico Way"–because that's where our jobs were going. Because I thought Senator Bentsen had to be part of the dropping of our provision, I sang "The Yellow Rose of Texas" just to get under his skin. As the evening wore on and turned into morning, I grew testier. I blasted Brother for threatening to shut down their plant if the circumvention provision was adopted. That was as good as saying, if we can't compete unfairly, we can't compete at all. I was sarcastic, angry, outrageous, and I was on my feet the whole time. If you sit down you lose the floor, and that's the end of the filibuster.

Some of my colleagues took offense at my remarks. Wendell Ford of Kentucky criticized me for calling Congress "a bunch of turkeys." He thought it was beneath the dignity of the Senate to talk that way.

At about ten o'clock the next morning, Senator Bentsen quizzed me about my singing "The Yellow Rose of Texas." Did I hold him personally responsible for dropping the provision? Of course I did. But I didn't say that to him. In the Senate, we fight battles every day and try not to be blatantly confrontational. In this case, I regret my lack of candor. I should have said, "Yes. You are the Senate Finance Committee chairman. You are responsible for everything that goes through your committee. Why did you shortchange New York workers by participating in this shabby spectacle?" I didn't say that, but I should have.

Filibusters can have a grating effect on other senators. I've been accused of using them to grandstand. Senator Mitchell called it one of D'Amato's "six-year filibusters." During my fifteen-hour ordeal, Mitchell complained audibly to an aide about having to listen to me harangue at three in the morning. He muttered that "watching baseball games was preferable to listening to Alfonse talk on and on and on." Well, someone overheard his remark and told someone else, and soon rumors were flying that Senator Mitchell was resigning to be the next baseball commissioner. Later that week some team owners even called to feel him out about the job.

I was on my feet for over six hours when Senator Moynihan came to the floor and, in an act of grace and courage that I will never forget, joined me in the filibuster. In a filibuster you can yield the floor only for the purpose of a question. Senator Moynihan came to my rescue by posing some of the longest and thoughtful questions I have ever been asked. He spoke passionately about having been a cosponsor of the provision and his shock and amazement that no one told him that it had been dropped. He then asked if I had been informed and I would answer no. We worked together in this manner for hours. Often his "questions" would involve reading long passages from the tariff act. At several times, the chair admonished Moynihan, reminding him that he could ask questions but not make speeches. He was giving me a chance to rest my voice.

Even with Pat Moynihan's generous strategy, I could not leave the chamber for any reason. Talking for fifteen hours makes you thirsty, but drinking water would have only made my life more difficult. I would moisten my lips occasionally, but that was it. At once point I had a coughing fit, but I went on.

From four in the morning until after noon the next day, the Al and Pat Show stopped the Senate in its tracks. A little after noon, we learned that the House had gone out of session and would not act on any new provisions or initiatives. Our amendment was dead. At this point, Pat suggested that there was no point of continuing.

At 1:15 P.M., I finally yielded the floor. Pat Moynihan, in an act of class, commented that "his friend and colleague from New York has fought a valiant fight. Nobody could do more." It took guts for Senator Moynihan to come to my side. I was in a tough reelection fight with Bob Abrams and some Democrats might hold his support for me against him. He added credibility to my efforts.

I didn't realize how long I had been speaking until I sat down. At fifteen hours and fifteen minutes, I had completed one of the longest filibusters in Senate history. Strom Thurmond holds the all-time record—more than twenty-four hours.

One of the first questions everyone asked was, "Alfonse, how did you do it? How did you hold it in? Did you have a catheter?" No, I didn't. I knew from around 7:00 P.M. that I was going to take the floor, so I drank no liquids from then on. I purged myself before taking the floor and after that I basically shut myself down. You can contract your muscles. After a while it's not a problem. In fact, I had done too good a job of shutting myself down. For some time after my speech, I was having difficulty getting my system going again. I panicked for a while, but finally, after a big bowl of chicken soup and a cup of coffee, I was back to normal.

The Al and Pat Show stopped the Senate in its tracks.

Back in New York, where my battle with Bob Abrams was going down to the wire, the Democrats assaulted my filibuster as election-year grandstanding. As usual, they were wrong. Wouldn't I have preferred to have saved the jobs? Wouldn't that have been better for the state *and* my campaign? Perhaps my filibuster—and to some degree Pat's participation in it—did demonstrate one of the qualities that helped get me reelected. It reminded people that while you may not agree with D'Amato on every issue, he's not afraid to take a position and fight.

MY FRIEND AND COLLEAGUE, PAT MOYNIHAN

I have served with Senator Pat Moynihan for the last fourteen years. He has served New York with distinction. He is a historian, scholar and statesman. I am proud to work with him and to be his friend.

I will never forget his concern when my brother Armand was unjustly found guilty of trumped-up charges in May 1993, a verdict that was eventually thrown out on appeal. We were both scheduled to speak at a rally to save Griffis Air Force Base in upstate New York. The federal commission on base closings was set to announce its decision, and we feared that Griffis was on the chopping block. When I got to the airport, Pat told me that he had just heard the news about my brother's conviction on the radio. Pat said, "Al, you don't really want to go to this rally, do you?" I told him I would rather be with my family–particularly my parents, who were devastated by this awful news. Pat agreed and he promised to represent me and tell the people that "Al D'Amato has been with you in the past and is with you now." And that's exactly what he said at the rally.

A few months later I had the chance to help Pat. As chairman of the Senate Finance Committee, he was saddled with the almost impossible task of passing President's Clinton's budget package. I offered to represent Pat at a rally to save the Plattsburgh Air Force Base and to read his statement to the crowd. Lieutenant Governor Stan Lundine, a Democrat, got wind of this and decided to preempt me by reading Pat's statement. I was ticked off that Lundine had bullied one of Pat's staff into letting him read the statement. This added fuel to an already simmering fire. Several months back, Lundine had publicly joked that "Al D'Amato belongs on the TV program *America's Most Wanted.*" I decided I wasn't going to let him publicly ridicule me and upset Pat's wishes. After I told Lundine that I was sick of his antics, he put his hands on my chest. I then said, "Take your hands off me and if you ever touch me again, I'll knock you on your ass."

The whole incident would have been remained a private tiff between Stan and me had the mayor of Plattsburgh not leaked his version of the incident to the press. To his credit, Stan Lundine played the whole matter down and even joked about it.

TAKING ON
NORIEGA

One of the things I'm most proud of is my successful war with the two-bit, drug-running dictator of Panama, Manuel Noriega, who is now spending the rest of his life behind bars in a federal penitentiary.

A good friend of mine and an early supporter from Long Island Harold Bernstein, chairman of Northville Industries, had been involved in building a pipeline across Panama. Because the Panama Canal was too small for supertankers, this pipeline would permit the shipment of Alaskan oil from the Pacific to the Atlantic. In 1981, I attended the pipeline's dedication with Senator Frank Murkowski of Alaska. On this trip I met Gabriel Lewis, the former Panamanian ambassador to the United States. Ambassador Lewis and other business leaders were concerned that following the death of Panamanian strongman Omar Torrijos in a plane crash, the Panama Defense Forces (PDF) under Noriega had effectively taken over the country. While the business community had tolerated the PDF's minor corruption, the defense forces under Noriega had become a vicious mafia bent on controlling the entire economy. The concerns of Ambassador Lewis and his friends struck home. Their stories of terror, including murder, rape, and sadism, were bloodcurdling.

Noriega had succeeded General Torrijos as the head of the PDF. Many prominent Panamanians, including Colonel Diaz Herrera, the deposed chief of staff of the Panamanian military, held Noriega personally responsible for the crash that killed Torrijos. When Dr. Hugo Spadafora, another Torrijos subordinate, refused to be silenced by Noriega's threats, he was murdered and his body was dumped in Costa Rica. Spadafora's corpse revealed Noriega's sadistic handiwork. His fingernails were removed and his testicles garroted. His groin muscles were slit to facilitate homosexual rape. And the quantity of blood in his stomach indicated that his head had been slowly cut from the still living body.

Noriega's sadism was matched only by his greed. The PDF's extortion tactics destroyed legitimate business while Noriega turned Panama into a money-laundering center for international drug cartels. Soon Noriega was receiving a cut of practically every dollar that changed hands. The government had its finger in every pie: clear-cutting of the rain forest for sale of lumber to the Far East; the sale of export-import end-user certificates so Cuba could avoid embargoes; kickbacks on every government purchase; the sale of guns to guerrilla groups; the sale of passports to nervous Hong Kong citizens wary of the upcoming 1997 Communist control; and, of course, the sale of drugs.

Noriega was not satisfied with "private sector" extortion. He made a fortune bilking foreign governments, including our own, for "intelligence" services. The Reagan administration reportedly paid $185,000 a year to Noriega, primarily for allowing Panama to become a transshipment point for arms to the Nicaraguan contras.

The United States had had Noriega on our payroll almost continually since 1959. He was also paid by the Japanese, Taiwanese, Israeli, Cuban, Nicaraguan, and French intelligence agencies. He mastered the art of making himself appear valuable to everyone, even as his regime was sinking deeper into corruption and decay.

In the course of bilking American taxpayers, Noriega co-opted the support of many high-ranking United States officials and former officials, including Admiral Dan Murphy, the former deputy director of the CIA, and Nestor Sanchez, assistant secretary of defense for Latin America in the International Security Affairs Division of the Pentagon. Sanchez had known Noriega for many years and was probably the person closest to Noriega in our government.

Of all the United States agencies that were bamboozled by Noriega, the Drug Enforcement Agency (DEA) takes the cake. In the midst of the Reagan administration's war on drugs, Noriega was smart enough to provide the DEA with its biggest success story in Central America. More drugs were seized, more cocaine-processing plants were shut down, and more dealers were busted in Panama than in any other Latin American country. The DEA refused to believe that Noriega was simply turning in his drug-dealing competitors or punishing Colombian operators who refused to pay him off. The DEA's director continued to write flowery letters praising the general long after everyone knew that Noriega was hip-deep in drug trafficking, money laundering, and much more.

By April 1987, I was convinced that Noriega had to go. He was a menace not only to his people, but to our country. I knew that Noriega had established his own cheering section in the CIA, Defense Department, and DEA. He would never be taken out without leadership from Congress. The previous year, I had led an effort to pass legislation requiring the President to certify that those countries receiving U.S. aid cooperated in our antidrug efforts. I subsequently supported a Senate resolution condemning Panama for failing to fully cooperate with our drug crackdown. Although the administration lobbied strenuously against the resolution, it passed with 58 votes. In the end, however, it had no effect. The President simply certified that Panama had cooperated in our drug-control efforts, and our aid was not stopped. Noriega's relationship with too many agencies was simply too cozy.

While the Reagan administration turned a blind eye toward Noriega, things in Panama were getting worse. I received a visit from Ambassador Lewis and an old friend, Colonel John "Riverboat" Campbell. Campbell had been the army liaison to the Senate and was knowledgeable about Panama's internal affairs. He told me how Noriega had just fired his chief of staff Diaz Herrera after Herrera had revealed many of the regime's outrageous crimes to the Panamanian media.

Noriega blasted my Senate resolution and attempted to stir up anti-American sentiment by accusing the United States of trying to renege on the Panama Canal treaty. In response to his nonsense, I sponsored an "open letter" to the people of Panama, in the hopes of bolstering dissent against Noriega and putting pressure on the Reagan administration to act. A bipartisan group of thirteen senators signed the letter. I also started to build support for a far tougher resolution.

Noriega's detractors in the Senate could not have been further apart: a group of conservatives, led by Jesse Helms, and a group of liberals, led by none other than Teddy Kennedy. These two senators openly disliked each other, so getting them to agree on anything was just short of impossible. I also knew that Ted Kennedy was not exactly thrilled with the prospect of working with Al D'Amato! To secure Kennedy's cooperation, I worked through Minnesota's Dave Durenberger, a Republican who was fairly close to Kennedy, to ask if he would support our efforts against Noriega. This strategy worked, and for the first (and perhaps last) time in history, Ted Kennedy, Jesse Helms, and Al D'Amato cosponsored a resolution. Unlike the administration's pussyfooting, this resolution was very specific and very intrusive. It called for Noriega to step down and for an independent investigation into the charges of murder, election fraud, drug dealing, and money laundering. On June 29, 1987, the Senate approved the resolution by a vote of 84 to 2. Some senators later told me that they voted for it because anything that could bring together Helms, Kennedy, and D'Amato had to be right.

The next day marked the beginning of the end for Manuel Noriega. In response to our resolution, he organized a demonstration during which his hoods stoned the American Embassy. After this act of audacity, no administration official would support him. Only Noriega's influence within our government allowed him to survive for as long as he did.

To keep the heat on Noriega, I proposed that the United States stop military and economic assistance to Panama unless certain conditions—concrete progress toward civilian control of the government, an independent investigation of crime and corruption within the PDF, and restoration of constitutional rights—were met. In September 1987, the Senate voted 97–0 to adopt legislation to terminate United States assistance to Noriega's Panama.

I followed up this resolution with tough letters to President Reagan, Secretary of State George Shultz, and Secretary of Defense Frank Carlucci demanding that we sever all ties with Noriega. Carlucci took my letter as a personal offense. He fired back a letter accusing me of charging that he and the Joint Chiefs were "cowards" who "supported a drug dealer." He then circulated this letter to Secretary of State Shultz, National Security Adviser Colin Powell, and White House Chief of Staff Howard Baker before having the courtesy of sending it to me. I was amazed by Carlucci's response. The United States had to stop this bully Noriega.

In late 1987, Panama's President Eric Arturo Delvalle had his ambassador, Juan Sosa, approach John Zagame, my former administrative assistant. Sosa told Zagame that Delvalle was a constitutionalist and a Democrat, and that he wanted us to help get rid of Noriega. I then met with Sosa and was impressed by his determination. These people were fighting for their country.

From that day on, John Zagame worked steadily with the pro-democracy forces in the Panamanian Embassy. I contacted George Shultz and his assistant secretary for Inter-American Affairs, Elliot Abrams, and started to build support within the Reagan administration for the anti-Noriega forces. In December 1987, Sosa summoned Zagame to the embassy. He wanted to talk, but they would have to do so outdoors. Walking in the bitter cold weather, Sosa informed Zagame that Delvalle was ready to throw down the gauntlet. As president, he would ask Noriega to resign as the head of the PDF. Of course he knew the dire consequences. He, Sosa, and their colleagues would have to set up a government in exile. The Washington embassy would become their base. He needed to know if we were behind him. While he could never speak for the Reagan administration, Zagame assured the ambassador that I would do all I could to back them up.

Delvalle was as good as his word. On February 26, 1988, he called for Noriega's removal and was instead ousted by the Noriega-controlled National Assembly. Delvalle fled into the jungle and Sosa established the Washington embassy as a headquarters of a government in exile. When Noriega's new ambassador tried to take residence, they were refused entrance in front of camera crews from CNN and the networks. We used CNN to flood Panama with images of real dissent.

With the Senate solidly against Noriega, and a Panamanian government in exile right on Washington's Embassy Row, the Reagan administration finally began to act. In April 1988, it ordered all American companies and their Panamanian subsidiaries not to pay fees to Noriega's illegitimate regime. The fees went instead to an account set up for the Delvalle regime at the Federal Reserve Bank of New York. This measure, which had been taken in the past only against Iran and Libya, was a serious step, but I warned that it was not enough to get rid of Noriega. He respected only force.

Meanwhile, encouraged by our actions in the Senate, and unbeknownst to the Departments of State and Defense or the CIA, aggressive federal prosecutors in Miami and Tampa were assembling a massive case against Noriega for drug trafficking and money laundering. By the time these cases reached the highest levels of the Justice Department they could not be squashed without a huge uproar.

Despite this activity, the Reagan administration continued to waffle. In May 1988, the idea was floated of dropping the drug charges against Noriega if he would resign. Putting a pretty face on this outrage, White House spokesman Marlin Fitzwater stated that "this amounts to a plea bargain." I was much blunter on the Senate floor and said, "What we have here is an administration that's set its hair on fire and is trying to put it out with a hammer." Not exactly Shakespeare, but the press carried it all week. The resulting outrage from the floor of the House and Senate, and from Democrats eager to run against George Bush in November, put an end to talk of plea bargaining.

I tried everything to persuade the Reagan administration to move more forcefully against Noriega. In late May I held a press conference with Ambassador Sosa to urge other Latin American governments to take action against Noriega. Two days later, Noriega approached the *New York Post* through lawyer Barry Slotnick, and in the story that ran, he invited me down to meet him, "mano a mano." I knew Noriega was bluffing, but I couldn't help being tempted by his offer. By singling me out as a foe, Noriega actually gave me one of the biggest compliments of my life. The next day, I rejected his invitation and replied with one of my own: I would be more than happy to arrange the general's surrender to the U.S. Attorney in Miami.

For the next year and a half, the sad stalemate wore on. Our economic sanctions squeezed the life out of the legitimate Panamanian economy while Noriega and his henchmen continued to cling to power. Well into the first year of the Bush administration, Noriega continued to thumb his nose at the drug indictment and our efforts to remove him. There were many dark days for the brave Panamanians who defied him. Many were in what seemed like permanent exile. Delvalle, once a prominent and wealthy businessman, was growing weary hiding for his life. I once had to send John Zagame down to Panama to meet with him in the hills and to assure him that we would not let them down. There were days when I could barely convince myself.

In October 1989, hopes were raised and dashed as a brave thirty-six-year-old Panamanian officer Moises Giroldi led a coup against Noriega. Giroldi and his men captured Noriega in his compound. They asked only that the U.S. military in Panama come to the roof and pick him up. As minutes ticked by, Noriega taunted the young officer that he didn't have the guts to kill him. When the United States failed to provide the helicopter, Noriega picked up a pistol and shot the brave young officer. He then had each of the coup plotters tortured and mutilated. It was a horrible atrocity, and not one of the Bush administration's finest moments.

Having humiliated Uncle Sam once again, Noriega went off the deep end. He began to harass and to detain American civilians. Some reports indicated that he was badly addicted to cocaine and that at times he had lost touch with reality.

What finally led us to war? In the case of Operation Just Cause, it really started with a trip to a bordello. One night in December, an American colonel and two enlisted men spent too long in the Torrijos section of Panama City. A curfew was on, and there was a roadblock, but the last thing they wanted was to be caught in an international incident and have to explain to their wives and families where they had been. So the colonel ran the roadblock, and a Panamanian soldier opened fire and killed him.

This time, the President finally had enough of Manuel Noriega. The U.S. government, which had coddled, paid, pampered, and stroked this villain for thirty-plus years, was ready to act. The government that wouldn't even send a helicopter in October would respond with overwhelming force and firepower by December. Colin Powell, Chairman of the Joint Chiefs of Staff, insisted on thirty thousand troops—a massive force. We hit on December 20, 1989, and laid waste to the entire neighborhood that housed the PDF. During this invasion hundreds, including twenty-four brave American soldiers, died. As George Bush's first year in office came to an end, the liberation of Panama became a symbol of his toughness and decisiveness. We should have acted much sooner.

PART III

CRISIS AND REDEMPTION

TAKING
HEAT AND
FIGHTING
BACK

In 1986, Democratic voters deserted Mark Green in droves. He lost by a landslide. Even Mario Cuomo, who was running for re-election used a quote from me in one of his TV commercials. Union voters, teachers, blue-collar workers, and voters of every ethnic and racial stripe repudiated Green's elitist brand of politics.

To be honest, I felt vindicated. My razor-thin margin of 1980 was now but a memory. I had worked tirelessly to get money for housing, bridges, roads, mass transit, and schools, and for projects to put New Yorkers to work by the tens of thousands. The voters approved my manic pace. The voters appreciated that I went the extra mile to keep my promise to fight for the forgotten middle class.

Having been in politics for twenty-five years, I had some sympathy for Mark Green. Losing is never easy. But I will never forgive Mark Green's disgusting campaign to reverse the voter's decision by attacking me, my family, and friends. He lost to Senator Pothole fair and square. But Green was a sore loser. He complained to the Senate Ethics Committee that my efforts for New York were only to raise contributions and line the pockets of my supporters. This was shown to be complete nonsense, but Green must have though that if he couldn't beat me at the polls, he would misuse the Senate Ethics Committee and make false charges in the media to try to destroy me.

To many people, the mere fact that I was investigated meant I was guilty. Green's charges, made in 1989, came when Congress was rocked with scandal. Speaker Jim Wright had been forced to resign. The Senate was investigating the "Keating 5." The savings and loan crisis was in the headlines. Respect for politicians, always shaky, was at an all-time low. The establishment press, never a friend of Al D'Amato, was under tremendous pressure from the tabloids to concoct outrageous stories.

But Mark Green did not choose tabloid television to launch his vindictive attack on me. Right after filing his ethics complaint, he wrote an article in *The New Republic,* a favorite of inside-the-beltway writers, reporters, and opinion molders. He began his article, not with a concrete establishment of the facts, but with a "conversation" between himself and an unidentified "Italian, Republican cabdriver" who allegedly referred to me as a "real sleaze, a lowlife." This fictitious cabbie tells Green that he wouldn't have voted for me if he knew about "all of the stories and scandals coming out."

Mark Green's litany of complaints filled the headlines with a steady drumbeat of doubt, accusation, and innuendo. Every day I was being cut a thousand little ways. I had done nothing wrong, but Green had turned my greatest strength, the delivering of services to my constituents, against me. He made being Senator Pothole seem sinister. My approval rate dropped while my negatives soared. I was slowly bleeding to death.

My friend and lawyer Mike Armstrong summed up my predicament when he told *Newsday* in April 1990: "Do you dignify the lies by answering them and thereby creating more stories? Or do you take the position 'I better answer this stuff or its going to look like I'm acquiescing.' It's a problem. You don't want to give more publicity to lies by trying to answer them, particularly when your answers don't get reported accurately by the publications that carry them."

People I had known for years were shying away from me. In

1986, when I had a 70 percent approval rating and won by a landslide, my phone never stopped ringing. Everyone–from congressional candidates to county committeemen–wanted my advice, support, and endorsement. I had my picture taken with every local candidate from Brooklyn to Buffalo. I spoke at local charity events, communion breakfasts, and high school and college commencements. I *was* a U.S. senator who was not too busy to speak at a local parish or to cut a ribbon or to raise money for a local United Way. After Green's smear campaign began, the phone stopped ringing and the invitations no longer arrived. Even though I was never charged with any crime, people expected me to be dragged off to jail at any moment.

The unfounded personal attacks hurt my parents and children. Even though they never said anything, I could sense they wished I had never become a U.S. senator.

Green was a sore loser.

Mark Green's complaint provided ammunition to the liberal press. *Newsday*'s Sydney Schanberg seemed fixated on destroying my reputation. Because Schanberg was a columnist, his utterances did not have to be supported by the facts. Schanberg was a pretty formidable opponent. He had won a Pulitzer Prize when he was at the *New York Times* for his reporting on Cambodia, which was later immortalized in the movie *The Killing Fields*. Schanberg was portrayed by Sam Waterston. But Schanberg's relentless and misguided war against the Westway project was his undoing at the *Times*.

Westway was an ambitious project to rebuild the dilapidated West Side Highway in New York City. Since the days when my grandpa Alfonso had run a restaurant near the docks, the West Side of Manhattan had lost most of its waterfront activity. The buildings, docks, and wharves had burned, rotted, or deteriorated. In 1974, a delivery truck fell through the elevated part of the West Side Highway. For many, this event symbolized the decay and near bankruptcy of New York City. Governors from Rockefeller to Cuomo supported Westway. The federal and state governments stood ready to allocate billions to restore the highway and to refurbish much of the waterfront.

Schanberg wrote a steady stream of inaccurate stories that mobilized local groups against Westway. In the end, Schanberg and the "just say no" wing of New York's liberal establishment killed a project that would have created thousands of jobs. To this day, the West Side Highway is still an eyesore and embarrassment to New York.

Schanberg may have beaten Westway, but he also enraged his boss, Arthur (Punch) Sulzberger. The *Times*'s publisher and his friend, Chase Manhattan Bank chairman David Rockefeller, adamantly supported Westway. According to the stories I've heard, the defeat of Westway earned Schanberg his pink slip.

Schanberg wasn't unemployed long when *Newsday* picked him up. Although this Long Island tabloid is the nation's sixth-largest newspaper, it must have seemed mighty local to Schanberg. After all, he had been to Vietnam and seen the horrors of Cambodia's Khmer Rouge. He had bashed Rockefellers and halted a multibillion-dollar project. What worlds could he conquer from Melville, Long Island?

Then Sydney Schanberg looked around and saw me. I was a self-righteous liberal do-gooder's dream come true. He described me as a "politician on the take from the crooked machine politics of Nassau County to the Court of Reagan and Bush." I was manna from heaven. As a *Newsday* columnist, Schanberg had an unchallenged soapbox to bash me in my home turf of Long Island. From the time of Mark Green's ethics charges until election day 1992, Schanberg wrote dozens of negative columns about me. Jack Newfield, the columnist for the *Voice* and later for the *New York Post,* remarked that "Al D'Amato broke Sydney's writer's block."

Every several days, Schanberg filled his column with vitriol and innuendo against me. There was no way for me to refute his steady drumbeat of charges. Although my staff was consumed with answering press inquiries, our explanations were buried in distorted stories that got blaring headlines.

Journalists all too often behave like a pack of vultures. A wounded senator makes a great target and good headlines. Dozens of reporters smelling blood went for the kill. *Newsday*'s Bob

Winter 1949: In front of fireplace at Mamma and Papa D'Amato's Island Park home: Grandpa and Grandma Cioffari, Alfonse D'Amato, age twelve, father Armand D'Amato, Sr.

1955: Chaminade High School Flyers track team. Al D'Amato is seated second from left.

The Flyers' mile relay team are, SITTING: W. LaBorne, A. D'Amato, J. McAuliffe, N. Sergi, J. Davis. STANDING: J. Ingarra, J. Schramm, J. McQuade, E. Skou, G. Clements, J. Derrick.

LEFT

1969: Hempstead Receiver of Taxes Alfonse D'Amato being congratulated on his new position by the outgoing Receiver Henry Von Elm (left with pipe) and D'Amato's grandfather, Alfonse Cioffari.

BELOW

September 1980: At Hempstead Holiday Inn campaign headquarters, senatorial candidate D'Amato declaring victory in Republican primary over Senator Jacob Javits.

LEFT

October 1981: Monsignor Hillary Franco (far left) holding a reception in honor of Senator D'Amato in Rome where he first told the Senator about the KGB involvement in the assassination attempt on the Pope. Also in photo: Cardinal Oddi (second from left) and Mrs. Maria Pia Fanfani, wife of Italian Senate President and later Prime Minister Amintore Fanfani.

1984: President Ronald Reagan and Nancy Reagan in New York, with New York Archbishop John Cardinal O'Connor, meet Mamma D'Amato.

BELOW

October 1985: New York City Columbus Day parade with Mayor Koch and Governor Cuomo.

LEFT

February 1986: Senator D'Amato as chairman of the Helsinki Commission on Human Rights meets with Elena Bonner (with glasses), the wife of Soviet dissident Andrei Sakharov, and David Rockefeller (sitting with glass) in NYC.

July 4, 1986: One hundredth anniversary of Statue of Liberty celebration in New York Harbor at Governors Island. It was also Mamma and Papa D'Amato's fiftieth wedding anniversary. Left to right: nephew Andrew, Papa, Mamma, the Senator, daughter Lisa Murphy, first grandson, Gregory, son-in-law, Jerry Murphy.

July 4, 1986: President Ronald Reagan and wife Nancy's surprise drop-in at Mamma and Papa D'Amato's fiftieth anniversary celebration. Left to right: Senator D'Amato's sons, Daniel and Christopher, brother Armand, Jr., with his son, Andrew, Papa D'Amato, Mamma D'Amato, President Reagan, Nancy Reagan, Senator D'Amato, grandson Gregory, daughter Lisa Murphy and son-in-law, Jerry Murphy.

Summer 1986: With President Reagan at the White House.

July 10, 1986: Benjamin Bear, chairman of the Federal Parole Commission, U.S. Attorney for the Southern District Rudolph Giuliani, and Senator D'Amato don undercover clothes to buy crack from a dealer up in Washington Heights. The three men drove up to the dealer in a sports car with blaring rock music.

January 5, 1987: D'Amato swearing-in reenactment with Senate President pro tempore Thurmond at Willard Hotel in Washington, D.C. Left to right: Christopher D'Amato, Senator D'Amato, Daniel D'Amato, Mamma, Jerry Murphy (behind Mamma), Lisa Murphy, Senator Strom Thurmond, nephew Andrew, Papa.

January 5, 1987: Victory cocktail celebration at Willard Hotel. Left to right: son-in-law, Jerry Murphy, daughter, Lisa Murphy, first grandson, Gregory Murphy, Senator D'Amato.

April 10, 1989: Senator D'Amato in Washington shaking hands with Prime Minister Yitzhak Shamir with Majority Leader Senator George Mitchell (left).

August 27, 1990: Senators
D'Amato and Nunn are briefed
by four-star General Norman
Schwarzkopf, commander of the
Central Command, about the
U.N. buildup of forces in Saudi
Arabia after Iraq's invasion of
Kuwait.

September 1, 1990: Senators
Robert Dole, John Warner, and
Alfonse D'Amato in Prague,
Czechoslovakia, where they met
with President Václev Havel.

September 5, 1990: Senator
D'Amato meets Soviet President
Mikhail Gorbachev at the
Kremlin in Moscow as part of
Senate delegation. Left to right:
Senators D'Amato, Steve Symms,
Soviet translator, President
Gorbachev.

June 10, 1991: Senator D'Amato with Chairman of the Joint Chiefs of Staff General Colin Powell at the reviewing stand of the New York City Operation Desert Storm ticker-tape parade.

February 1992: New York Governor Cuomo and Senator D'Amato in "The Battle for the Mike" debate at the New York Association of Towns meeting at the New York Hilton.

August 1992: Senator D'Amato with grandchildren on Long Island.

August 1992: Republican convention in Houston. D'Amato said, "It was a disaster."

Early 1990s: Senator D'Amato at the keyboard of his piano in Washington office.

July 1993: Senator D'Amato with soon-to-be FBI Director Louis Freeh. D'Amato had proposed Freeh to President Bush as a nominee to the federal bench in New York.

August 1993: Senator D'Amato with youngest daughter Lorraine Paton and granddaughters Blair (in center) and Janet at Island Park public beach. It was the Senator's birthday party.

April 18, 1994:
Senator D'Amato with a catheter presented by (later New York State Public Service Commissioner) John O'Mara at Chemung County Republican dinner. D'Amato was given catheter by Alonso Borja, a heart surgeon, when he heard about the Senator's 1992 filibuster on behalf of Smith-Corona Company and thought this would give D'Amato even greater staying power. Senate Republican Leader Robert Dole is seated right.

June 4, 1994:
Salute to Israel parade in New York City with (left to right) future governor George E. Pataki, Senator D'Amato, comedian Jackie Mason, and Dr. Joe Frager, president of the Jerusalem Reclamation Project.

Autumn 1991:
"D'Amato Kiss Your 'Seat' Goodbye" man holding up poster is Mahmud Abouhalima, convicted in World Trade Center bombing. Photo is at an anti-Israel rally in New York City.

Greene, joined the "get D'Amato" hunt. His "Greene Team" put me under a microscope. One Friday afternoon, my press secretary Zenia Mucha called to say that Bob Greene insisted on talking to me. He had a story about me for Sunday and was on deadline.

Six weeks earlier, Greene had been working on a story about the scandals surrounding HUD, and asked me if I had requested any Moderate Rehab HUD funding for Sackets Harbor or any other community in New York. I told him I had not. Sackets Harbor is a village located on Lake Ontario, near the Canadian border with a population of 1,200. It had one of the highest unemployment rates in the state and was in desperate shape. Sackets Harbor's Mayor Vincent Cappazella had requested help from my Syracuse district office. My assistant there, Gretchen Ralph, made it her business to bring the plight of often overlooked rural communities to my attention. At Mayor Cappazella's request, Gretchen drove up to Sackets Harbor. What she discovered was heartbreaking. Situated on Lake Ontario were original barracks from the War of 1812. This historical treasure, on the National Registry as a historic site, was now rotting away. The mayor and local officials were seeking economic assistance to restore the barracks and turn this eyesore into a tourist attraction.

Gretchen promised help. When the village submitted an application for a federal grant, Gretchen sent a letter of support, under my signature, to the HUD secretary. This was normal practice, and the letter requested nothing out of the ordinary. Senators regularly send these kinds of letters. Gretchen was doing her job and doing it well.

Bob Greene accused me of lying about Sackets Harbor and offered Gretchen's letter as direct "evidence." I told him that I had no idea that my office had sent this routine letter, that the letter did not relate to the troubled Moderate Rehab HUD program, and that Gretchen had done the right thing.

On Monday, November 6, 1989, *Newsday* devoted a front-page article, complete with a picture of the letter, to say that I had deliberately lied about Sackets Harbor. They even doctored the letter, whiting out the address of my Syracuse office to create the false impression that the letter had been sent by my Washington office.

I got so angry at Greene for distorting Gretchen's letter that I broke a cardinal rule of politics. I spoke on local television and called Greene a "sleaze bucket." I should have known that it is never wise to attack a journalist. It didn't matter that I was right, or that *Newsday*'s alteration of Gretchen's letter was dishonest. I was further appalled by *Newsday*'s halfhearted attempt to defend its fabrication on "artistic" grounds.

By making Bob Greene a victim, I ensured that the Greene Team would join Schanberg's personal vendetta. Greene and Schanberg wrote about me with the kind of disdain and assumption of guilt usually reserved for mobsters.

It pained me that my family would read these fabricated stories. Children cannot understand why people would say such awful things about their father. When my daughter Lorraine was only sixteen, she turned to me in tears, and asked, "Daddy, are you connected?" I said, "Lorraine, what do you mean?" And she said, "You know, to the mafia?" I told her of course not and asked where she could get such an idea. She reluctantly told me that some of the kids at school said I was tied in with the Mob. It was awful to hear Lorraine say such things. We lived in modest circumstances. I had worked honestly for every penny I ever earned. I had to clean toilets to pay for law school. The D'Amatos had nothing to hide or be ashamed of.

During the twenty awful months of the Senate Ethics investigation, my son Dan's college graduation in 1991 was the darkest moment. Dan had attended Siena College, a small Catholic school run by the Franciscans near Albany. Dan and I liked the school from the first time we visited.

In the spring of 1986, the year before Dan entered, I gave the commencement address at Siena and received an honorary degree. It was a great day. I told the students and faculty one of my favorite stories—a valuable lesson with a touch of humor. It concerned a family with three sons. The parents had worked seven days a week to put their boys through school. Their effort was not in vain. Their oldest boy had become a doctor, the middle son an engineer, and the youngest an attorney. One day, after the boys had all become successful, the parents decided to go on a well-deserved vacation to Europe. Unfortunately, when they figured out the cost of such a trip, they realized that they could never afford it. The father turned to the mother and told her, "Don't worry, I'll ask the boys. They'll be glad to help us"—or so he thought. When he turned to his son the doctor, he told him he'd be glad to help out but all of his money was spent on his house. Then he asked the engineer, who replied, "I'd love to help, Dad, but I just bought a new car and the kids are all going to summer camp and you know how it is." That night he asked the third son, the lawyer, and he told the father that he'd love to send them to Europe but that he had just sunk his last penny in a new business venture.

That night the mother and father called the boys together and told them they had something to confess. "You see, your mother and I worked two jobs seven days a week to give you a good education, and while we were so busy scrimping and saving for you, we didn't even take out the time to get married." Well, the lawyer blushed and said, "Do you know what that makes us?" And the father replied, "Yes, and cheap ones too."

This little fable brought the house down and hopefully it made a few of the students more appreciative of their parents' sacrifices.

Parents are emotional at graduations, and I'm certainly no exception. The ceremony represents the sum of all your dreams for your child. They are adults now and on their own. You'd have to be a rock not to get a little choked up.

At Dan's graduation from Siena in 1991, I was more than choked up, I was hurt. You see, earlier in the year Dan had been asked to find out if I would be commencement speaker. I told him, "Yes, absolutely." I heard nothing further from him. Now months later, at his graduation, college officials treated me like the invisible man.

After rain threatened, the ceremony was moved into an overcrowded field house. I stood at the back and listened as the vicar of the Franciscans droned on and on about liberal education. My heart was never heavier. This should have been one of the proudest days of my life, but it was ruined. I felt like I had become an embarrassment to my son. I was crying inside.

And then sometime during that long and boring ceremony, a light went off inside my head. If I let things burn up inside me, I would be a defeated man. I had to turn my hurt and anger into determination. I made up my mind and said, "Stop feeling sorry for yourself, Alfonse. Stand up and fight." I vowed that I wouldn't let the Schanbergs, the Bob Greenes, and the Mark Greens run me out of office without a fight. I owed it to my family to fight for my reputation. I was filled with a new sense of purpose. I wasn't going to hold my punches any longer.

In early 1991, I learned that Mike Wallace and the celebrated program *60 Minutes* planned to do a show about my record and Mark Green's allegations. *60 Minutes* knew how to destroy people's reputations. While they had exposed their share of shady wheeler-dealers over the years, their tactics were often biased. They ambushed people with cameras and then edited those segments to make their subjects look guilty. More than five years earlier, I spoke with Barbara Walters at a party thrown by the lawyer Roy Cohn. Roy had just been mercilessly grilled on *60 Minutes* about having AIDS. He denied being gay or having the disease. His inquisitors then produced evidence from the National Institutes of Health that he had received treatment for AIDS. *60 Minutes* had no business badgering an obviously sick man, and invading his privacy. Roy Cohn was as politically incorrect as they came, and *60 Minutes* knew they could savage him and get away with it. Who would have sympathy for Cohn even if he was dying? It is ironic that *60 Minutes,* a program that purports to carry on the tradition of the celebrated newsman Edward R. Murrow, the man who cut Senator Joseph McCarthy down to size, had used McCarthyite tactics to attack McCarthy's protégé, Roy Cohn.

After seeing *60 Minutes*'s treatment of Cohn, Barbara Walters gave me some friendly advice, "Don't go on that program, Al, unless you do it live. Never, never, never."

Barbara Walters's warning was on my mind when I received

a call from Mike Wallace to tell me that *60 Minutes* was going to run a story containing some pretty nasty allegations, including charges tying me to organized crime. He asked me if I wanted to defend myself. I told Wallace that I had already known that *60 Minutes* was targeting me, and that a guy named Marty Bergman who raised money for Rudy Giuliani was producing the segment. The fact that *60 Minutes* was letting a fund-raiser for one of my political rivals produce a "news" show about me was incredible. I told Wallace that Bergman had been peddling this story all over town.

Three weeks later Wallace called again. He offered an "opportunity" to clear the air. Fat chance. "Would you like to try on this noose, sir," was more like it. I agreed to appear if I could speak live and unedited. I wasn't going to have them cut me up and spit me out and make me look like an idiot. I told Wallace that a live appearance was fair. Then my car phone disconnected.

I called Wallace back immediately and had at least two additional conversations with him. He asked me to come on, and I repeated my request to do it live and unedited. Then he told me that they never allowed anyone to appear live or unedited. "Not for you, Alfonse, not for the President, not the Pope." That's pretty much how we left it. Less than a year later, *60 Minutes* allowed Bill and Hillary Clinton to appear live to counter the Gennifer Flowers story. So much for equal treatment.

CBS ran promos for the *60 Minutes* segment with a clip making it look like I had hung up on Wallace. I had expected treachery from *60 Minutes* but now they were running phony footage of me supposedly hanging up on Wallace. It never happened. If this was only the commercial, God knows what they had in store for the actual "news" segment.

The show turned out to be a shabby moment in television journalism. *60 Minutes* quoted from such objective characters as Mark Green's campaign aide Mark Waldman. Without regard for the truth, *60 Minutes* trotted out Mark Green's baseless charges. But *60 Minutes* set new lows when they produced Henry Hill, who had gotten my friend Phil Basil in trouble, to level charges at me. Nick Pileggi's famous book *Wiseguys,* which inspired the film

GoodFellas, was based on Henry Hill's career in the mob. On *60 Minutes* Henry Hill, with his gravelly voice and mobster wannabe demeanor, declared that "the word on the street is that you can get to D'Amato." It made for great theater but it was totally false.

Right after the segment aired, Nick Pileggi was quoted in Jerry Capeici's "Gangland" column in the *Daily News*: "Henry Hill never met D'Amato, he never knew who he was," Pileggi said. "I went backwards and forwards with [Hill] on that, and he could never give me one detail I could pursue.' " The *Daily News* also quoted Edward McDonald, head of the federal Organized Crime Strike Force, who had also questioned Hill repeatedly about me and determined that he had no information about me.

60 Minutes did not bother to check Hill's story out. They simply allowed a convicted felon to slander a United States senator on national television. *60 Minutes* never wanted the truth.

Don't take my word for it. On April 30, 1991, Jerry Krupnick, television critic for the *Newark Star Ledger,* said it best:

> The word "fair" never entered into Mike [Wallace]'s report. We found it to be pure "gonzo journalism," totally hostile, with no intent whatsoever to do anything but repeat damaging innuendos that Mike's researchers found in the files on D'Amato, most of which already have been found wanting.
>
> Wallace made a big deal out of the senator's "refusal to appear on the program," but that's not how the Senator has been telling it. According to Big Al, he told Wallace he would submit to the (what obviously would be a hostile) interview provided a) it was done live and b) it was aired unedited.
>
> Mike, in a rather self-righteous indignation, declared that *60 Minutes* almost never would allow such an interview. In fact, according to D'Amato, Wallace told him, "We wouldn't even do that for the Pope."
>
> Well why not? Why should D'Amato expect he would get evenhanded treatment from Wallace if the broadcaster was allowed to take whatever he wanted out of context and edit it so that it would say just what he wanted it to say? Editing a friendly interview, sure, it's done all the time. But D'Amato knew Mike was out to get him and would have been a fool to

allow it, except on his own terms. . . . Again, we are certainly not defending D'Amato. He is far from our favorite politician. . . . On the other hand he was right about one thing. This was a pure and simple not-much-new hatchet job. Shame on you, Mike!

After falsely accusing me of hanging up on Mike Wallace, it seems the CBS brass didn't exactly like the tables turned. When the *New York Post* badgered them about the Bergman connection, a *60 Minutes* producer "slammed down the phone." They could dish it out, but they sure couldn't take it.

To put it simply, the *60 Minutes* experience was ugly and unfair. It was journalism at its worst. The Tuesday after *60 Minutes* aired, we rented a room in New York's Grand Hyatt Hotel and challenged my accusers—Mike Wallace, Mark Green, and Sydney Schanberg—to offer proof of their absurd charges. The room was jammed with TV and radio crews from every network. But guess what? None of my accusers accepted my challenge. None of them showed up. This was probably the first and only time Green ever passed up the chance to speak into an open mike. I went on the offensive. We held numerous press conferences. *PrimeTime Live*'s producer called and said, "Since *60 Minutes* wouldn't give you the chance to appear live, we will." I had complained so loudly about the unfairness of not being permitted to go on live that I had to do this interview. I was not exactly thrilled with the prospect of being grilled by Sam Donaldson. We sat within arm's reach of each other. He peppered me with vicious questions and continually interrupted me, never allowing me to complete an answer without firing off another question. I thought, "This is a disaster, this pompous ass is destroying me." For a moment I actually considered reaching over and lifting his hairpiece off his head and then saying to viewers, "If you want the truth, here's the real Sam." It certainly would have made headlines. I fantasized about a *Time* magazine cover of Donaldson's bold dome next to me holding his hairpiece. It would have been disastrous if he had one of those pieces woven into his head. Even my mother would never have forgiven me.

When I returned to my New York office from *PrimeTime Live*'s studios I was depressed. To my amazement, our switchboard was lighting up with calls congratulating me for standing up to Donaldson. Callers complained, "He just wouldn't let you answer the question." The public was finally catching on.

We then took an unusual step. We bought time on WOR-TV, an independent station in New York, to rebut the *60 Minutes* charges and to clear the air about the ethics allegations. While many politicians buy time during a campaign, we took my case to the people almost two years before the 1992 election.

The program cost more than $100,000 to air. It was a complete success. We not only got the truth out but our ratings were pretty good. We purchased time at ten o'clock on Saturday night, the half hour before Howard Stern's television show. And we got better ratings than Howard. While this book might not sell as many copies as Howard's best-seller, I'm proud to have beaten him in the Nielsens.

For thirty minutes, I made a point-by-point rebuttal of the unsubstantiated charges that had been hurled at me for the previous two years. It felt good finally to go on the offensive against the lies, libels, and innuendos.

Most viewers didn't know that the ethics charges against me were not brought by any law enforcement agency, but by none other that Mark Green, my defeated and bitter 1986 opponent. I looked the camera in the eye and said:

"It's ironic that the charges that he lays against me are the ones that I am most proud of. That is being the best constituent senator in the state of New York. In fact that is why I believe you elected me, to fight for New York and to get things done."

I then turned to each of Green's charges.

On the Allegations That I Gave My Cousin a HUD House:

"My cousin. It's been said that he unfairly received a HUD house. This allegation is outrageous. They would have you believe that I was the senator who used my office to help him. The fact is [when he got his house] Jimmy Carter was the president of the U.S., the Democrats not the Republicans controlled the White House and the Department of Housing and Urban Development, and I was not, repeat not, [yet] a United States senator.

"Now let me tell you about my cousin. He had two children and a full-time job earning $13,000 and a part-time job earning $5,000, and his wife worked. She drove a school bus part-time and earned $4,800 a year. Their combined income was less than $25,000 per year. They were perfectly within HUD guidelines. They were well below the level. The real scandal in HUD and that kind of housing [concerns] those people who had huge incomes, who didn't qualify, who unfairly got a house. That wasn't my cousin. The real scandal [occurred when] those people who bought these houses, lived in them a short period of time, and then sold them and made windfall profits. Again, in 1980, before I was a senator, my cousin bought that house. Again, in 1991, today, my cousin still lives in that house. He never sold it. He never profited. In fact,

They simply allowed a convicted felon to slander a United States senator on national television.

the only thing that's different, that's changed, is that he now has four children instead of two. Now would those who criticize me like me to tell my cousin that he should leave his house, that I should put him out in the street because it looks bad? Well that's not me. And I'm proud to fight for New York, and certainly that includes my cousin. He was qualified. Well, maybe Mark Green would throw his relatives out on the street, but I wouldn't."

On the Allegation That I Had Undue Influence at HUD:

"Duboice Guilliam, a convicted felon who worked at the Department of Housing and Urban Development, appeared on *60 Minutes* and he says that they rolled out the red carpet for Senator D'Amato. Sometimes they referred to him as the secretary of HUD. He had great influence. Well, let me tell you something: I'm proud if I had great influence because I used that to bring home billions and billions of dollars for New York. In the Transportation Department, for the Welfare [Health and Human Services] Department, the Education Department, Labor, etc., I fought to get New York its fair share and through that influence I was able to make a difference. I was able to get money for drug rehabilitation centers, Mother Hale, Daytop Village, money for roads, for bridges, for treatment for drug-addicted kids. In the town of Brookhaven alone I got more than $6 million. That was half of the discretionary money that I brought back to New York. And do you know why? Because there were over 3,300 homes in Rocky Point, Mastic, and Shirley, Long Island. These are small communities that didn't have clean drinking water. Let me tell you, they shouldn't be ashamed that I did this. I'm not. I fought so that they could have drinking water. And you know we built senior citizen houses and low-income houses. They were needed. Am I supposed to apologize for being successful for getting these projects for the people of New York? Of course not.

On the Allegation That I Favor Big Contributors:

"Ask the mayor and the former mayor of New York whether the office of Senator D'Amato was available to fight for their needs, for their fair share. Now Mark Green in his complaint said that my contributors had access to my office. Now let me tell you something, I help the people who contributed to me, I certainly do, and I help the people who don't contribute to me. I certainly do. I try to help *everybody* who comes to my office and I even help people who supported my opponents. We try to make a difference. [My office looked into] tens and tens of thousands of cases from the little guy to the big guy. [We've helped] people who need help with Social Security or the immigration department. We've fought for big projects, for General Electric, for Carrier, Grumman, you better believe it. They employ thousands and thousands of New Yorkers. And as far as contributors are concerned, the people of New York have a right to support their senator, and I hope they support me. And the fact is that more than 35,000 have contributed to my campaigns. Does that mean that they or I have done anything wrong? Of course not. Should people who contributed to me be denied access? Or, if I am to be denied giving them help, isn't something wrong? The fact is that we have fought for everyone and we are going to continue to do that and there has never, ever, been a quid pro quo for doing the work that we are supposed to do. . . . The fact of the matter is that recently I went to bat for a contract that involved almost a billion dollars and we got it for Grumman. Now you think that we did that because people may or may not have contributed to me. Well, I did it because there are thousands and thousands of jobs at stake. Seventeen thousand Long Islanders work for Grumman. And they asked for my help and they were entitled to it and I'm proud of that."

On the Allegation That I Help Only Wall Street Contributors:

"The allegation is made that I helped to pass a bill just days after Drexel Burnham held a fund-raiser on my behalf. Now Drexel Burnham was a major securities firm in New York. And the financial industry is among New York State's most important. It literally employs hundreds of thousands of people. And I've gone to bat for that industry time and time again."

On the Allegations Against My Dear Friend and Next-Door Neighbor Geraldine McGann:

"Let me tell you how really terrible the situation has gotten. I have a very dear friend, Geraldine McGann, who lived next door to me for many years. She was employed by HUD and moved up to become the regional administrator with my support. Now when all of these stories broke and the headlines blared throughout the state, her name was dragged through the mud. She was sullied. It was incredible. But she fought back. She didn't quit. Then they transferred her to Newark. And then they tried to reduce her pay. And they did. All based on allegations. No facts, no proof, no substance. But the headlines blared and her reputation was ruined and her family embarrassed and her friends looked at her strangely. And you know what happened? Just a couple of weeks ago a judge finally looked at the case and he said there was no evidence and no wrongdoing took place. And he demanded that her job be given back and her full salary be restored and that she be given her rightful place in the administration for which she had done no wrong. Now how do you give back her reputation? How do you give her back those months and months of anguish that she and her family shared? How do you think they felt?

"And what were the reasons for those attacks on her by the press and by politicians? You know why, it was because Geraldine was my friend. Well you know what, I'm not backing away from my support for Geraldine McGann [or for] the people who support me."

VINDICATION

On August 2, 1991, after a twenty-month investigation, the Senate Ethics Committee cleared me of all of Green's charges. To say that I had been thoroughly investigated would be the understatement of the century. The committee's special counsel, Henry F. Schuelke III, reviewed approximately one million documents, including more than 250 boxes of files and papers supplied from my office. The panel subpoenaed documents from seventy-one individuals.

After two years of anguish, my colleagues had cleared my name. Most of the charges were dismissed out of hand as "frivolous" by New Hampshire Senator Warren Rudman. In fact, upon announcing my exoneration, both Rudman and Senator Terry Sanford of North Carolina took a not too subtle jab at Mark Green for wasting their time and the taxpayer's money. "We're going to have to require more in the way of affidavits and sworn statements before we accept this kind of complaint again," Senator Rudman said. He also declared that the investigation's cost of $686,000 had persuaded him of the need for the committee to adopt rules to prevent the waste of time on spurious charges.

The committee did, however, admonish me for allowing my brother to obtain two letters under my signature requesting information from the Defense Department sought by a New York company he represented. While no law was broken, this was a mistake. The buck stops with me. I've learned a valuable lesson. It's important that even the appearance of undue influence be avoided. It's not always easy, but it's essential, particularly when family members are involved.

I was relieved. For God's sake, I jumped for joy. Coming a day after my birthday, the committee's findings were the greatest present I could have received. With *60 Minutes* and the Senate ethics charges behind me, our polls began to show that I was no longer in a free fall. My "negatives" had stabilized, and I was beginning to get my message across.

I was getting ready for the toughest campaign of my life.

LITHUANIA

One of the most moving moments of my Senate career was the stirring speech that Lech Walesa gave to a joint session of Congress on November 15, 1989. As the Iron Curtain fell, Walesa spoke of America as a beacon of freedom to oppressed people all over the world:

> I too remember these words; I, a shipyard worker from Gdansk, who has devoted his entire life–alongside other members of the Solidarity movement–to the service of this idea: "government of the people, by the people, for the people." Against privilege and monopoly, against violations of the law, against the trampling of human dignity, against contempt and injustice.

Walesa chastised those in the West who, in their desire to keep peace with the Soviets, were willing to forget Poland.

> At the beginning, many warnings, admonitions, and even condemnations reached us from many parts of the world. "What are those Poles up to?" we heard. "They are mad, they are jeopardizing world peace and European stability. They ought to stay quiet and not get on anybody's nerves."
> We gathered from these voices that the other nations have

the right to live in comfort and well-being, they have the right to democracy and freedom, and it is only the Poles who should give up these rights so as not to disturb the peace of others.

The Poles were mindful of the tragic irony that even though World War II had started over Poland, it had ended with a deal subjugating them to more than forty years of Soviet domination. After starting the Solidarity revolution in 1980, the Poles were in no mood for lectures by the West on "not rocking the boat." Or as Lech Walesa put it:

> Is there any sensible man understanding the world around him who could now say that it would be any better if the Poles kept quiet because what they were doing was jeopardizing world peace? Couldn't we rather say that the Poles are doing more to preserve and consolidate world peace than many of their frightened advisers?

Here was a man after my own heart. Walesa was not afraid, in his own way, to tell the assembled leaders of the world's greatest democracy that we were all too willing to sell out the cause of freedom. It was moving to be lectured by a real working-class hero.

In March 1990, less than six months after Lech's speech, I had the chance to put into action my commitment to his ideals. Vytautas Landsbergis, the new president of Lithuania, had invited me to the capital city of Vilnius. The Lithuanians had just declared their independence from the Soviet Union. In retaliation, Moscow had cut off Lithuania's oil supply. It also still had more than 100,000 troops stationed there.

Lithuania's bold declaration of independence came at a dramatic time. The Berlin Wall had just been torn down. The Eastern European nations were repudiating their Communist governments. Mikhail Gorbachev could barely maintain control over the Soviet Union itself. Unlike Hungary, Poland, and East Germany, Moscow considered the Baltic states of Lithuania, Latvia, and Estonia to be part of the Soviet Union. It did not matter that Stalin had boldly seized these nations in 1940. It was obvious to

Gorbachev and everyone else that the whole Soviet Union would unravel if Lithuania bolted.

The Bush administration's public posture was cool to Lithuania. To the folks in the White House and Jim Baker's State Department, Lithuania had put Gorbachev in a tough spot. They were rocking the boat. I thought our foreign policy establishment was blinded by their admiration of Gorbachev. They ignored that he was desperate to keep the Communist Party in power. They were suffering from Gorbymania.

The struggling independence movement in Vilnius needed a tangible symbol of U.S. support. I decided to go with members of the Committee for the Liberation of Lithuania, and I took along my tough and brilliant press secretary Zenia Mucha. It took four bus hours to travel from Warsaw to the Lithuanian border.

The Soviet guards at the border rejected my Lithuanian visa and invitation from Lithuanian President Landsbergis. I had been escorted to the border from Warsaw by the new Lithuanian foreign minister, Algirdas Saudargas. The Soviet guard, Major Vitas Buchis, allowed Saudargas to pass through, but denied me entry. He wouldn't recognize my visa and told me that I would have to be a Soviet or a Polish citizen. I asked him "if a nice Italian boy could be granted a one-day Soviet visa to go into Lithuania." I don't know if they could translate the joke. The major disappeared into the guardhouse to telephone my request to Moscow. After a few nervous minutes he reappeared and told us that my request was denied, and that "this is a decision straight from the Kremlin." Before turning away, I made a brief statement condemning "the Soviet Union's stranglehold on the Lithuanian people. . . . These artificial barriers cannot keep the Lithuanian people from freedom."

Back in the United States, my trip was treated as both a nuisance and a bit of a joke. The press accused me of grandstanding and treating Gorbachev with less respect than he deserved. President Bush made it clear that I had been completely on my own and did not speak for the United States government. The *New York Post* summed up my trip as "Al to Gorby: I'll Kick Him in the Baltics." Upon arrival at Kennedy Airport I was greeted by hundreds of Lithuanian-Americans chanting thanks. When asked by reporters why I went, I answered bluntly: "I went because there never, ever, was a better time to answer the cry of freedom. Never a better place to be in the cause of freedom." Both President Bush and *my mother* didn't want me to go. Even while I was at the border, the administration tried to mollify the Soviets, explaining that the President could not control crazy, renegade senators. My mother's concern was easier to understand: "What, are you crazy? You'd better not get hurt over in that place."

Looking back, I'm more certain than ever that I was right to go to Lithuania. With the putsch of August 1991, Gorbymania came to an abrupt end. It fell to Boris Yeltsin, the man who experts claimed to be a drunk and a fool, to fight for freedom. In 1991, independence for Lithuania became a reality as the Soviet Union disintegrated. The U.S. officially recognized the independence of Lithuania on September 2, 1991. I'm proud to have listened to Lech Walesa. I tried to offer Lithuania whatever help I could.

A few years later, I was attending Senator Larry Pressler's Bible study class. William Safire spoke to us about his book *The First Dissident: The Book of Job and Today's Politics.* I have a problem with many in the establishment press and the *Times* in particular, but I have always admired Bill Safire for being smart, insightful, and not afraid to tell it like it is. To my surprise and delight, he took me aside and gave me a copy of his book with the inscription "To Alfonse D'Amato, who showed uncommon courage in standing up for the people of Lithuania."

GEORGE
BUSH

J ust how did George Bush become president? While he had an impressive résumé of appointed jobs–GOP chairman, head of the U.S. Liaison Office in China, and CIA Director–he was not a big winner at the ballot box. He served two terms in the House, but lost a Senate race to Lloyd Bentsen in 1970. How did this nice man, not a proven vote-getter, get into the big time?

George Bush owes much to a certain boy from Long Island named Rich Bond. A political junkie from the time he was in short pants, Bond was only twenty-nine when he organized Bush's campaign in the 1980 Iowa caucus. Although he had the exalted title of Deputy Campaign Director, Bond made only $450 a week. He uprooted his young family to Ames, Iowa, and canvassed the state morning, noon, and night. As he spent years softening up Iowa for Bush, Bond made more than 300 personal appearances. No gathering of Republicans was too small or obscure. He haunted Kiwanis Clubs, Grange Halls, and American Legions. In the late 1970s, George Bush was known only to readers of the *New York Times* and *The Washington Post*. But Rich Bond knew that the Iowa caucus could turn that around. After all, in 1976, Iowa had transformed Jimmy Carter, a one-term Georgia governor, from a nonentity into the front-runner, and he rode that momentum all the way to the White House.

Rich Bond's years of work paid off. To everyone's surprise Bush won 33 percent of the Iowa vote. Ronald Reagan gathered 31 percent, and the rest was split among Howard Baker, John Connally, Bob Dole, Phil Crane, and John Anderson. Bush suddenly had political momentum or as he called it, "big mo." Rich Bond, the Hempstead boy wonder, had beaten the pros.

But Bush hit a wall in New Hampshire, when Ronald Reagan took charge of the microphone at the Nashua debate. Reagan won New Hampshire and eventually the nomination, but Iowa had transformed George Bush from just one of many contenders to Reagan's only serious opponent. Without Iowa, Bush never would have been nominated vice president, his stepping-stone to the White House. Iowa had made Bush, and Rich Bond had made that victory possible.

Once Bush became Vice President, Bond's political savvy was wasted. He became deputy chief of staff but soon found himself frozen out of the loop. He had not been on the job six months when he saw Bush having lunch with George Clark, who had become the chairman of New York State's Republican Party. Clark, an early supporter of Ronald Reagan, had been part of the 1976 insurgency that almost wrested the nomination from President Gerald Ford. Bond wondered how his own home state party chairman could meet with the Vice President without his knowledge? What the heck was going on?

Puzzled by this incident, Bond confronted Clark. Why was he the last to know? Clark took him aside for a little friendly advice. "Listen, Rich," he said. "Everybody knows that if you want to reach the vice president, you've got to go through Jennifer. She's the power here." Clark was referring to Jennifer Fitzgerald, who, although her official title was Senate Liaison, was truly the gatekeeper of the Bush office. Nothing happened without her knowledge or approval. Bond was frozen out. That's why he and everyone in the office referred to her as the "Ice Lady."

As a smart and aggressive young man, Bond had no choice

but to leave the office and become a political consultant. Bush never should have allowed a man who had been so essential to his rise simply walk away. Bond just didn't pass muster with the "Ice Lady." To his credit, Bond would later return to try to salvage the Bush presidency in 1992, when he became Republican Party chairman. By then, not even Rich's political savvy could pull off another miracle for Bush.

My only encounter with George Bush's famous "Ice Lady" was in 1987, when the Vice President summoned me to his official office in the Capitol, located just off the Senate floor. He was lining up support for his 1988 presidential bid and made a very candid, personal plea for my support. "This is it, Alfonse," he said. "It's now or never. I'd like your support. There's no second chance. If I don't make it this time, it's the end of the road." Impressed by Bush's frankness, I asked him why Lee Atwater was his political guru when Atwater's business partner, Roger Stone, was a Kemp supporter. To Bush's credit, he expressed total faith in Atwater's fidelity to him and his ability. He wasn't at all concerned about his campaign being compromised.

While we were having this intimate political heart-to-heart, I couldn't help but notice that Fitzgerald was in the room with us all along. Bush seemed to think nothing of her presence, but I considered it peculiar. He was pleading for my support and felt perfectly comfortable doing so in her company. She was his right hand.

Years later, the tabloids would drag Jennifer Fitzgerald into the limelight by trying to turn her into the "other Jennifer" of the 1992 campaign. While some might try to misinterpret their professional relationship, this was total nonsense. George and Barbara Bush seemed to have a great marriage.

With or without Jennifer Fitzgerald in the room, I was a little uncomfortable listening to Bush pour his heart out about needing to win in 1988. I was in Bob Dole's camp. I was in a tough spot. Bush, as Vice President, was the heir apparent to Ronald Reagan. Bush had done an impressive job of nearly locking up the nomination.

New York exemplified the Bush organization's clout. Since

1980, Bush's younger brother, Jonathan, had courted every Republican Party chairman and operative in New York. He tirelessly promoted his brother, thinking nothing of speaking in Rochester in the morning and then having dinner on Long Island. He wined, dined, and charmed in every county and district. He became one of our party's best fund-raisers. The Bush operation in New York was a steamroller that owed its success to the genuine decency and friendliness of Jonathan Bush. No one could have a more faithful brother or loyal supporter. By 1987, New York was wrapped up tight for George Bush. On the eve of the campaign, the state's potential favorite son Jack Kemp had no organization. He could field delegate slates in only five or six counties.

With New York all but locked up for Bush, and most of the national GOP establishment leaning toward the affable veep, it would have been very safe to join the Bush stampede. When I decided to back Bob Dole in 1988, he was a long shot—probably impossible. But I was convinced he would make a great president. I still feel that way. If Bob Dole had been elected by pledging not to raise taxes, he never would have allowed the likes of John Sununu and Dick Darman to bamboozle him into their kamikaze tax "compromise" of 1990. I thought Bob Dole, a wounded war veteran, would make the better commander-in-chief. As for foreign trade, he would have stood up to the Japanese when they tried to make a joke out of our import laws. And, as a hard-boiled Kansan, Bob Dole would have had more rapport with the American people than George Bush when the economy was hurting in 1991 and 1992.

In December 1987, I hosted the most successful fund-raiser of the entire Dole campaign at the Grand Hyatt Hotel in Manhattan. Organized by my friend Ambassador Charles Gargano, we raised more than a million dollars for Dole. The Bush people had heavily courted Charlie. Together we had run the very successful reelection campaign for Ronald Reagan in 1984—the President carried New York by half a million votes. We held an outdoor rally near Binghamton that drew more than 40,000 people to see President Reagan. The sheer enthusiasm of the crowd was unforgettable. This high became a painful memory for me in 1992, when I witnessed personal appearances by President Bush that drew sparse crowds and little enthusiasm.

When Bob Dole ended his candidacy, I did whatever I could to help George Bush campaign. The 1988 campaign was somewhat frustrating. With more advertising dollars we could have carried New York for Bush, instead of losing by a quarter million votes. After Reagan's triumph of 1984, I took this defeat personally. Together with George Junior and Jonathan, the candidate and I had spent two days together barnstorming the state in a small plane. While the Bushes and the D'Amatos come from very different worlds, they are a very close family and easy to get along with.

Two years later, Jonathan sent letters of support to tens of thousands of Republicans in New York blasting the charges against me as politically motivated and baseless. At a time when many politicians (not all of them Democrats) hoped that I would simply disappear, Jonathan Bush was deeply committed to my reelection. I've never met a more decent and honorable guy than Jonathan Bush.

If George Bush's advisers were as astute and hardworking as his brother, I'm convinced he would be in the White House today. Many of the Bush administration's key mistakes were the result of his baffling chorus of self-serving aides.

I'm not alone in thinking that Bush's advisers were without political acumen and out of touch with middle-class Americans. His closest advisers included such political "geniuses" as Jim Baker, Treasury Secretary Nicholas Brady, and Dick Darman, the head of the Office of Management and Budget (OMB). Each was born into a world of privilege and power. As one of my friends, a former Bush staffer, once said, "they were born on home plate, and thought they hit a home run."

Perhaps one of Bush's worst appointment was his chief of staff, John Sununu. While Sununu, the governor of New Hampshire, may have felt that his assistance was essential to Bush's 1988 primary victory, the Bush campaign there was won by Congressman Judd Gregg and his father, Hugh Gregg. The Greggs were a very old New Hampshire family, and they enjoyed a close relationship with the Bushes. Sununu did his best to take credit for Bush's win. The Greggs never tried to take credit for anything.

Sununu was convinced of his own genius. He really thought that everyone should just stand in awe of his IQ. He was a bright guy, but he was never wise enough to know that being smart is never a guarantee of anything in Washington. After all, the Clinton White House is now filled with Rhodes Scholars.

Sununu suffered from the delusion that *he* was deputy president–that he had gone from being governor of a small state to being the president for domestic affairs. He didn't really seem to stand for anything. With Sununu at the helm, the Bush administration became known as an "in box" presidency. Sununu reacted to daily events, but didn't establish an agenda. This philosophy permeated the Bush administration and explains his defeat in 1992.

HOW BUSH LOST

Late in 1991, I was heading into a reelection year with polls showing me with high negatives. Unlike 1986, more than a half dozen Democrats were eager to take me on. My personal political woes were compounded by what was already beginning to look like a tough year for the Republicans. The economy was in the tank. George Bush, who was so decisive in Desert Storm, could not inspire leadership at home. The day after Thanksgiving in 1991, he tried to stimulate the economy by buying a pair of socks at a mall. The fact that he was completely baffled by the workings of a cash register's scanner only reinforced most voters' suspicion that he was out of touch.

The President's unfortunate bout with nausea during a state visit in Tokyo that January symbolized his bad luck. From time to time, unfortunate snapshots get burned into the public imagination. In 1979, the photo of Jimmy Carter collapsing while jogging seemed all too appropriate for the malaise-plagued Georgian. The photo of Bush getting sick in front of the Japanese prime minister similarly became a metaphor for the shaky state of our economy.

After the Gulf War, George Bush had approval ratings of 90 percent. His subsequent free fall in the polls mystified his advisers. They didn't have a clue. I'm certain that the seeds of his defeat were sown when he was talked into raising taxes in the summer of 1990. It was a political killer. The Democrats were quick to jump on Bush's abandonment of his campaign no-new-taxes pledge and Republicans were saddled with a president who had broken a key promise. Saddam Hussein's invasion of Kuwait, less than a month after the budget deal, did much to quiet the outrage. But when the last Iraqis were driven from Kuwait seven months later, the glory of military victory could not erase the damage done by this political and economic fiasco.

John Sununu deserves the lion's share of the blame for the "deal" that killed the Bush presidency. We knew that the Democrats would never vote for spending cuts and would demand more taxes. That's when the President should have said, "No way." Sununu knew nothing about negotiating with Congress. When the administration met with the congressional leadership at Andrews Air Force Base to discuss the budget, Dick Darman wanted to propose a budget that called for spending cuts. That way the Democrats would have gotten the blame for proposing a tax hike. But Sununu, who was not the day-to-day negotiator and who liked to hear the sound of his own voice, just talked and talked. No fools, the Democrats let him talk himself into a deal that had the Bush administration agree to a tax hike.

I have heard that Sununu made this move to "pull one off for the President" and avoid confrontation. Sununu was feeling heat for being too combative and felt that this agreement would show that he could make a deal without creating a terrible row. In his attempt to show the President that he could deliver, Sununu handed Bush his greatest defeat.

The tax cave-in of 1990 was not only bad politics, it was bad for the economy. The deal called for a "spending cap," allowing discretionary spending to increase by 13 percent—some cap. When you raise taxes and don't cut spending, you obviously hurt economic growth. I refused to vote for this tax increase. It was a turkey, and I knew the people would say "Enough is enough" in 1992.

By January 1992, George Bush was dogged by Pat Buchanan's insurgent campaign. Most people had believed George Bush when he said, "Read my lips: No new taxes." That forceful speech, written by Peggy Noonan, spelled out a clear difference between Bush and Dukakis. That's why he was elected president in 1988. George Bush wouldn't raise your taxes. When he said so, that was it.

If Bush had taken on Congress in 1990, and stuck to his guns, he'd still be president. Maybe the government would have run out of money for a few days. The networks might show pictures of the Washington Memorial closed to tourists. The liberals would have attacked his assault on government, but the people would have supported him. Bush's failure to stand firm reminded the voters that he

By then, not even Rich's political savvy could pull off another miracle for Bush.

had no political compass. Despite his experience, his bravery in war, his success in business, his wonderful family, and his popular wife, George Bush couldn't convince voters that he believed the script he was reading. That's deadly for any politician.

In November 1991, the Bush administration and I split over capping interest rates for credit cards. During a speech in New York, the President criticized banks for charging too much interest on credit cards. I had first introduced a bill to cap interest in 1986. Armed with the President's statement, I reintroduced my bill the next day. There was absolutely no correlation between credit card rates and the banks' actual cost of money. The big banks were using the cards to subsidize other, less profitable operations. Of the ten largest banks, seven charged the exact same rate—21.8 percent!

My bill caused a panic on Capitol Hill. I blasted the banks for gouging the middle class: "Jesse James at least wore a mask. These guys want you to say thank you." My amendment sailed through the Senate with 74 votes.

That very day the Dow Jones average dropped more than 120 points. Lobbyists for Citibank and every other bank and credit card company wasted no time blaming me for the sharp decline in the Dow. I was stunned when Treasury Secretary Nick Brady blamed my bill for the market collapse. This was not only untrue, it was politically stupid. At the first sign of trouble, you don't attack a senator of your own party for acting on the President's own stated position! Who was in charge at the White House?

My bill was introduced on a day of what turned out to be great stock market volatility. Some major firms, including Aetna and Boeing, had just released some poor quarterly earnings. A number of biotech companies were being slapped with some unanticipated action by the FDA. These events occurred on a "double witching" day, when options on stock indexes and individual stocks expire at the same time. Many investors sell off on such days, and this, more than anything, contributed to the Dow's dive. A Securities and Exchange Commission study later confirmed that my credit card legislation was not the culprit.

The banking interests pulled out all the stops to crush my legislation. The bankers did a good job of shouting "the Dow is falling, the Dow is falling," and the President's men ran from my bill as fast as they could. The bank lobby eventually won, and the House passed a tame bill calling for an eighteen-month "study" of credit card rates. While I generally oppose interfering with free markets, my bill did push banks toward more competition, and credit card rates have since come down.

Meanwhile, John Sununu lamely tried to suggest that President Bush had ad-libbed his remarks about credit card rates. Imagine, instead of taking the heat, Sununu blamed his boss! It was obvious now that the White House was completely adrift and politically out of touch. The White House ignored me and columnist George Will called me "a publicity mongering practitioner of smash-and-grab opportunism." Pretty strong words for a man who had been called "Nancy Reagan's lapdog."

Things never got better for George Bush. For Bush and his friends, a senator like D'Amato was to be endured at best, humored when need be, and ignored most of the time. The Bush team never bothered to ask for my advice or support. Ronald Reagan had called me many times. Perhaps my nasal voice, my frank style of speech, rubbed the Bush people the wrong way. Perhaps it was my habit of telling them what I thought.

I was on the outs during Bush's miserable 1992 reelection campaign. On July 27, 1992, weeks before the Republican convention, I appeared at the New York State Broadcasters Association Meeting in Saratoga. Larry King also spoke. He received $10,000 and I got more coverage than I ever expected.

I candidly observed that there was a slight chance that Bush might not run again. I figured the odds against him running had lowered from a million to one immediately after the Gulf War to one hundred to one. I also suggested that Bush fire Nicholas Brady as Treasury Secretary and bring in Jack Kemp to show that he was serious about the economy. I also suggested that it might not be prudent for the party to print Bush-Quayle buttons just yet.

These unvarnished observations got me into plenty of hot water with the White House. The *New York Post* played them up for all they were worth. Later that week, Bush visited Bob Dole's office to discuss the campaign with Republican senators. Once again everyone assured him that the campaign was going just fine. We all smiled and agreed how well things were going. I had the strangest feeling that we were on the *Titanic* after it had hit the iceberg, and no one wanted to admit we were sinking.

OUR UNFINISHED BUSINESS WITH SADDAM HUSSEIN

CODDLING A TYRANT

As the lone senator to commend Israel in 1981 when her jets destroyed Iraqi's nuclear reactor, I was not surprised when, in 1990, Saddam Hussein emerged from his rat hole to become lead bully on the world stage. What angered me was how the United States coddled and encouraged Saddam right up until the very week that his tanks rolled into Kuwait.

Our support of Saddam—a murderous tyrant whom even the most cynical State Department or CIA bureaucrat had no illusions about—must be put in context. After Ayatollah Khomeini's mullahs seized Iran in 1979 and militants held fifty-three American Embassy personnel hostage, Iran emerged as our primary enemy in the Middle East.

In September 1980, Saddam Hussein launched a surprise attack on Iran. He charged that the Ayatollah had fomented revolution among Iraq's Shiite majority. Saddam foolishly believed he would win a quick victory. But the Iran-Iraq War would last eight years and cost hundreds of thousands of lives. Saddam financed this insane war by blackmailing his neighbors. He claimed Iraq was the only barrier between Iran's radical fundamentalism and the vulnerable, oil-rich sheikdoms of the Persian Gulf. Saudi Arabia and its neighbors responded by giving Iraq billions to fund his war.

The United States adopted the foolhardy policy "the enemy of my enemy is my friend." Our navy defended Kuwaiti tankers. When an Exocet missile fired from an Iraqi jet killed dozens of American sailors on the U.S.S. *Stark*, you would have thought it was the Ayatollah himself had pulled the trigger.

But the situation only got stranger when the Iran-Iraq War ended in stalemate in 1989. Most analysts expected Saddam to lay low to lick his wounds. Fat chance. By March 1990, after a farcical trial, his regime executed a British journalist for spying for Israel. On April 2, he threatened to annihilate half of Israel with chemical weapons. The Bush administration still treated Saddam with kid gloves. I did not. After I called Saddam the "butcher of Baghdad," the Iraqi ambassador complained to several senators and the State Department. I saw him as the new Noriega. He had to be stopped.

As early as April 19, 1990, Bill Safire blasted the Bush administration for ignoring Saddam. Mounting evidence showed that Saddam was buying technology for chemical and nuclear weapons. Mysterious weapons designer Gerald Bull was building a super cannon in Iraq that would launch missiles at Israel. And the United States was still funneling billions of loans to Baghdad via an obscure Atlanta branch of an Italian bank.

Amazingly, just six weeks before Saddam's tanks crushed Kuwait, Assistant Secretary of State John H. Kelly urged Congress not to impose sanctions against Iraq. Kelly feared sanctions would worsen our trade deficit. What stupid testimony! As it was, the Senate cut off only $700 million in agricultural assistance.

THE GULF WAR: HEROES AND VILLAINS

The Bush administration's rather shameful coddling of Saddam ended when Kuwait was invaded. The President's resolve and determination surprised Saddam. The war proved that the United States was the world's *only* superpower. We would not let a megalomaniac blackmail the free world.

George Bush was the hero of the Gulf War. He made the tough calls. Most of his advisers, especially Brent Scowcroft and Jim Baker, favored "diplomacy." The President understood that Saddam would respect only force. Words would mean nothing to a bully.

I suspect the chief villain, after Saddam himself, was Jordan's King Hussein. I learned from confidential sources, including the Saudi ambassador in Washington, Prince Bandar bin Sultan, that King Hussein counseled Saddam that the coast was clear to invade Kuwait. As a Soviet client, Saddam was not familiar with our strategic thinking. King Hussein was his link to the West.

To make matters worse, our "friend" King Hussein has since thumbed his nose at the United States by circumventing United Nations sanctions against Iraq. Now, four years after the Gulf War, Jordan is the principal hole in the U.N. embargo on Iraq. It is wrong that Jordan is *still* a major recipient of U.S. aide. For almost forty years, we have propped King Hussein up, bailed him out, and made excuses for his actions. But he is not our loyal ally. The proper place for a Palestinian state is Jordan. Most of Jordan's population *is* Palestinian. It wouldn't be a hard transition. Don't be surprised if moves toward Palestinian autonomy in the West Bank and Gaza spread eastward and overtake King Hussein's miserable kingdom.

George Bush's decision to use force to oust the Iraqis from Kuwait was not an easy one. When the White House briefed the Senate Appropriations Committee, National Security Adviser Brent Scowcroft defended the official propaganda of the moment that an embargo would force Saddam to leave Kuwait. To Scowcroft's amazement, I responded with a tale about bully behavior. I recounted how I took on Johnny the bully when I was seven years old. Both Scowcroft and Colin Powell, who was also at the briefing, looked at me as if I were crazy, but I held my ground. You have to be tough with bullies, I explained, because that's the only language they understand. I reminded them that our embargo of

Noriega had been a fiasco. After two years of sanctions, we only hurt the poor, the middle class, and the business community–the very people who supported democracy. Our embargo against Noriega did nothing to his entourage of drug dealers, thugs, and criminals. Why, I argued, would an embargo hurt Saddam? He thought nothing of killing thousands of his own citizens.

A dictator doesn't have to answer to a free press or angry constituents. A Noriega, Saddam, or Castro shoots his way into power and will kill anyone who is a threat. Will such dictators resign because the price of milk goes up? Because babies are dying? Because gas is hard to find? I had worked day and night to put the pressure on Bush to go in and take out Noriega by force. I was hoping to do the same to Saddam.

Colin Powell was reluctant to use force and wanted to give sanctions a chance. I did not want to second-guess Powell. He knew what it meant to send men into combat. When the President finally decided to use force, Powell worked to bring about our triumph in the Gulf.

The same cannot be said for Jim Baker. Reportedly, Baker was so put off by Bush's decision to fight that he went on vacation. Baker always saw himself as the next Henry Kissinger and wanted to negotiate peace in Kuwait. If the secretary of state licked his wounds during the greatest crisis of the Bush presidency, it says something very telling about Jim Baker.

PRINCE BANDAR–SAUDI HERO

The unsung hero of the Gulf War was Prince Bandar, the Saudi ambassador to the United States. He persuaded King Fahd to support the U.N. coalition. The king feared foreign troops might destabilize the Saudi population. But, as Bandar told me, Saddam left the king no choice. Iraqi tanks had rolled right to the Saudi border, and beyond. If Saddam had desired only Kuwait, the Saudis might have appeased him, as the French and English had with Hitler in Czechoslovakia. Saddam, however, was a lousy Hitler. Instead of bamboozling the Saudis with peace talks, he poised Iraqi tanks to invade Saudi oil fields.

Saddam's brazen aggression shocked the Saudis. They had provided billions—in reality, protection money—for his war with Iran. Even as Iraqi troops were occupying Kuwait, the Saudis still maintained links to Saddam's military. Prince Bandar advised me that when the Iraqis first crossed the Saudi border, a Saudi officer *telephoned* his Iraqi counterpart, who promised that the tanks would be withdrawn. Hours later, the same thing happened. This time an Iraqi lieutenant answered and promised to pass the message along. Once again the tanks withdrew. The third time it happened, the Saudi military commander called and the line was dead. These three incursions, along with satellite surveillance, were the ammunition Prince Bandar needed to persuade the king to permit the stationing of U.S. troops on Saudi soil.

The introduction of U.S. troops prevented Saddam from seizing control of the world's oil. The Saudi army would not have stopped Saddam. And the Saudi oil fields were only several hours by tank from the Kuwait border. If Saddam controlled Saudi Arabia, the world's economy would have plunged into depression. If Saddam would have secured the revenues to acquire nuclear weapons, I suspect the Middle East, if not the world, might have been plunged into nuclear conflict.

THE GULF WAR COMES TO ISRAEL

When our air war began against Saddam on January 16, 1991, he struck back at Israel. This attack was intended to inflame the Arab masses and to demonstrate that Israel, as well as the United States, was the enemy. The Israelis deserve great credit for their restraint. Had Israel retaliated, Iraq might have divided our Arab allies.

I wanted to show my support for Israel while she was under attack, to visit the brave U.S. soldiers who manned the Patriot missile batteries in northern Israel and to meet with the Israeli leadership. I knew from experience on the Senate Intelligence Committee that the Israelis would have excellent insights into Saddam's objectives.

With these goals in mind, we began organizing our trip to a

war zone. I took two close and trusted aides: Mike Hathaway, my counsel on the Intelligence Committee in Washington, and John Sitilides, my executive assistant for communications and public affairs.

Mike had only recently married, and his wife, Therese, was upset that I was dragging her new husband into a war zone. John was still a happy bachelor, but his father was even more concerned that I was risking his son's life. He cursed a blue streak before John assured him that we would be spending most of our time in Jerusalem, which Saddam had spared from attack due to the fact that it was also a holy city of Islam. It was cold comfort, but the best excuse he could come up with.

On January 24, we met at Kennedy Airport and were joined by Malcolm Hoenlein, the executive director of the Conference of Presidents of Major American Jewish Organizations. We landed at David Ben-Gurion Airport at ten A.M. the next day and were met by Yossi Orian, a young man from the Israeli Foreign Ministry. John had packed a week's worth of meetings into our three-day trip, so we set off without the benefit of sleep.

Before leaving the airport, we were each handed a small corrugated cardboard box with a shoulder strap. After close inspection of the Hebrew lettering on the box, I saw a drawing of a gas mask and other devices. We were assured that Saddam fired his Scuds only at night and that we would receive complete instructions in the use of our gas masks before darkness fell. We were told never to be without our little box. It was the latest law in Israel.

We met with Israeli Foreign Minister David Levy at 11:45 A.M. He wasted no time in telling us that the Israelis would not withstand Saddam's attacks indefinitely. It was clear he wanted to communicate to Washington that Israel would eventually have to retaliate. He also advised me that the United States was being lulled into a false sense of security about Syria. While Syria had joined in the anti-Iraqi coalition, Levy warned that Hafez al-Assad was a craftier and more patient version of Saddam. Levy outlined a scenario in which the Syrian president, having taken effective control over the Lebanese government, mobilized the

Lebanese army and drove it south toward Israel.

At one P.M. we met with Israeli Prime Minister Yitzhak Shamir, with whom I had established a close relationship. He strongly urged that the United States make an example of Saddam and to conduct war crimes trials when the war was over. He also warned that Israel would eventually have to retaliate for Saddam's Scud attacks. He repeated Israel's concern about Syria's intentions. After meeting with Shamir, we ran into another New Yorker, reporter Gabe Pressman. We then met with Justice Minister Dan Meridor, who also stressed that Syria could not be trusted. While we were in Israel to observe one war, the Israelis were contemplating steps to avoid the next conflict.

It was almost five in the afternoon, before we finally got to our rooms at the Jerusalem Hyatt. But before we could unwind, our guide Yossi gathered us for one last bit of official business—learning how to use our gas mask. The latex rubber masks were to be worn from the time sirens announced the first Scud attack to the ringing of the official "all clear." Each mask had two small nozzles in front. One for speaking and the other—in event of chemical or biological weapon attack—for a large green canister that filtered out contaminants or viruses.

After we tried on these eerie masks, Yossi went through some of the other goodies in our kit. The first was talcum powder to be used if any liquid droplets or other signs of biological contamination appeared on our skin. The powder was to be placed directly on the droplets, drying them into little balls to be flicked off the skin. Then came a six-inch metal tube containing a four-inch needle. If any contaminant penetrated the rim of our mask, reached our skin, or we became dizzy or nauseated, we were to drive this needle into our inner thigh. This medicine would ward off temporarily the lethal effects of Saddam's poison until medical assistance arrived. I took a deep breath and prayed that none of us would have to use these needles.

It was almost six, the beginning of what the Israelis called prime-hour range, the time between six and ten P.M. when the Iraqis were most likely to strike. We had plans for dinner at seven, so there was little time to unwind. I wanted to look up my old friend Bebe Netanyahu, the Israeli ambassador to the United Nations, at the King David Hotel.

I hopped in a cab without thinking. The streets were all but deserted. At exactly 6:05, a piercing sound split the night. The horrible noise changed from high pitched to low and back again. It was several seconds before I realized that we were under attack.

Fortunately, the King David Hotel was close by. We quickly jumped out and went to the King David's shelter. In a sealed-off basement, we put on our gas masks and waited for further instructions. I wondered for a minute if John Sitilides's dad hadn't been right all along. But I was moved by the sight of Israeli families standing together with their gas masks on. Mothers were hovering over their babies in small shelters no bigger than incubators. It was an awful sight that brought home the reality of this war and the treachery of our enemy.

After the longest half hour of my life, the all clear sounded. Informing us that it was safe to return to our rooms. The Scuds did not contain chemical or biological warheads. I watched some elderly couples take off their masks and walk out hand in hand. I wondered if they were haunted by memories of the gas the Nazis had used almost fifty years before.

I rushed back to the Hyatt. I wanted to eat, but John had arranged for half a dozen telephone interviews. John then told me that I would be on *Larry King Live*. That sounded great until I heard the hitch. Live from Washington at nine P.M. meant four A.M. in Israel. It was going to be a trip without sleep.

I met John at 3:30 A.M. and waited for CNN's car to pick us up. Fifteen minutes passed and no one showed. With the studio ten minutes away, we were quickly running out of time. We asked the hotel clerk to drive us to the studio, but he was concerned about possible Scud attacks. We then heard the screeching wheels of CNN's driver. Fewer than thirty seconds after arriving at the studio and getting a microphone clipped to my lapel, I heard that gruff, familiar voice: "Live from Jerusalem, U.S. Senator Alfonse D'Amato. Good morning, Senator." And I responded, "Good morning, Larry."

On Saturday morning we drove to Tel Aviv to meet Mayor Shlomo "Cheech" Lahat, a warm and outspoken politician who has been called "the Ed Koch of Israel." In Tel Aviv we saw the devastation caused by the Scud attack the night before. Saddam had launched three missiles against Tel Aviv and one against Haifa. While Patriot missiles had disabled all four, the Scuds still caused massive damage.

Mayor Lahat led us on a tour of Ramat Ghen, a small community on the outskirts of Tel Aviv. The remains of a Scud had leveled several homes, blasted a hole in streets and sidewalks, and blown out hundreds of windows. I shuddered to think of the damage the Scuds would have caused if they had not been disabled by the Patriots.

The mayor then took us to the small Arab village of Abu Nassar, several miles south of Tel Aviv on the Mediterranean coast. The Israelis had spent a great deal of money on attractive and affordable housing in this village. They had hoped Abu Nassar could be a model to demonstrate that Arabs could live peacefully and prosperously within Israel.

We stopped at a seaside restaurant for a delicious lunch of Arab food and desserts. The mayor lived up to his reputation, regaling us with many jokes. My favorite goes something like this: A pollster approached four men, a Pole, a Russian, an American, and an Israeli, and asked them, "Excuse me, what is your opinion regarding the shortage of meat?" To which the Pole replies, "What is meat?," the Russian asks, "What is an opinion?," the American wonders, "What is a shortage?," and the Israeli snaps "What is 'Excuse me'?"

It was late afternoon when we finally left Abu Nassar. I had an appointment at six-thirty with Benjamin Begin, the son of former Prime Minister Menachem Begin and a rising political star in his own right. I had expected a frank, insightful conversation with Benny, and I wasn't disappointed. He insisted that Israel could never participate in an international peace conference where its security would be traded away. He felt that Israel could engage only in direct, bilateral negotiations with her neighbors. Such talks would have to take place without precondition and include the explicit goals of contractual peace between the negotiating parties. Two years later, in September 1993, Benjamin Begin's foresight was realized when the PLO and Israel signed a once unimaginable peace accord.

We had dinner that night with Eliahu Ben-Elizar of the Foreign Affairs and Defense Committee of the Israeli Knesset. We discussed the possibility that Israel's foes might one day come to terms with her existence. Unfortunately, our talk of peace was rudely interrupted by the distant sound of Scud attacks. We soon heard hundreds of people in the floors above us making their way en masse through the hotel. I looked at my watch. It was 10:04 P.M.

Once again, we made our way to the basement shelter. Although we were headed the next day for the relative safety of New York, for these brave Israelis this was home, and they had no way of knowing how long Saddam's attacks would go on. No wonder Prime Minister Shamir was so adamant that Israeli patience could not last forever. What country could take this kind of punishment and not retaliate?

When the all clear sounded at 10:30 P.M., we were all too tired and upset to continue. My desire for sleep was interrupted when John Sitilides, telephone in hand, explained I had to do another interview "live from Jerusalem." This pattern of Scud attack, interview, Scud attack, interview, was surreal.

We were up Sunday morning, January 27, at six to meet my friend Housing Minister Ariel Sharon. Although he has a reputation for being ruthless, Ariel has been very warm to me. He was justifiably proud that Israel had provided shelter for the hundreds of thousands of new immigrants flooding in from the Soviet Union. Israel had to build three hundred new apartments every single day to keep up with her newest immigrants. The Scuds, however, were destroying hundreds of housing units every evening. More than two thousand had been damaged the night before.

As a former general, Ariel was full of questions we had no way of answering. How would the United States respond to a gas attack on Israel? Would the United States agree to a cease-fire that liberated Kuwait but allowed Saddam to stay in power? Would he be allowed to keep his air force? He cautioned that the United States had to act swiftly to keep Saddam off balance. We could not afford to allow the war to drag on.

Before we finished, Sharon brought up the controversial matter of Israel's request to the United States for a $10 billion loan guarantee to build housing for new immigrants. Some in Washington considered this request a form of Israeli extortion for not retaliating against Iraq. I cautioned Sharon that Israel's timing was terrible. Many Americans misunderstood the issue and considered the loan guarantee to be an outright grant to Israel.

Our next excursion was perhaps the most rewarding of the entire mission. We took off for the northern port of Haifa to visit with the American military personnel who manned our Patriot missiles. The Patriots had an astounding success rate against Saddam's Scuds and these men and women were justifiably America's and Israel's newest heroes. We were met at the base by William Brown, the U.S. ambassador to Israel, and dozens of enthusiastic American and Israeli soldiers. They showed us the Patriot missile launchers, some of which had been fired only hours earlier. Their pride was contagious.

That night was particularly poignant. Back in the United States, it was Super Bowl Sunday. Whitney Houston was belting out a heart-stopping rendition of "The Star-Spangled Banner." I had brought a couple of dozen football caps to Israel. New England Patriot caps were of course the biggest hit. We provided New York Giants caps to the New Yorkers in the crowd. This bunch of selfless kids deserved to be sitting on the fifty-yard line. Whenever I hear some loudmouth putting down America's youth, I remember those soldiers. There are entirely too many dreary stories about the malaise of the "twentysomething" generation. I wish at least one writer for *Time* or *Newsweek* would focus on the spirit of the men and women who fought and won the Gulf War.

On our trip to the airport, we could see thousands of cars jammed on the highways outside of Tel Aviv. We learned that the entire thirty-mile eastbound stretch connecting Tel Aviv and Jerusalem was bumper-to-bumper with families leaving the danger of imminent missile attack. Families were fleeing for their lives.

I left Israel determined to do what I could to see that our government did everything possible to rid the world of Saddam Hussein. On the El Al flight back to New York, I bumped into Jimmy Breslin. While Breslin is no D'Amato fan, at least he's funny about it. Once, he quipped, "When Al D'Amato walks by a bank, the alarms go off." At least he's not as humorless as my other critics. Breslin had his own view of the Gulf War. Breslin knew I had attended Chaminade, so he started listing the names of Catholic high schools on Queens and Long Island. He feared that seniors from those schools would be dying in the desert sands of Saudi Arabia. Breslin was sure the United States was entering a quagmire. We would be tied down by Saddam's army and then all of the Arab nations would rise up against us in an Islamic jihad. He was nothing but doom and gloom all the way back to JFK. After I had witnessed the bravery of the Israelis and the spirit of the Patriot missile battery, Breslin's scenario was a little difficult to take. But it was instructive. To Jimmy Breslin and his politically correct neighbors on the Upper West Side, the Gulf was Vietnam all over again. They could bash the President and relive their glory days at antiwar rallies.

I wonder what Jimmy Breslin thought when we won that war in one hundred hours? Was he happy? Disappointed? Or just confused?

THE LIBERATION OF KUWAIT

I was in Washington when I heard that U.S. Ambassador Edward "Chip" Gnehm had returned to Kuwait City under the security shield of U.S. Army Rangers. Kuwait was free! Saddam was in hiding, his army smashed on the Basra road.

I was so excited, I had a U.S. flag flown over the Capitol on Kuwait's liberation day, February 28, 1991, and planned to send it to General Norman Schwarzkopf to raise over our embassy when he returned to the freed city.

I did not then know I would be sending more than a flag to

Kuwait City. I would be going myself. At ten that morning, Kuwait's ambassador, Saud Nasir al-Sabah, came to express his nation's gratitude for my early and enthusiastic championing of the Kuwaiti cause. "As the first American to support Kuwait, you are the first American thanked," he declared, and invited me to Kuwait, "even before the President."

I was touched by his gratitude, but could not help remembering the days when no one listened to our warnings about Saddam. From March through July 1990, Ambassador al-Sabah had used my office as his command center on Capitol Hill. He was more than a diplomat in trouble, he was a man whose nation was on the verge of obliteration.

I was filled with tears of both joy and despair when Ambassador "Al" came to thank me. But I suspect the ambassador was a little surprised when I immediately accepted his invitation. My administrative assistant, Mike Kinsella, was concerned that Kuwait City was still a war zone. There were chemical fires. Renegade factions of the PLO and Iraqi units might still be in the city.

I told Mike to forget about it. With hundreds of New York troops in the vanguard of the liberating forces, I was going. I also wanted to see the devastation that our policy of appeasement had created. Convinced of my determination, al-Sabah agreed that "the first shall be first" and offered his nation's cooperation in welcoming me.

Bob Dole was a little taken aback by my impromptu travel plans. He thought Kuwait City was still a little dicey for a visit. Then the State Department tried to throw a roadblock in front of me. They had no time to arrange anything—"perhaps some time later, when things were settled" was their response. Now Bob Dole was behind me 100 percent: "Go if you must. You represent the Senate."

Undeterred by the State Department, I called my old friend Saudi Ambassador Prince Bandar. He immediately agreed to put a Royal Saudi Air Force jet at my disposal. Now we had a plane to Kuwait, but only if we could get to Saudi Arabia.

At a lunch that day with the New York State Medical Society, I publicly confirmed my travel plans for the following day: New

York to London to Abu Dhabi to Bahrain to Dhahran, Saudi Arabia, and then on to Kuwait City. When Mike Kinsella and I hopped aboard the British Concorde early Friday morning, which would connect us to a red-eye flight to Abu Dhabi, visas, hotels, land travel, guides, and agendas were still unsettled. By the time we reached Heathrow, our arrangements were in order. But we also learned that my nemesis Jim Baker was trying to intercept our mission, supposedly out of concern for our safety.

Early Saturday morning we met with U.S. officials in Abu Dhabi who briefed us on the situation in liberated Kuwait. A thousand fires burned all over the countryside, and sabotaged Kuwaiti oil wells were spewing a noxious plume of black smoke downwind to Saudi Arabia, Bahrain, and the whole Persian Gulf, so that white flags flying four hundred miles south of Kuwait were stained gray. Saddam had added environmental crime of untold proportion to his many atrocities.

> Our military response to Saddam's savagery was masterfully selective.

At the Saudi border we were greeted by Major General Sultan Mutari, commander of Saudi forces in eastern Saudi Arabia. It was 10:30 A.M., but this did not stop General Mutari from throwing an elaborate banquet at a lavish palace. Sumptuous food and comfy bedrooms were laid out for us tired sojourners. I was grateful for the hospitality, but we had not traveled halfway around the world to drink tea, eat goat, and take naps. Suddenly, we learned that the plane for our last leg to Kuwait City was "not yet available." I thought we were being deliberately delayed. After a fourth cup of tea, I told the Saudi general in no uncertain terms that either we got the plane or I was hitchhiking on the nest convoy to Kuwait.

That seemed to do the trick. The plane was suddenly freed up and the final leg of our journey began between the takeoffs of armed F-16s and A-10s. I thought this short flight might allow me a chance for a little shut-eye, but after ten minutes I was rudely awakened by the smell of burning oil. I looked out the window and could see nothing at all. Two hundred miles south of the liberated capital, blackened clouds pressed against the windows. Saddam's satanic oil fires blocked the sun and bathed our plane in vaporous oil slick fifteen thousand feet above the ground.

Approaching the airport, the pilot warned us that the airport was without radar, radio, lights, or secured runways. We had to complete our visit by sundown or be trapped in battlefield conditions.

We were greeted on the runway by twin U.S. Ranger helicopters—one would transport us, the other would be a decoy/defender in case of enemy fire. We were warmly welcomed by the American Embassy staff—a marked departure from the State Department's official stance. The Ranger helicopters provided us with an airborne tour of the line of Iraqi defense that our forces had breached to liberate the city. We flew over the strategic sites: the phone complex, the radio and television relay stations, the port facilities, and the sabotaged oil fields surrounding the city. This short tour convinced me that our military response to Saddam's savagery was masterfully selective and almost merciful in its application of force. We did what we had to do and no more. The obvious devastation visited on the city came not from our firepower but from the seven-month occupation by Iraqi forces. The destruction of the city's buildings, port facilities, water system, and storehouses exposed Saddam's goal of eradicating all traces of modern civilization in Kuwait. It was as if Saddam wanted to return Kuwait to the desert sands.

We landed on the parking lot of the American Embassy and met Ambassador Chip Gnehm and the special forces commander. The embassy's offices and residences had been looted and ruined. Everything possible had been stolen and shipped north. A single AT&T phone line was being installed as we landed. Electricity was provided by an auxiliary generator. Coffee was black and instant. We were giddy with victory, but we were frightened by the devastation on the ground and in the skies. It was apocalyptic. But U.S. military morale was unstoppable. After six months in the desert, these men and women were on top of the world. I didn't hear a single complaint. Their only request was a call to their husband or their wife, to "tell them I'm O.K.!" I had come on an official mission to show my solidarity with our troops, but I left inspired by their attitude and sacrifice.

I had a hard time concentrating on my military briefing about the rout of the Iraqi army on the Basra road. Sporadic gunfire was all around. Celebrating Kuwaitis were firing their guns into the air. Some Iraqi and PLO forces were still being flushed out. Bob Dole was right—it was still a very dangerous place.

I presented the ambassador with the American flag I had flown over the Capitol, which then replaced the battle flag that had proudly flown all during the Iraqi occupation. This tattered flag was given a place of honor in the embassy.

I met with Kuwait's ministers of public health and domestic security, who were the first officials to return. They were shocked by Saddam's destruction and feared disease would spread throughout Kuwait City. They were also plainly frightened that some Kuwaitis might use the armaments left by the Iraqis to extract revenge on those Kuwaitis who collaborated with Saddam. There was even some fear that an armed minority might try to oust the ruling family.

As we drove through Kuwait City under heavy security, the enthusiasm of the people was beginning to emerge. The streets were already festooned with American and Kuwaiti flags, and walls were covered with graffiti declaring "We Love USA" and "God Bless George Bush." As a little boy, I had watched news-reels of GIs marching into liberated Rome, Paris, and Berlin. For the last forty years, we'd had to watch too many news reports of American flags being burned in foreign capitals. I was proud to be an American. We were the liberators again.

But my euphoria was quickly dampened at the beachfront. Saddam had expected the U.S. forces to land here. What was intended to be a solid wall of death for American forces was now a salvage yard for munitions. Kuwaiti bathers had frolicked on those same white sands only seven months before.

Back at the embassy, the ambassador and I were greeted with shouts of gratitude and kisses on both cheeks from delirious Kuwaitis. Daylight dwindled quickly as the clouds of burning oil competed with the sun. On top of the Kuwaiti Sheraton, CNN was broadcasting live to the world with a single camera, one klieg light, and a diesel generator. As I made some hurried comments to CNN, I was keenly aware that the celebratory gunfire was increasing as daylight waned.

We were hurried from the Sheraton's roof to our helicopters. We barely reached our plane in time to catch the last dying light before fumes and darkness engulfed the city. The hundreds of burning wells spread out before us like 3-D holograms from hell stretching from one horizon to the other and spewing forth smoke clouds ten to twelve layers deep. No painter, poet, or filmmaker could have envisioned a more harrowing portrait of the end of the world. And at the same time there was a twisted logic to the awful scene. Oil was what this was all about. And Saddam had to destroy what he couldn't plunder.

The rest of the trip was an anticlimactic. Back to Riyadh for meetings with U.S. officials, a conference with the U.S. ambassador to Saudi Arabia, calls to Washington and New York. General Schwarzkopf could not see us. He was in a tent accepting the surrender of Iraq's surviving officer corps. Then a flight back to Bahrain, London, and home.

Recalling those days is not easy, seeing what a mess we've made of our victory in the Gulf. No sooner had we chased the Iraqis out of Kuwait than the press started pounding President Bush with the charge that we had killed innocent Iraqi troops. I'm sorry, but it was my position that we should have forced the Iraqi generals to deliver Saddam to us. The forces close to Saddam had only a few options. Their best bet would have been to deliver him to us. Saddam deserved to stand trial for his crimes. He ran roughshod over a neighboring nation. He slaughtered thousands of innocent civilians both in Kuwait and Iran. He had declared war on the *world*'s environment, flooding the Persian Gulf with oil and setting fire to hundreds of Kuwaiti oil wells.

I suspect that Saddam's generals would have killed him to save their own skins. Faced with imminent destruction, I am sure that any number of Saddam's henchmen would have wiped him out to stop the bombing and to try to emerge as the next strongman. Either way, the people of Iraq and the community of nations would be rid of the butcher of Baghdad, and we would all be better for it.

One of the weakest excuses for our failure to take out Saddam was the purported need for a strong Iraq to counter Iran. This was precisely the strategy that led us to coddle Saddam in the first place. With permanent military bases in Saudi Arabia and throughout the Gulf, we don't need to prop up Saddam. Did Saddam ever stop Iran from spreading Islamic terror to Lebanon, Algeria, Egypt, or Jersey City? We should have taken out Saddam dead or alive. Would we have kept Hitler around after World War II to maintain a strong Germany to counter the Soviet threat? Of course not.

The White House and State Department bureaucrats blew it. We stopped short of total victory and watched as defeat replaced our military triumph. Within weeks of being kicked out of Kuwait, the Iraqis were slaughtering Kurds. And it was only the media coverage that shamed the Bush administration into taking action. And where are we now? The United States and the United Nations are still playing cat and mouse games with a conniving Baghdad regime that shows no sign of weakening or disappearing after four years of the very sanctions that Baker, Powell, and many of my Senate colleagues assured us would bring Saddam to his knees! So much for the conventional thinking.

WINNING THE WAR, LOSING THE PEACE

George Bush turned his greatest triumph into a quagmire of indecision and stalemate. I don't think he ever really recovered from letting Saddam off the hook. One of the earliest and most effective lines the Democrats used in 1992 was "Saddam Hussein still has his job—do you?" This might not have been fair, but it captured the public's frustrations.

Following the Gulf War, George Bush had an approval rating of 90 percent. He looked unbeatable in 1992. He had a golden opportunity to set the country marching to his agenda. The problem was, he didn't have one.

In September 1991, the Bush administration committed a

blunder that permanently destroyed its relations with the American Jewish community. It was a completely avoidable situation resulting from the arrogance and shortsightedness of Secretary of State James Baker. The $10 billion loan guarantee that I had discussed with Ariel Sharon was now a controversial topic on Capitol Hill. The United States would guarantee a $10 billion loan to Israel to pay for infrastructure and housing for the thousands of Russian Jewish immigrants. This was not an outright loan, but a loan guarantee. It would not cost U.S. taxpayers one penny unless Israel defaulted.

In the months following the Gulf War, many Americans feared the loss of their own jobs and were wary of spending billions overseas. The fact that Israel wanted only a loan guarantee was ignored in the heat of debate. Many Americans heard the words "$10 billion" and thought it was wasteful foreign aid.

Given the politics, the issue of loan guarantees for Israel had to be handled very diplomatically. But the President and the secretary of state poisoned the atmosphere between Israel and the United States. Even worse, their comments caused many American Jews to wonder whether the White House was actively anti-Jewish, or worse. When asked about the loan guarantee at a White House news conference, the President made an offhand crack that "thousands of lobbyists" were working for the loans and "I'm all alone up here." If the President intended to be funny, he missed the mark. His joke snidely insinuated that thousands of "Jewish" or "foreign" lobbyists were trying to take over our foreign policy. Coming from a man known for the country club company he kept, it was construed by many as an anti-Semitic remark.

And it got worse, much worse. When Israeli Prime Minister Shamir attempted to press Secretary of State Baker on the subject of the loan guarantees, Baker publicly rebuffed Shamir by saying that if Shamir wanted to reach the President on the issue he could call the White House. Incredibly, Baker gave the prime minister the phone number of the White House switchboard. Then the *New York Post* printed a story which quoted Secretary of State Baker uttering the phrase "F––k the Jews" at a cabinet meeting. It may or may not have been true, but it was perfectly consistent with the James Baker III I knew.

I was disgusted by these sad events. The White House had gone out of its way to belittle and to humiliate the prime minister of Israel and the dispute had taken on an atmosphere of "us vs. the Jews." This was dumb, this was nasty, and it was politically stupid. While I wholeheartedly supported the loan guarantees, I could understand the reluctance of many people to fund expansion in the West Bank. What I could not understand, and what I could not silently condone, were the mean-spirited, bigoted noises coming from the secretary of state.

I confronted Secretary Baker at a Banking Committee hearing on the loan guarantees. I gave him a piece of my mind in loud, angry tones. I didn't like him, and I know he didn't like me. He was personally repelled by Yitzhak Shamir. And he thought he was vastly superior to some Italian-American senator from Long Island. Jim Baker is a blue blood, a snob, and he didn't hide the fact that he really didn't care for ethnic Americans of any stripe. While he was free to dislike me, it was a dereliction of duty for the secretary of state to treat the prime minister of Israel like a panhandler.

As the controversy mounted, more and more Jewish Americans were outraged by Baker. Senator Dole arranged a meeting with Baker and six other Republican senators to see if there was a way to stop some of the bad blood between the White House and the Jewish community. I was still steamed at Baker, so I wasn't about to pull any punches at this more intimate meeting. Larry Pressler could tell how worked up I was and goaded me. "Hey, Alfonse," he said, in earshot of the secretary of state, "tell Baker the story about Haman." Baker looked at us with obvious confusion. "Who," he asked in his iciest Texas drawl, "is Haman?" I turned to him and blurted out, "You're Haman," but that didn't seem to register, so I told him and everyone else in the room the biblical tale of Haman and Queen Esther, which is the basis for the Jewish holiday of Purim. Haman was an evil counselor to the king of Persia. Haman had advised the Persian king to kill all of the Jews, and he was on the verge of succeeding when Queen

Esther used all of her womanly charms to turn the king against Haman. Esther succeeded in saving the Jews while Haman was cast out as a traitor and hung.

Baker went absolutely nuts. How dare I compare him to Haman? Baker's usually smooth, Ivy League temperament went out the window. I had finally gotten to him. But I didn't let up. I made my case loudly and forcefully that he had completely insulted the Jewish people in New York, and that I was their spokesman in the Senate. All the goodwill the Bush administration had won with its valiant efforts in the Gulf War was gone. Jewish voters would never forget his remark.

As it turned out, I was right–they did remember. In New York the Jewish vote turned out against George Bush, but provided me with my margin of victory. Nationwide, the President plummeted from his 90 percent approval rating to go down to defeat with only 38 percent of the popular vote.

And Jim Baker ran his campaign.

1992—
THE REAL
COMEBACK
KID

When I look back on my reelection to the Senate in 1992, I still get shivers. I rode to my swearing in on January 4, 1993, in the little Senate subway with Joseph Lieberman, the Democratic senator from Connecticut, a friend of mine. "You're the real comeback kid," he assured me. "You made one of the greatest political comebacks of all time. Maybe the *greatest* comeback ever." Joe then compared my win to the Buffalo Bills' comeback on January 3, 1993, when they beat the Houston Oilers after being down 35–3 at the half. "Besides that, Alfonse, no one can touch you."

After thanking Joe, I got off the car, took my oath of office, and began my third term as U.S. senator from New York. As I entered my office, I still couldn't get over how close I had come to political oblivion. It had been a wild ride.

My victory in 1992 surprised everyone, and to some extent, even me. The experts gave me next to no chance to win. Some called me "Rocky" and "the real comeback kid," but I thought of myself as the Carmen Basilio of New York politics. Basilio was a great welterweight and middleweight world champion boxer. He fought some of the greatest fights of all time against Sugar Ray Robinson. There are some classic photos of Carmen Basilio after a few of his victories with his nose and his ears bashed in. He could take pounding like no other fighter. Raised on an onion farm in upstate New York, Basilio was given little to no chance of becoming a professional boxer, but he persevered. Most of the time, when his bouts were over, he'd be battered and bloodied and bruised beyond recognition, but he would still be standing at the end of fifteen rounds and emerge triumphant.

On August 3, 1991, the day after I was cleared by the Senate Ethics Committee, I had an outdoor lunch in at the Ristorante Marionetta in Little Italy with two of my greatest supporters, my mamma and former mayor Ed Koch. Ed is no fair-weather friend. He supported me when almost no one else would. Some of the reporters who covered that lunch called it the unofficial kickoff to my 1992 reelection campaign. In many ways, they were correct. Having beaten Mark Green's frivolous charges, I was now ready to fight for my seat, and to regain the respect of the millions of New Yorkers who had put me in the Senate. Most of all, I was determined to defend my family's name. Many political experts urged me to step aside to allow a stronger Republican candidate to run for my seat. But I was not going to go quietly into retirement, or fade into some law firm and have people say, "There's Al D'Amato. He had to leave the Senate under some ethical cloud." My parents and grandparents had given me a good name and reputation. Even if I lost, I was going to go down throwing punches.

Two years before any election, I give up alcohol entirely. You have to get in fighting form to campaign day and night. I had been eating too much pasta, and my weight was up to 180. My good friend Larry Elovich helped me get into shape. Larry is a former Democratic leader from Long Beach and a health nut. We worked out in his basement and walked and bicycled up and down the Long Beach boardwalk. I don't know how many times he called me in Washington to make sure I was still working out. Thanks to Larry, my personal trainer and drill sergeant, my weight dropped to 165.

As we entered 1992, I was considered politically dead. In politics, a 30 percent negative rating is often considered fatal. In my case, after being unfairly tarred for three years, my negative ratings exceeded *50 percent*. By all rights, I should have been looking for another job.

But even if I was dead, the press didn't mind beating up on my corpse for good measure. By January 1992, *Newsday*'s coverage of me had grown so blatantly biased and hostile that even some on that paper's staff had to admit it. After more than two years of accusing me of criminal wrongdoing in connection with the sale of Roosevelt Raceway to private investors in 1984, the paper had to report on January 14, 1992, that a State Investigation Commission, ordered by Governor Mario Cuomo, had found no evidence of wrongdoing on my part. In fact the commission supported what I had been saying all along: "[D'Amato's] actions in this matter appear to have been based on his ardent belief in the use of Industrial Development Bonds as a means of economic development, and a genuine desire to save this harness racing facility, located in his former home district, because of its economic and social importance to the surrounding community."

Now, after dragging my name through the mud for more than three years, how did *Newsday* report my exoneration? Did they call me for a response? Did they declare in their headline that D'Amato had been cleared? Of course not. *Newsday* buried the story on page 25 along with the classifieds and the comics.

I immediately called a press conference. With the cameras running, I tore two copies of *Newsday* in half and blasted its editors for running completely biased coverage of me and my actions. "I'm objecting to the fact," I said, "that after you harangue me for three years, vilify me for three years, accuse me of misdeeds for three years, you do little to give me back my name. It's one thing to have a political philosophy. But this is a political agenda aimed to do me in politically and to do it in a matter that is not acceptable."

Newsday Editor Anthony Marro had to agree: "He's right that we should have given more prominence to the SIC findings concerning him, and that we should have called him for comment. There's no excuse for our not having done so."

Newsday's Bob Greene and Sydney Schanberg dogged me throughout the campaign, and they were hardly alone. It got so bad that even the most obscure events were magnified to vilify me. In September 1992, less than eight weeks before election day, the *New York Times* ran a headline in bold one-inch caps, "D'Amato Letter Appeared to Aid Reputed Mob Figure." But the facts did not support the headline. My office routinely sent such computerized form letters to agencies in response to constituent complaints. The *Times* did not make clear that this sinister letter was in reality a well-photocopied form letter:

> BECAUSE OF THE DESIRE OF THIS OFFICE TO BE RESPONSIVE TO ALL INQUIRIES AND COMMUNICATIONS, YOUR CONSIDERATION OF THE ATTACHED IS REQUESTED.
>
> PLEASE TRY TO RESPOND WITHIN 4 WEEKS OF YOUR RECEIPT OF THIS REQUEST. YOUR FINDINGS AND VIEWS, IN DUPLICATE, ALONG WITH RETURN OF THIS MEMO PLUS ENCLOSURE, WILL BE APPRECIATED.

It was a low blow, even for the *Times,* to characterize a letter that I knew nothing about as a special demand from my office on behalf of a mafioso. While the *Times* goes to all sorts of lengths to appear sensitive to every "politically correct" group or lifestyle, its editors thought nothing of tying an Italian-American senator with the Mob only weeks before a tight election.

In April 1992 we ran a series of radio ads that were short vignettes of people who had asked me to fight the government on their behalf. These were true stories of people whom the government had failed, or in some cases, even hurt. These highly effective spots halted my slide in the polls. My favorite radio ad told the story of Captain Hand:

> ANNOUNCER: Senator Al D'Amato. Getting it done. Making waves. Taking them on.
>
> Captain Dan Hand is a Long Island fisherman. He was off the coast of Long Island, doing his job, when he accidentally caught a World War II torpedo in his fishing net.
>
> He did what he should do. He told the navy.
>
> His reward? The navy blew up his boat, taking away his livelihood.

The government promised they would replace Daniel Hand's boat. But they didn't. They lied.

For seven months Captain Hand couldn't earn a living. For seven months he looked for help. He didn't get anywhere until Al D'Amato got involved.

Senator D'Amato went to work. He got the secretary of the navy on the phone and forced the government to make good on its promise.

And when that wasn't enough, he went to the U.S. Senate and passed a special amendment to make sure Captain Hand got a new boat.

Today, off the shores of Long Island, Captain Dan Hand is back earning a living as a fisherman.

CAPTAIN HAND: I'm Captain Danny Hand. Al D'Amato restored my livelihood. Thanks, Senator D'Amato.

ANNOUNCER: Senator Al D'Amato. Getting it done. Making waves. Taking them on.

D'AMATO: Paid for by friends of Senator D'Amato.

At first, people thought the ad was a spoof and called to find out if the story was true. As we highlighted more cases of New Yorkers who had turned to my office for help, the morale of my campaign picked up. Hundreds of people called offering to tell how Senator D'Amato had helped them.

We ran more than a dozen such constituent ads that spring. Another one told how I helped Marine Corporal Chuck Kleckner, who had lost the use of his right hand in service and was discharged with 70 percent disability benefits. Not long after returning to Bayside, Queens, he was mugged and lost the use of his other hand. Now a virtual cripple, Kleckner turned to the government that he had served so proudly. Incredibly, instead of increasing his veteran's benefits, the Veterans Administration cut his benefits by more than half! We got involved and not only restored his benefits, but obtained the full 100 percent disability he deserved.

We also told how I helped to obtain clean drinking water for the town of Brookhaven; how I helped an AIDS patient travel to France for treatment; how I helped a middle school in Manhattan save twelve teaching jobs; how I helped Barbara Harless find her missing children; and how I forced the federal Centers for Disease Control to finally take seriously the breast cancer epidemic on Long Island. All of the ads ended with the same combative tag line, "Al D'Amato. Getting it done. Making waves. Taking them on."

It was great to get our message across after so many months of fending off negative stories. A friend of mine even made a parody tape about "Al Tomato: Blowin' smoke. Takin' names." If our poll numbers weren't so bad, I would have given it to Don Imus or Howard Stern to air. But my reelection prospects were no laughing matter.

It seemed that every major Democrat in the state was considering or planning to run against me. With my low approval rating, it was not like 1986, when most ran the other way. National pollsters targeted me as the most vulnerable Republican senator up for reelection. As the Democratic primary neared, the announced candidates included the Reverend Al Sharpton; former vice presidential candidate Geraldine Ferraro; my 1980 opponent, Liz Holtzman; State Attorney General Bob Abrams; and Long Island congressman Bob Mrazek.

Early in the year, we considered Mrazek the most formidable opponent. While relatively unknown, he was a moderate and had support in the business community. He was also from Long Island, relatively popular, and capable of cutting into my home base. As it turned out, we never had to worry about Mrazek. Along with other House members, he admitted to writing hundreds of bad checks against the House bank. With the electorate in a dark and unforgiving mood, Mrazek found himself bounced out of the race.

With Mrazek gone, Geraldine Ferraro loomed as the strongest and most likely opponent. Ferraro's liberal base and her appeal among women who remember her as Walter Mondale's running mate made her more formidable than the bland and colorless Bob Abrams. As the primary wore on, Ferraro opened a commanding 20-point lead over Abrams, with Holtzman trailing badly. This drove Holtzman crazy. After all, she viewed herself as the real liberal. In her mind, Ferraro was not the rightful nominee. She started a kamikaze mission to destroy Ferraro. Holtzman hoped to emerge as the woman candidate in the "Year of the Woman." She launched a series of brutal attacks on Ferraro that were broad smears linking her to organized crime. Aware that he would probably benefit from this character assassination of his chief rival, Bob Abrams did nothing to distance himself from Holtzman's hatchet job. Holtzman's tactics succeeded in turning the Democratic primary into an ugly affair. In the candidate's final debate, Al Sharpton, long considered an irresponsible publicity hound, emerged as the most calm and statesmanlike of the bunch. Abrams won the nomination in a squeaker over Ferraro but there was bad blood on all sides.

> **Voters were so disgusted by Holtzman's tactics that she finished dead last.**

In the final count, voters were so disgusted by Holtzman's tactics that she finished dead last. In her blind and furious quest to destroy another woman's candidacy she had destroyed herself.

Less than a year later, in June 1993, as Holtzman geared up for a reelection campaign as New York City's comptroller, her career would end for good. It was revealed that the comptroller's office had given business to the Fleet Bank, which had provided her shady financing for her 1992 Senate primary battle. Holtzman, who had always presented herself as holier than thou, obtained loans from Fleet Bank at interest rates that were well below the market. Even worse, Fleet had made little effort to collect on the loans. Facing what looked like an easy primary fight, Liz, the ever sanctimonious one, was knocked off her high horse and defeated by Alan Hevesi. The *Daily News* printed a brutal photo of Liz crying in public accompanied by the headline "Time to Go." The extraordinary thing about Liz's Fleet Bank debacle is that she had taken these loans to continue a campaign she had no chance of winning. She did it just to try and trash another woman's reputation, and she wound up ruining her own. She deserved everything she got. Imagine the furor if Al D'Amato had done what she had done.

Ferraro took weeks to concede defeat to Bob Abrams. It was understandably difficult for Geraldine to support someone who was complicit in the destruction of her reputation. The embitterment of the Ferraro people was good news for my campaign. She certainly would have had appeal among Italian-American voters. Now I was running against Abrams, who was associated with an anti-Italian smear. Twenty-four hours after the primary, I called on Bob Abrams to apologize publicly to Geraldine. He didn't.

This set the tone for the whole campaign. We put Abrams on the defensive and kept him there. He had joined in the disgraceful treatment of Ferraro. A significant number of liberals were so turned off by Abrams that they voted for Clinton and then did not vote in the Senate race at all. I may not have won liberal Ferraro voters, but Abrams lost many of them. As I learned in Island Park as a young boy, in a close election every vote *and* every *non*-vote counts.

We blasted Abrams with the tag line "Bob Abrams, Hopelessly Liberal." Senator Pat Moynihan's former administrative assistant, Dick Eaton, told me that our ads were so effective that when someone mentioned Bob Abrams's name, his eight-year-old daughter responded immediately with the punchline "hopelessly liberal." In what became a war over ethics, Abrams called me "Senator Shakedown" and "Senator Sleaze." We informed New Yorkers of the Ferris Commission report, which had criticized Abrams for collecting campaign contributions from the very people his office was supposed to regulate. In fact, Abrams personally solicited a $15,000 contribution from a developer with $43 million to gain from a favorable decision by his office. In our TV ads, we reminded voters of Abrams's attacks on Ferraro while providing new details on Abrams less-than-pristine record: "We are not going to let mudslide Bob Abrams throw manure at Al D'Amato the way he threw it at Geraldine Ferraro and get away with it. Two can play at this game, Bob. So try to stick to the issues."

Bob Abrams had barely gotten out of the starting gate and we were hitting him hard on his negatives and neutralizing his ability to attack. My campaign was smart, fast, and focused. It had to be if we were going to have any chance of winning.

We were still in a deep hole. The Friday after Abrams's victory, we took a poll to get a sense of where I stood. I was trailing Abrams by 25 points.

My first debate with Abrams was nothing to be proud of. We both entered the event hostile and testy, and it quickly descended into a shouting match. But Abrams was the man with the 25-point lead. For me, time was slipping away.

The second debate was televised, and I did a better job of defining the race to my advantage by accurately painting Abrams as a taxer and a spender out of touch with the problems of New Yorkers. My daughter Lisa, her husband, Jerry Murphy, and their three children (Lisa was then pregnant with her fourth at the time) had driven more than 150 miles to watch the debate. When it was over, Lisa and all the kids bounded up on stage to kiss their grandpa Al. There was nothing like the sight of my daughter Lisa and three cute grandkids—Greg, 6; Dennis, 4; and 18-month-old Katie—to dispel my opponent's portrait of me as a corrupt monster. The credit goes to my son-in-law Jerry. He had watched the Democratic primary debate between Abrams, Ferraro, Sharpton, and Holtzman. When it was over, Abrams's daughters came running up and kissed their daddy. Abrams appeared warm and human, while his opponents seemed stiff and lost. Jerry was sure the Abrams kids would repeat their performance and insisted that Lisa and the kids come up so the same thing wouldn't happen to me. As it turned out, Abrams didn't bring his daughters, so Alfonse and the Murphy kids had the stage all to themselves!

After the debate, I had dinner with my family, my staff, and my campaign strategist and political guru Arthur Finkelstein. Arthur and I talked into the night about the campaign. He was upbeat, saying that the debate had gone well, that I had tagged Abrams with the hopelessly liberal line, and that it had stuck. I wasn't so positive. In fact, I was miserable. Maybe it was seeing Lisa and the grandchildren and the obvious concern they had for me. Wild charges had been hurled at me daily and I often wondered to myself, "Who needs this?" I should have kept my feelings to myself, but I didn't. Right after the debate, when the press surrounded me and started their usual ritual of shooting obnoxious questions, I blurted out, "This is the last time I'm running." The pundits thought this was a political ploy hatched to gain sympathy and support. But it wasn't. I was just one tired human being who had decided "enough is enough."

Arthur was very disappointed at my announcement. It was a mistake, but I meant it at the time. He told me I had clearly won the debate and, in spite of my doubts, thought I could still win the race. I was sure he was just saying this to make me feel better.

Despite my apprehension, the polls began to move our way. Maybe Arthur was right. Maybe the debates had made a difference. As much as we gained, a 25-point hole is almost impossible to climb out of, and we were still substantially behind Abrams in a state where polls showed Bush trailing Clinton badly. Ross Perot's reentry into the presidential race helped us. It would be easier for us pick off Perot voters than win in the face of what looked like a certain Clinton blowout. For us to win the Democratic voters who supported me in 1986, we had to count on their voting for Clinton and then crossing over on the ballot to my place on the Republican ticket. That was a lot to ask for. With Perot voters, it would not be quite as difficult.

Then Abrams blundered publicly. He labeled me a fascist in front of a group of about one hundred college kids in Binghamton, New York. It was now a regular part of his stump speech to call me "Senator Shakedown," but then he added, "D'Amato is a fascist," not thinking any reporters were in the crowd.

When the remark was reported, Abrams tried at first to deny it. After he was confronted with a tape, he claimed that he had been heckled by my people. But when the reporter pointed out that there were no D'Amato hecklers at the rally, he fell back to a story that in Elmira earlier in the day he had encountered people with D'Amato signs trying to disrupt him. The more he wiggled, the wimpier he looked.

Within forty-eight hours, we were on the air criticizing

Abrams for his "fascist" remark as an irresponsible insult to all Italian-Americans. Our ad showed a film of Benito Mussolini speaking in slow motion. The news media immediately jumped on our ad. One round table of "experts" on the *Today* show declared our Mussolini ad to be the worst commercial of the political season. So much for the experts. More than anything, that ad put Bob Abrams on the defensive, if not on the ropes. It proved to the voters that Abrams was not as nice a person as most people thought. Voters who thought they could turn to bland but safe Bob Abrams were now having second thoughts. Even after taking well-deserved heat for his "fascist" remark, Abrams never could keep his remarks, or those of his supporters, in check. I knew he had been using the fascist charge for months to private groups. In fact, a week after his public blunder, he appeared at a rally with Bella Abzug and Gloria Steinem. In Abrams's presence, the two of them called me a fascist. He stood by mutely. Two years later, I made a terrible mistake when I mimicked Judge Lance Ito on Don Imus's radio show. People were justifiably outraged. I saw that my remarks were hurtful, insensitive, and stupid. My family taught me to take responsibility for my mistakes. I took to the Senate floor to offer my apologies to Judge Ito and everyone I might have offended. As an Italian-American I have a special responsibility to be sensitive to ethnic slights and stereotyping.

As much as I love a good fight, I regret that the battle with Abrams got as ugly as it did. It didn't have to be that way. As far back as the spring of 1991, Abrams was engaging in a not so subtle whispering campaign. He went from fund-raiser to fund-raiser saying that there was an "ethical cloud over D'Amato." On issues, he knew from nothing. He was a spend-and-tax liberal and wasn't about to debate me on that. Although New Yorkers were overwhelmingly for a death penalty (as I was), Abrams wasn't. New Yorkers were suspicious of Abrams's schemes to pay for health care with higher taxes. One of our ads said that if we adopted Abrams's big government, single-payer health care plan it would result in a "tax on everything that moved and some things that didn't." While we tried to stick to the issues, Abrams's campaign centered on his personal attacks on me as "Senator Shakedown." For all intents and purposes, he was a bald version of my 1986 opponent, Mark Green.

In June 1991, during the Gulf War parade on lower Broadway for General Norman Schwarzkopf and his triumphant troops, I shared the platform with Attorney General Abrams. With four million tumultuous New Yorkers, falling ticker tape, and beautiful sunshine, it was hard to maintain a political grudge. I turned and offered Bob Abrams an olive branch. I said, "Bob, I know you're running, and I know we have legitimate differences on the issues. So let's stick to them and have a good campaign. Because if you continue this business of calling me Senator Sleaze, and Shakedown, I'm going to be forced to respond, and neither of us will look very good. We both have families, and at the end of the day, that's what's really important. Do we really want to put them through hell, or do we want to run a good campaign?" I was calm, nonconfrontational, almost collegial. I told him that we were like two boxers, so why didn't we fight a good and clean fight. The low blows don't count in the eventual scoring, they would only hurt us both.

Abrams was clearly uncomfortable in my presence and never really acknowledged my remarks.

Months later, at a political gathering in Rockland County, I had another chance to speak with Abrams. I again told him I didn't appreciate his persistent discussion of my so-called ethical lapses. This time my tone was more in the way of a warning than a friendly chat. Again, he chose to ignore me.

Our third encounter occurred two weeks before the general election, at a Plaza Hotel reception for Israel's new prime minister, Yitzhak Rabin. It was a very awkward occasion. A lot of bad blood had already been spilled between Abrams and me. He had run the same ugly campaign against me that he had against Ferraro. He had watched his once seemingly insurmountable lead shrink to 3 or 4 points. Yet Abrams acted like he was already elected. He had positioned himself, with a big grin on his face, at the entranceway to the reception so that everyone had to pass by him to get to Rabin. When I passed, he was no longer grinning.

"You don't get it, do you?" I asked. Abrams turned to me with a sneer and said in a loud voice for everyone to hear, "I resent you talking to me that way." It was our last private conversation before the election.

During our last televised debate, we were asked if we regretted the nasty, personal nature the race had assumed. I described my three encounters with Bob and my requests that we both stop the personal attacks. Abrams looked at me and told the cameras, "You threatened me." He looked pathetic.

As the days dwindled down, we stuck to a simple strategy: one press event a day while we pounded Abrams with radio and TV commercials. Abrams continued to attack me based on my "ethical cloud." While Abrams talked about ethics, we focused on the economy. We painted him as a hopeless liberal who would raise taxes.

In the last week, we ran a television commercial that drove a stake through the heart of Abrams's hypocritical campaign. It simply stated that Abrams, a millionaire with a home on Park Avenue and a Dutchess County estate, had been fined $1,000 for taking an illegal tax deduction when he declared that his bedroom was his office. He had also not paid school taxes on time on his Dutchess County home. It was simple but devastating. It began with the line, "Bob Abrams wants to raise your taxes—but millionaire Bob Abrams doesn't want to pay his own," and it concluded with "Bob Abrams never met a tax he didn't like, except his own."

Now that Abrams was caught in his own ethical lapse, our tracking numbers showed us moving into a statistical dead heat, which is where we were on election night. This was nothing short of a miracle. We had moved 25 points in the course of seven weeks, while George Bush, the head of the ticket, was projected to lose New York State by roughly one million votes.

Election day 1992 in New York was a miserable day. And I don't just mean for Republicans. It was pouring rain—cold, typical November weather. I took my granddaughter Katie into the voting booth in Island Park, and a local reporter took our picture. My mother's friend had a painting made out of that photograph, which now hangs in my Washington office.

The evening was to be impossible. I wasn't too sure I was going to be able to keep my composure in front of my family, my friends, and my supporters. That evening, I spent hours at a midtown Italian restaurant, with my closest friends and advisers. Ed Koch was there. So were Arthur Finkelstein and my old friends Marty Bernstein, who had raised the money for my first Senate campaign, and my friend and campaign treasurer Ambassador Charles Gargano. I was so nervous, I can't recall what we ate. Everyone was doing their best to keep my spirits up. They were my friends. Arthur insisted that I had a good chance of winning even though exit polls showed Bush being walloped. As of six P.M. those same polls showed me dead even with Abrams. Arthur was upbeat: "You're ahead, Alfonse." I told him he was full of it. I turned to Ed Koch and said, "Do me a favor and take care of Mamma." Ed Koch and my mamma have a wonderful relationship going back to my first swearing-in in 1981. In fact, not more than a month after his stroke in 1988, when his doctor put him on a strict diet, he had made a pilgrimage to my parents' house in Island Park. She fixed him a feast that could have put him back in the hospital. *Newsday* wrote a nice article about it. Nobody breaks a diet like Ed Koch.

As the evening wore on and the waiters took our plates away, I didn't want to leave. It was safe here with my friends to encourage me, and to tell me that we could pull it out. A couple from across the restaurant waved at us, told us, "Way to go, Alfonse!" and bought us a bottle of wine. They were young and probably weren't old enough to vote when I first won in 1980. Here they were cheering me on. It helped.

We had already won one victory that evening. A heavy turnout had resulted in long lines and delays in many polling places, and Abrams tried to keep New York City's polls open for an extra hour. Of course, according to Bob Abrams, New York's heavily Democratic precincts should have an extra hour to vote. Why not two? Why not a week? Luckily, a fair judge put the kibosh on that nonsense.

Arthur Finkelstein walked around the restaurant as if it was his own campaign headquarters. For all practical purposes, it *was* his command post. Hours seemed to tick by while Marty Bernstein told jokes and kept me from becoming too maudlin. Finkelstein came back to say that my friend Lauch Faircloth was ahead in North Carolina. He was going to win. If he won, so could we. Finkelstein was a human computer with trends, projections, and exit polls. We had been down a couple of points during the day, but had pulled even by the time we entered the restaurant. Ed Koch wondered if Clinton would take the state by a million or more votes. He didn't say it, but I knew what he meant. Who could survive against that kind of landslide? Arthur saw things differently. He came back to us with another exit poll. We were up by eight tenths of a percent–.8 percent! We could do it. Turnout would be key. Clinton was a factor, but my race with Abrams had been so personal, so bruising, and so loud that it had its own dynamic. Arthur argued that the Perot votes could swing it for us. It would be a long night, but we could pull it off.

It was 9:30 P.M. before we went to my campaign headquarters at the Hilton. As I entered the ballroom and looked at the crowd, my worst feelings resurfaced. My mother and father were there, my sons and daughters and grandchildren. My uncle Alfonse had come from Nutley, New Jersey. He was eighty-two years old. He should be home, not staying up all night in New York City. I had to stay strong for my family. I had to keep their spirits up, but how could I when I wasn't too sure I could keep my own feelings in check?

As a candidate, you have to project confidence when you are not sure of the outcome. Keeping everyone calm and confident is part of the game. It's a little like being the father of the bride at a wedding banquet. You have to beam with happiness no matter what you think of the groom!

At the same time you have a squad of experts upstairs working every possible phone and calling every key precinct in the state for the latest returns. It's as frantic as a trading pit on Wall Street in one room, even while a party is going on downstairs in the ballroom. It's enough to drive you out of your mind. I live for election nights. It's excitement, nerves, and more nerves.

In the Hilton ballroom were the hundreds of friends and neighbors who had worked endless hours on the campaign. While media attention was focused on our television ads and campaign strategies, my neighbors worked nights and weekends at our little Oceanside storefront headquarters. My neighbor Jackie Papatsos, the mayor of Island Park, spent nights there making phone calls, reminding people to vote and raising funds. Mike Scarlata, the Republican leader of Oceanside, was at the storefront every night, and was indispensable in maintaining a high level of energy and enthusiasm. Mike helped make the Nassau campaign a social event, a good time. Making calls can often be a tedious task, and there were times when my reelection chances looked like a longshot at best, but Mike kept everyone's spirits up, with jokes, stories, and coffee cake. There were times when I would get to the headquarters at ten at night and the place would still be filled with laughter. During a grueling campaign, I came to see the Oceanside office as my sanctuary and I derived an emotional high just from my visits there. Larry Elovich and his wife, Helen, would bring their friends from Long Beach. My friends Bob and Irma Schatz would be there, along with Frank McGinty and his son Michael. Andy Parisi and his wife, Lillian, would always bring some friends from the Five Towns section of Long Island.

They all came from Long Island to the Hilton to be with me, win or lose. I regretted that my friends Tony and Donna Gioa could not make it down from Buffalo, where they had shown me so much hospitality over the years, putting me up at their house and campaigning tirelessly when everyone else had given up on me. During my last swing through the state, Tony met me at the airport. It gave me such a lift to see a friendly face there. Only months later did he tell me that he came to the airport because he feared he would never see me again as a U.S. senator. He worked day and night for my campaign even though he feared I would lose. Friends like Tony are priceless.

I was happy to see that John O'Mara and his wife, Ann, could come. During my 1980 race, John had been the center of my campaign in Chemung, Steuben, and the counties in southwestern New York known as the Southern Tier. My executive assistant Margie Dillon was there. She had worked for me back when I was Hempstead Receiver of Taxes. Along with Miriam Madden, who has worked with me since 1962, Margie is an indispensable part of my New York office. I couldn't function without them.

The crowd at the Hilton was unusually buoyant, and I soon learned why. The local news showed us ahead of Abrams. Early returns, I thought, and Arthur agreed with me. Probably Island Park. At least I could count on Island Park. This early lead, I thought, would evaporate soon enough.

But it didn't. Three points up. Five points. Eight points. It was unreal. It couldn't last. Unbelievable. Here I had steeled myself to stay calm in defeat, and I was getting the greatest charge of my political lifetime. Bush was getting shellacked in New York. Only Massachusetts and Arkansas provided Bill Clinton with larger margins. But we were running ahead.

At 10:30 P.M. the incredible occurred. Associated Press, and then all three networks, declared Alfonse D'Amato the winner in the biggest upset of the night. I grabbed Arthur and conferred with my campaign manager, Kieran Mahoney. Could it be true? Was this victory?

Suddenly the whole night shifted gears. Now the band, the music, and the hoopla didn't sound like a cruel joke. This was a celebration. Ed Koch had disappeared after dinner to write his newspaper column and now he had returned to bask in the glow of unexpected triumph. Together we schmoozed with what seemed like every rabbi in New York State. Peter Kalikow, the owner of the *New York Post*, was there. He was working his contacts to get us more complete election results. I went upstairs to the private room where my family could watch the results. I hugged my daughter Lisa, whose face was soaked with tears. She had always been a sensitive kid, and this election and all the things the press and my political opponents had said about me had hurt her much more than me. To me it was just politics. To her, they were attacking her daddy.

As always, my father worked the room. With his refined voice and elegant carriage, he always seems larger than five foot six. I embraced him and the room applauded.

I don't know what time it was or if I was upstairs or downstairs when Arthur took me aside to say that the networks had called back their projections. It was now officially too close to call. It was a wake again. My family, friends, and supporters were in shock. The euphoria created by the early projections had swept away all of their emotional armor. Downstairs, the band played on.

But the crowd was somber now. Defeat seemed possible and you could taste it in the air.

Arthur and my campaign manager Kieran Mahony worked harder than ever to track down every last unreported precinct. As midnight approached, we still had a 100,000-vote lead. With most of the evening's races over, the television news teams remained glued to the festivities in Little Rock, where the beaming families of the Clintons and the Gores swayed incessantly to the babyboomer anthem "Don't Stop (Thinking About Tomorrow)." We still had tonight to get through, and it was going to be a long one.

Meanwhile, Bob Abrams's staff declared that he would win. They were behind by 100,000 votes and declaring victory. Would their arrogance never end? The biggest difference between the people in my hotel room and those in Abrams's camp was that my people had come to be with me win or lose, and his had come to watch him win. As the evening wore on and I began to grow more philosophical about my possible defeat, I could appreciate more and more the wonderful people who had made my career possible.

Downstairs, Conservative Party chairman Mike Long acted as my unofficial emcee. We had grown close since he initially opposed me back in 1980. Even when Mark Green, *Newsday, 60 Minutes,* and Sydney Schanberg were throwing everything at me, Mike Long gave me his total support for reelection.

Kathleen Mahoney was there too. With her husband, Dan, she had worked for generations to build a real Conservative Party in New York. Her son Kieran had started working for me as a researcher during my 1980 campaign and now he was my campaign manager. Kieran never lost his cool. He calculated that our victory was never in doubt. My press secretary, Zenia Mucha, repeatedly reminded me that while the networks were fence-sitting, AP was sticking to their prediction of a D'Amato victory. Jack O'Leary, Conservative Party chairman of Nassau County, and Terry Anderson, my local Island Park Conservative Party leader, hoisted a glass in an exaggerated toast. They had been key to each of my elections to the Senate. They were there for me tonight. My old friend from my days at Syracuse University, Walter Caligaro, came up to me, punched me in the arm, and said, "Hang in there, Al. We're going to make it." I thanked him for coming from New Jersey to be with me.

There was a piano in our family suite. At about one A.M. I sat down and started to sing. My piano playing is rusty and my voice is nothing to speak of, so it was a good thing that I got the room to join together for some old corny tunes and Broadway favorites. To everyone's relief, my father volunteered to take over at the keys.

I was listening to my dad when Arthur came up to me and put his hand on my shoulder. We'd been through hell together many times and tonight certainly qualified as a new circle of political hell. Normally gregarious and full of energy, his voice was low and somber and full of concern. He knew the last thing I needed was to be jerked around again. He spoke with calm assurance and told me that we had won.

He and Kieran were pulling out all the stops. They called John O'Mara about the state's southern tier. They crunched numbers with Assemblyman Tom Reynolds from Buffalo. By identifying the unreported precincts, we were trying to determine, even before the official tally, what the result would be. Half of Staten Island hadn't been counted, nor parts of Nassau, Suffolk, and Erie Counties. Based on that information, Arthur was sure that even though more than 200 precincts in heavily Democratic Brooklyn had not been reported and paper ballots and absentee ballots from Manhattan were outstanding, we would win at least an 80,000-vote victory. "Alfonse," he told me, "it's time to go address your supporters. You're a senator for another six years."

I reminded Arthur of the last time we had been through this. Back in 1980, he told me I had a sure 5 percent lead over Holtzman, and that I should go down and give a speech. But by the time I reached the podium, my 5 percent lead had shrunk to 1 percent! I told Arthur I couldn't afford to lose 4 percent again. Arthur would not listen to my superstitious concerns and insisted that I declare victory. There were still two thousand people milling about—old people, priests and rabbis, and party stalwarts from as far away as Buffalo. Win or lose, they had come. It was time for them to see me win.

My son Danny heard the news that we had won, and he ran across the room to embrace his weary father. When I won in 1980, I lifted him over my shoulder and above the crowd. He was twelve years old then. Now he was twenty-four, six feet two, and 180 pounds, and I should have known better. I threw caution to the wind and tried to throw Danny over my shoulder. This time, I collapsed with a sharp, shooting pain from my right knee. So much for trying to relive your fondest memories.

I didn't have much of a victory speech prepared, and I don't really recall what I said. I do remember, however, who gave the shortest, most eloquent talk of the late evening. My mother stood up there, just five feet, and she had the crowd in the palm of her hand. "You know they call my son the pothole senator. The pothole senator. Well you know they're wrong. He's the people senator. The people's senator." The crowd went wild once again for Mamma D'Amato.

Looking at my mom and my pop, my children, and the faces of hundreds of my friends and neighbors, I realized that I had triumphed and would serve for another six years. But thoughts of power and office paled beside the feelings of warmth and love I felt from the people who were surrounding me. Most of them had known me for years. I saw faces from law school, high school, even grammar school. Some I had known since I was a little boy on the streets of Newark and Island Park. A boy few would have expected to grow up to be a United States senator.

REGRETS

Politics is a very rough game, and I've taken my fair share of hits. But of all the cheap shots and low blows, I've been personally hurt only by those directed at my family and friends. As a three-term senator, I know I am fair game. But when people I know and love suffer because of efforts to demean or disgrace me, the game has gone too far. Certainly the *Village Voice*'s vicious attacks on my father's reputation during the 1980 campaign were uncalled for. Mark Green's use of the Senate Ethics Committee to settle a political score also set a new low standard for political sportsmanship.

But the two meanest examples of dirty politics run amok are the criminal prosecutions brought against my brother Armand and my friend Jack Libert. In both of these cases, the criminal justice system was used and abused for transparently political purposes. Neither of these prosecutions would ever have been brought if Armand and Jack had not been very close to me. Both Armand and Jack suffered greatly because they knew me, and for that I am deeply sorry. What happened to these two men should never happen in America. But it did.

JACK LIBERT

Jack Libert and I go back together to the early 1970s, when I was Hempstead Supervisor and he was an attorney for the Nassau County Board of Supervisors. Jack eventually became the board's counsel. After fifteen years in public service, he went into private practice and later merged his firm with my brother's law firm. This new firm, D'Amato, Forchelli, Libert, Schwartz and Mineo, was one of the best on Long Island.

Shortly after entering private practice, Jack was approached by two individuals who promoted Israeli tax shelters. They asked Jack to review their investment programs to see if they would satisfy the IRS. After careful analysis, Jack warned that these tax shelters could raise a red flag.

And Jack turned out to be correct. The IRS did audit the shelters and discovered fraud. And beyond that, the two individuals had misappropriated funds, which came to the attention of the FBI. When the Justice Department began to examine the case, they seized upon the fact that Jack Libert was tangentially involved and began to target Jack. The prosecutor behind this action was an assistant United States attorney in New York's Southern District, James McGuire. According to many who worked with McGuire, he had a real fixation on me. He wanted Libert to get me. He tried to get the two tax shelter operators to finger Libert in exchange for immunity. In prosecutor slang, this is known as "working your way up the ladder." You get a small fry you are not interested in and threaten to charge him with a crime unless he cooperates in helping you get the "big fish." This is perfectly acceptable when crimes have been committed, but to manufacture a crime is reprehensible.

There was absolutely no case against Libert. When Libert's lawyer, Robert Fink, met with McGuire to ask what the case was all about, McGuire reportedly responded that all charges against Libert would be dropped if he would "give us D'Amato." Fink relayed McGuire's offer to Jack Libert, who was stunned. When Fink returned to McGuire and told him his client was "not aware of any wrongdoing by either Alfonse or Armand D'Amato," McGuire made it clear that he was not interested in what Libert knew or didn't know. According to Fink, McGuire simply said, "Have [Libert] come in and talk to us. After we hear what Libert has to say, we'll talk about a deal for him."

It's amazing this actually happened in America.

At first, Libert could not quite comprehend the sheer cynicism of McGuire's offer. "You mean to say," he asked Fink, "that the government is proposing to tell me what they want said about the D'Amatos? If I agree to say what they want, they will be lenient with me. The truth is irrelevant to them."

"You understand it correctly," Fink replied.

Libert flatly refused McGuire's corrupt offer and suffered the Justice Department's groundless prosecution.

McGuire's irrational prosecutions were not limited to Jack Libert and the

If the system worked, why wasn't James McGuire in jail?

D'Amato brothers. At the same time that McGuire was pursuing these cases, he was censured for trying to launch an undercover investigation of his own boss, U.S. Attorney Otto Obermaier. After that, he then began a personal vendetta against gays and minorities in the U.S. Attorney's Office that finally got him fired.

After McGuire was given the boot for such vindictive and paranoid behavior, you would think that his very dubious prosecution of Jack would be dropped. Unfortunately, that's not how bureaucracies work. Because it involved Jack Libert, a law partner of a U.S. senator's brother, this was a high-profile case. Having gone as far as it did under McGuire, it would have taken someone at the Justice Department a great deal of guts to admit that it was wrong. Dropping such a case would result in a lot of media stories, and some might be spun that pressure was brought to bear to leave Al D'Amato's friend alone. The high profile of the case guaranteed that it would go forward.

And Jack Libert was put through the ringer. His phone was tapped. His tax records were subpoenaed. Every law firm and financial institution that he had ever done business with was informed of the case against him and interrogated. If the Justice Department had taken out a full-page ad in the *Wall Street Journal* saying, "We think Jack Libert is a crook!," they could not have done more damage to his reputation.

After two years of legal fees, intimidation, and public humiliation, Jack Libert's trial took place before Judge Jack Mishler. It lasted two weeks. Two assistant U.S. attorneys, four special agents, and several support people attended the trial each day. They were all lodged at taxpayer's expense at the five-star Garden City Hotel.

On June 25, 1992, the jury took less than three hours to find Jack Libert innocent on all counts. A case that should never have gone to court was finally over. When interviewed by a local newspaper, Libert graciously said that he was "gratified in the final analysis [that] the system works!"

I have to disagree with my dear friend. If the system worked, why did he have to spend more than $700,000 to defend himself? If the system worked, why wasn't James McGuire in jail for abusing his privileged position as an assistant U.S. attorney? If the system worked, somebody would pay my friend Jack Libert back for the suspicious stares of his neighbors, the whispers behind his back, and the damage done to his reputation. It took courage to fight a Justice Department that had terrorized him and his family. A lesser man would have crumbled.

THE CASE AGAINST MY BROTHER ARMAND

The prosecution of my brother Armand was ultimately exposed as one of the weakest and most blatantly political actions ever brought in the long history of New York State. In reversing my brother's conviction, the United States Court of Appeals for the Second Circuit unanimously ruled that it was "inconceivable" that a civil suit against Armand could have survived, "even under the lower burden of proof applicable to civil cases." The court also excoriated the prosecution for misstating the evidence and for repeatedly "block[ing]" Armand's defense at trial. It was an unprecedented and well-deserved reprimand.

My brother Armand is a distinguished attorney who served in the New York Assembly from 1972 to 1992. While my detractors love to depict Armand as my little brother, that is simply not true. For many years, Armand had far more clout and visibility as a legislator in Albany than I ever did as a Hempstead Town Supervisor. Armand is a smart and capable attorney. He never needed any connection to me or anyone else to succeed.

The prosecution of my brother was legally unprecedented. It rested on the convoluted claim that Armand had used the U.S. mails to defraud the shareholders of Unisys Corporation, a military contractor with a large facility on Long Island, of the "right to control" legal fees paid to him.

My brother was charged with mail fraud, but he never sent a false legal bill to Unisys. In fact, every bill his firm sent sought payment "For Professional Services Rendered re: Monthly Retainer." The prosecution created a crime by claiming that Armand's bills did not expressly state each and every service he provided, including a complete description of some lawful lobbying of my office on behalf of Unisys. Several bills had also been sent out on the letterhead of a partner in the firm.

The prosecution created a crime by claiming that Unisys shareholders somehow had the right to control retainer payment of no more than $6,500 per month to a lawyer. The appeals court ruled this was absurd. Shareholders don't control such payments, and Unisys management had approved every penny paid to Armand's firm.

Armand provided all sorts of lawful legal services to Unisys. He met with management in his office; he was briefed on major defense contracts; he reported to management on the status of such contracts; and he met with congressional staff.

Lobbying has all sorts of bad connotations, but it is protected by the First Amendment. Many distinguished former officials–Republicans and Democrats–lobby as part of their law practices. Armand was a former assemblyman, and many of his former colleagues were now in Congress. Everything that he did was perfectly legal.

Armand did make a mistake. He asked my office to send two routine letters to the Navy inquiring into the status of a government contract. There was simply nothing illegal, or underhanded with these letters. Each year, I send hundreds of such letters on behalf of constituents. And Unisys was a big Long Island employer. They didn't need Armand to obtain a letter.

But the two letters had absolutely nothing to do with the prosecution of Armand. While the prosecution and press falsely created the impression that Armand was indicted for political corruption, nothing was further from the truth. While, in retrospect, he should not have contacted my office, he violated no laws.

Robert Jackson, who served as attorney general to President Franklin D. Roosevelt and went on to be a justice of the U.S. Supreme Court, once warned that prosecutors violate their sacred duty most when they pick on people they think they "should get," rather than cases that need to be prosecuted. Clearly, Armand's prosecution was a case of prosecuting first and creating some theory for doing so later.

My brother's prosecution rested on a very controversial theory developed in prosecuting E. Robert Wallach, who was a lawyer for former Attorney General Edwin Meese. Wallach had sent two letters to a client acknowledging payment for work on the company's initial public offering and shipyard acquisition. His supposed crime was failing to mention his lobbying of Meese on behalf of the client in these letters.

After Wallach was convicted of racketeering, his conviction was thrown out on appeal. The court's reasons for exonerating Wallach were a shocking rebuke to his prosecutors: perjury by the main witness against him, and the conclusion that prosecutors knew or should have known about the perjury. The court did, however, uphold the theory that incomplete legal bills could deprive shareholders of their right to control corporate spending, even if the company's directors and officers weren't deceived at all. Wallach's seven-year-long legal nightmare finally ended when, after he chose to represent himself at his retrial, the jury deadlocked.

Relying on broadly stated principles announced in the much

criticized Wallach case, the Justice Department went after Armand. He was unjustly forced to spend thousands of dollars on his defense that he had set aside for his children's education. Our elderly parents were wrongfully put through unimaginable hell. Armand was falsely branded a felon for almost two years.

Before the indictment was brought against Armand, his lawyers, Paul Rooney and Mike Armstrong, were convinced that the government had no case. The government had pushed the envelope with the Wallach case and the case against Armand was far weaker. At least against Wallach the government had produced witnesses—albeit admitted perjurers—who testified that the defendant to a scheme to misstate a public company's books of account and SEC filings to shareholders. The evidence was undisputed in Armand's case that all payments to his firm were properly accounted for. My brother's "for services rendered" bills were no different from bills sent by lawyers, doctors, and plumbers every day.

The Justice Department permits a potential defendant to make a presentation why an indictment should not be brought. To make this presentation, my brother's defense team brought in one of the country's most respected lawyers, Robert Fiske. (If Bob's name sounds familiar, it should. He served as special counsel in the Whitewater affair until replaced by Kenneth Starr.) Fiske would represent Armand only if he were convinced of his innocence. After carefully reviewing the facts, Fiske strenuously argued that the government wanted to go far beyond the Wallach precedent in trying to find my brother guilty of something—anything.

Despite Fiske's powerful argument (which ultimately was proven right on appeal), the Justice Department indicted Armand on March 11, 1992. It was one of the saddest days of my life. Like the Libert case, the case against Armand was too hot a potato to drop.

Prior to trial, *Newsday* reported inflammatory grand jury testimony. *Newsday*'s repeated editorials accusing the D'Amato brothers of political corruption—when no such charges were ever brought—confused Armand's jury about the narrow and technical charges against him and made it impossible for him to get a fair trial.

The news of Armand's indictment brought much joy to my political opponents. Less than eight months before election day, it provided the perfect fodder for Bob Abrams to talk about "an ethical cloud" over my head. Liz Holtzman went so far as to taunt me about the matter during a parade in Queens (more on that in the next chapter). I refused to become obsessed over my brother's case. It wasn't easy to do.

On May 7, 1993, after a year of public humiliation and a two-week trial, Armand was convicted of seven of the twenty-four counts of mail fraud alleged in the indictment. The jury never understood the actual charges. Prosecutors Larry Noyer and Joshua Hochberg had succeeded in their strategy of capitalizing on inflammatory pretrial publicity and public distrust of politicians and lobbyists. Although the conviction was a setback and a personal blow to my entire family, Armand left the courtroom convinced that he would win on appeal. He maintained his dignity throughout this ordeal. He showed class.

Seven months later, Judge Jack Mishler gave my brother the lightest possible sentence–five months. Mishler saw the unfairness of Armand's prosecution. He remarked that "maybe one out of 100 [lawyers] would say no" to the billing arrangement for which Armand faced imprisonment and disbarment. Well into his eighties, Mishler left it up to the appeals court to throw the case out.

The press had a field day with Armand's sentencing. *Newsday* saw fit to print a blazing "D'Amato Sentenced" headline on page one, so millions of Long Islanders and Armand's neighbors could read all about it. It was disgusting. To make matters worse, *Newsday* even sent a reporter to call on my mother and badger her about why she didn't show up for Armand's sentencing. What kind of person would want to torment a seventy-eight-year-old mother? I had seen a lot of low blows from *Newsday,* but this was the lowest.

A few weeks later I expressed my feelings about this coverage to *Newsweek*'s publisher. Along with about two thousand others, I had been invited to Donald Trump's wedding to Marla Maples at the Plaza Hotel.

Donald and I have shared some great times together. To his credit, he never gave up on me when I was down in the polls and lambasted by the press. As someone who has been on the brink of bankruptcy and back, Donald has a great perspective on the fickle nature of public notoriety. In 1992, my campaign produced an ad blasting the Abrams campaign for taking tens of thousands of dollars from major contractors who had business pending with the Attorney General's office. Bob Abrams had accused me of being "Senator Shakedown," but he sought contributions from construction people who depended on the goodwill of his office. We wanted the people to know what a hypocrite Abrams was. The ad showed a bald-headed man from behind, seated at a large cash register ringing up the large amounts of $10,000, $15,000, and $25,000 along with the name of his major contributors. One of the contributors mentioned was Donald Trump, whom I called to explain what we were considering. To his credit, Donald said, "While I don't need this kind of publicity, I know you're in the campaign of your life, and if this is going to help, then use it." We never ran the ad but Donald Trump showed guts for understanding why we might.

The Trump wedding was a media frenzy. At one point, I ran into my old friend Bernadette Castro, who is now New York State's parks commissioner. Many New Yorkers of my generation remember Bernadette in ads for her father's famous convertible couches. She was a four-year-old girl who showed that even a child could pull the mattress from the couch. At Trump's wedding, she took me by the hand and led me directly to her friend *Newsday* publisher Robert Johnson. She told me I simply had to say hello. I didn't want to, but Bernadette made me feel as if I were being an unreasonable boy.

Good manners would dictate that I smile and extend my hand. I had recently endured a similar situation when Mike Wallace greeted me during the intermission of the New York opening of Jackie Mason's *Politically Incorrect* and extended his hand. I smiled and thought what a phony he was. I knew darned well that while Mike Wallace was saying, "Hello, Alfonse," he was really waiting for the day when he could ambush me again. Such are the necessary hypocrisies of public life.

If Yitzhak Rabin could shake Yasir Arafat's hand, I guess I could shake Bob Johnson's.

To his credit, Johnson didn't try to smooth over my obvious discomfort with idle small talk. He immediately reminded me of an earlier occasion at which I had publicly stated that I thought *Newsday*'s coverage of Armand's trial was fair. "That's right," I said. "But your front-page coverage of my brother receiving a five-month sentence was completely out of line."

As my voice grew louder, both Bernadette and Johnson got the impression that maybe this wasn't the right time to try to bury the hatchet. But since the fat was in the fire, I was not to be deterred.

"You'd think my brother was Jack the Ripper!" There was no stopping me now. "And then you go and have a reporter call my mother! She's almost eighty years old! You have the nerve to ask her why she didn't attend the sentencing? Have you no shame, no decency?"

Johnson conceded that harassing my mother was not in the best taste. But, he said, the news was not his province. My beef was with editor Anthony Marro.

After my tirade, Johnson quickly moved on. I realized right then that while it felt good for about five seconds to get it all off my chest, my little talk with Johnson had accomplished nothing. Would this outburst change *Newsday*'s unfair coverage of the D'Amatos? Of course not.

A few minutes later I was chatting with *All My Children*'s Susan Lucci and her husband, Helmut, marveling at the size of Donald and Marla's wedding cake. It was a fantastic cake and became the focus of everyone's attention. We were trying to figure out just how much it weighed when Johnson and Bernadette joined us. Then boxing's Don King approached our group, and was introduced to everyone, including Johnson. King had recently been the subject of a series of scathing articles in *Newsday* focusing on his criminal record, alleging that he swindled money from his fighters and that he was the consort of notorious criminals. I wondered how King would handle meeting Johnson. To my surprise, upon hearing the publisher's name, King's face lit up with the most infectious smile I have ever seen. He grasped Johnson's hand and shook it like the handle of a water pump. "Oh, Mr. Bob Johnson, sir, the most wonderful publisher. What an honor it is to finally make your acquaintance. Oh, Mr. Johnson, sir, let me extend my sincere congratulations on the fabulous series of stories in your newspaper about me. I can only tell you how I read each and every *word* with complete attention, sir. Oh, Mr. Johnson, let me shake your hand."

King gushed, crooned, and ladled it on so thick that we all stood in awe as Johnson was reduced to a quivering, humiliated bystander at his own execution. It was a beautiful moment. I have no idea if half of the things written about Don King are true, but I take my hat off to him for having shown me the fine art of public decimation. It was an absolute knockout! Johnson barely said a word, and after King and his entourage moved on, he slipped away from our group.

In February 1994, I had another public encounter about Armand's case at the annual dinner of the Alfalfa Club. This club's membership of 232 includes many Supreme Court justices, legislative leaders, business executives, and other members of Washington's power elite. Although I have never spent much time ingratiating myself with this crowd, it was fun to be invited once for the annual dinner. The club has no sponsor, no building, and no real reason for existing—except for their annual dinner at which members pretend to be the "Alfalfa Party" and to nominate their candidate for president. This night's nominee was House Speaker Tom Foley. The dinner also marked the very first time that women were inducted into the club. *Washington Post* publisher Kay Graham, Supreme Court Justice Sandra Day O'Connor, and former secretary of labor and transportation Elizabeth Dole were all attending their first dinner as Alfalfa members.

I had been invited by good friend Senator Pete Domenici of New Mexico, who was elected president of the club. I was happy to see Pete elected president of such a distinguished group.

While making the predinner rounds, I chatted with Colin Powell, Senator John Danforth, and others before I heard someone calling my name. I turned around to see Arthur Liman. He is an outstanding lawyer, best known for his role as the Democratic counsel during the Iran-contra hearings. I had no idea why he was so eager to talk to me at this very public function.

Arthur told me he had been following Armand's case quite closely and was appalled by his conviction. He had just read the post-trial briefs prepared by my brother's appellate lawyers and was eager to help write an amicus brief on behalf of my brother. (In cases raising important legal principles, distinguished groups sometimes submit such briefs as "friends of the court.") I realized that this meant Armand's case had become a cause célèbre in the legal community. His conviction threatened to criminalize widely accepted practices, such as "for services rendered" bills and monthly retainer agreements. This was an ominous development for the bar.

There are many instances when a client may want a lawyer to send a "for services rendered" bill. Armand's billing of lawful lobbying services for Unisys was no different from the bills sent by other lawyers who render services in connection with take-overs, criminal investigations, bankruptcies, and other sensitive matters. "For services rendered" bills protect the confidentiality of services. Such bills ensure that clerical employees do not disclose such confidential information to the press or chatter about it with their friends to the company's detriment.

Arthur Liman told me emphatically, "Alfonse, your brother's case will be reversed. Your brother will win." I had just heard the same thing from Armand's young appeals lawyer, Bob Giuffra, but was not convinced. The government wins more than 90 percent of all criminal appeals and the judges might not want to take any flack for reversing Armand's conviction. But Liman was adamant. "Alfonse, I don't care who the panel is. Your brother will win."

I can be emotional, and I was greatly moved by Liman. Here was an establishment liberal Democrat who wanted to write a brief on Armand's behalf. This was an extraordinarily decent thing for Liman to do. Ultimately, Liman and a young lawyer, George Conway, prepared a very persuasive brief for the New York State Bar Association and four other prestigious bar associations. Even more remarkably, the New York Civil Liberties Union advised in an amicus brief that the Justice Department had violated "fundamental principles of due process" in convicting Armand. None of these groups came forward out of love for me or my brother. They did so because of the terrible implications of the case against him for lawyers everywhere.

After this uplifting moment, my emotional high was temporarily ruined when I ran into former Secretary of State James Baker III at the Alfalfa dinner. I could not look at him without thinking of the botched 1992 race. I wondered why the Bush campaign never took on Clinton for some pretty questionable behavior in Arkansas. Some people, including *Newsday* columnist Lars Erik Nelson, have speculated that Bush feared his son Neal's involvement in the Silverado Savings & Loan would more than overshadow the questionable loans and write-offs of the Clintons, James McDougal, and their friends at Madison Guaranty. Still, it struck me as the height of insanity for the Bush campaign to roll over and die the way it had in 1992.

> "Alfonse, I don't care who the panel is. Your brother will win."

If only all the Alfalfas could be as decent and honorable as Pete Domenici and Arthur Liman.

THE NIGHTMARE ENDS

I became somewhat more confident as the date for Armand's oral argument approached. His lawyers, John Warden and Bob Giuffra of Sullivan & Cromwell, had prepared an excellent brief that exposed the government's case for what it was–a thinly veiled political prosecution of absolutely no merit. The amicus briefs added further legal support and, more important, credibility to Armand's case.

I knew the D'Amato family nightmare would have a happy

conclusion when I listened to the tape of the oral argument of the appeal. John Warden made a powerful presentation in his deep southern voice. He was asked only a single question. Then, when the prosecutor's time to speak finally arrived, the questions started coming from all directions. Experienced courtroom observers had never seen anything quite like it.

Before the prosecutor could even utter her name, Judge Milton Pollack thundered down from the bench, "Had the government introduced any accounting records indicating that Armand D'Amato had committed fraud?" The prosecutor was flustered. Then, the presiding judge, Ralph Winter, observed that a mining company might want to conceal the hiring of a geologist. That wasn't criminal, was it? For the next thirty minutes, the judges pounded the prosecutor's case. Judge Pollack was particularly disturbed by the prosecution's improper summation to Armand's jury and had counted more than twenty improper references.

On October 31, 1994, the federal appeals court issued a thirty-seven-page opinion completely exonerating Armand. The court unanimously ruled that, even under the view of the evidence most favorable to the prosecution, Armand did not violate any law. In fact, the court made it clear that Armand's case never should have come to trial, much less to jury. It agreed with Armand's lawyers and the friends of the court that lawyers do not commit mail fraud simply by submitting a "for services rendered" bill or a bill in the name of one partner in a firm.

I started crying when Bob Giuffra called with the news. But we could not locate Armand. It turned out that he was swimming at the Y. Exercise had helped him endure this terrible ordeal, and it was fitting that when the news came that he had won, he was working out. I was even more happy for our parents. They had attended the trial and been subjected to the hordes of reporters. The pain had taken its toll.

The press could not ignore the magnitude of Armand's vindication. The *Times* called the decision a "strong rebuke to federal prosecutors." The *New York Post* said: "It's outrageous that Armand D'Amato had to suffer this lengthy ordeal. Still his vindication is complete—based not on a legal technicality but, rather, on a determination that he never should have been charged." The *Wall Street Journal* praised the case as "withering in its rebuke of the federal prosecutors who brought the case." The court had refused to "let ambitious prosecutors twist the mail fraud statute into a rubber hose to go after whomever they chose."

In all fairness, I have to admit that the Long Island edition of *Newsday* did carry the story of my brother's exoneration on page one. They didn't send any reporters to interview my parents about their joy and vindication, but perhaps they knew they might not be welcome. In a strange coincidence, just days after Armand's reversal *Newsday* publisher Robert Johnson, to whom I had given a piece of my mind at the Plaza, was let go by the parent company, Times Mirror. While I do not gloat at any man's misfortune, I cannot help but think that life works in very strange ways.

Just as in the case of Jack Libert, the system had finally worked for my brother Armand, but at a horrendous personal, professional, and financial cost. It was a political prosecution undertaken solely to hurt me and my family. We had won a total victory, but when I see the lines of worry on my mother's face, I know that the cost of battle was too high. I'm also reminded of the statement of former Labor Secretary Ray Donovan upon being exonerated after eight years of hell: "Which office do I go to to get my reputation back?" Armand rightly asked the same question.

PART IV

POLITICS, NEW YORK STYLE

PARADES
AND
POLITICS

T he old song "I Love a Parade" must have been written by a New Yorker. Every single year there are just so many parades in New York. One of the detectives assigned to protect me, Brian Ahern, used to complain that he couldn't turn on the television without seeing one. I told him that's a good thing, because New York's parades reflects its tremendous diversity.

It's no secret that parades are perfect for politicians to express their solidarity with different ethnic groups. I try to march every year in our famous St. Patrick's Day parade. It's great to be Irish for a day, or to march with the Greeks, or in the Israel Day parade or in the festive West Indian Day parade that turns Brooklyn's Eastern Parkway into a carnival every Labor Day. If you march in one parade, you should try to march in them all.

ED KOCH AND AL D'AMATO: GERMANS FOR A DAY

The one parade that is second to none in terms of efficiency is the German-American Steuben Day parade, which is held every October. It starts at 12:00 sharp. It doesn't matter who the grand marshal is. It could be the President of the United States, but if he got there one minute after twelve, the parade would have started without him. It's an orderly parade and even more orderly crowd, and the streets seem to be cleaner after the parade takes place.

It was in October 1980 during the Steuben Day parade that I first met New York's number-one parader, Mayor Ed Koch. I thought I loved parades, but Koch, with his trademark "How'm I doin'?" at every block, gathered energy with each wave. I was in the midst of a heated race for the Senate when I rather timidly introduced myself to His Honor. I shook his hand and mentioned that since he had met with Republican presidential candidate Ronald Reagan the week before, I wondered if he would like to meet with me to discuss those federal issues most important to New York City.

I was well aware that Koch, a Democrat, had taken incredible heat for meeting with Reagan while he was challenging Jimmy Carter for the White House. To his credit, Koch responded with the common sense that endeared him to most fair-minded New Yorkers: "Ronald Reagan may be the next president and certainly I should meet with him." I was hoping that Koch would show me the same nonpartisan hospitality. I was trailing Liz Holtzman by more than 20 points with less than five weeks to go. Koch had been a five-term Democratic congressman, and he certainly had no obligation to give me a boost.

To my delight, he responded without hesitation, "Absolutely. Have your press person contact my scheduler and we'll arrange it." Thus began a political friendship that has benefited the city and state of New York. Not only did we work closely for the remaining nine years of the Koch administration, we began a friendship that has grown closer over the years.

My visit with Koch could not have come at a more opportune time. It provided millions of dollars worth of free publicity and added legitimacy in the eyes of Koch voters who might have been on the fence. When grilled by the media after meeting with me, Koch wasted no time defending his decision to keep his options open. "Al D'Amato may be the next United States senator from New York, and I want him to know what our problems are and want to know that we can call on him for help." Having served in the House with Holtzman, Ed Koch had no use for her and made it clear that he wanted me to succeed Jacob Javits.

TANGLING WITH LIZ AT THE PURIM PARADE

Parades attract politicians of all stripes, even those who might be running against each other, and generally the festive nature of the occasion keeps hostility and naked political vindictiveness from creeping in. No one wants to see would-be statesmen brawl at a parade. I tried to avoid any nasty encounters, but there was one incident involving Liz Holtzman when I simply couldn't help myself.

It took place in May 1992, when two of my Democratic rivals, Liz Holtzman and Bob Abrams, had made an election-year pilgrimage to Kew Gardens, Queens, to march in the Purim parade. I had marched in this parade every year. As a result of so much parade experience, I had developed my D'Amato Rule for Maximum Parade Visibility: run like hell for the head of the parade. This was no mean feat, and thank God for my years of track at Chaminade and Syracuse. One year, as I was making my mad dash, I was suddenly stunned with a hip check that sent me flying twenty feet into the crowd. Had I been blocked by Dick Butkus? Had Wayne Gretzky arrived? In my confusion and considerable pain I realized none other than former Congresswoman Bella "the Hat" Abzug had upended me. This agonizing encounter forced me to amend my visibility rule: always steer clear of swinging hips and walk in the clear.

Now every rule has its exception, and the exception to my parade rule is if you can latch on to a popular nonpolitician who is willing to walk with you, do so at all costs. I was more than happy to follow this exception at the 1992 Purim parade. I had the fortune of walking through Kew Gardens with Jackie Mason, perhaps the most beloved Jewish entertainer in New York, if not America. Holtzman and Abrams could only look on in envy as the crowds mobbed us. Mason rubbed it in by repeating, "Vote for Al D'Amato, the best friend Israel ever had."

This goodwill brought out Liz Holtzman's nasty streak. When we took our seats, she came up to me and actually said, "Well, they finally got your brother." She was referring to Armand's indictment. If she were a man, I would have knocked her flat. Instead, I whispered to her, "Liz, you are as ugly on the inside as you are on the outside." At this, Liz, the Wicked Witch of the Left, started to scream, "I dare you to repeat what you said. I dare you to tell these people what you said." Like most bullies, she could dish it out but she could not take it. When I left the bandstand, she was still sputtering, and would continue to do so until her sanctimonious reputation came crashing down with the Fleet Bank scandal a year and a half later.

Jackie Mason was cold, so we both made a beeline for the warmth and comfort of Benjy's Kosher Pizza and Falafel Restaurant a block away. The neighborhood went wild. I even heard one person ask, "Who's that guy standing next to Jackie?" You've got to have a pretty thick hide in this business.

Bless his heart, Jackie never let the crowd's obvious enthusiasm for him get in the way of his nonstop plugs for me. At one point, he grabbed me and shouted out to the gathered crowd, "How could they call this guy Al D'Amato a thief? Look at this guy's clothes! I've seen better clothes on *tzebrochen* [broken-down] and *tzehget* [dead-looking] bums!"

St. Patrick's Day Politics

Sadly, one of New York's oldest and most celebrated parades has become embroiled in controversy. Gay activists have demanded the right to carry banners and placards identifying themselves as gay Irish. The parade organizers refused, and the uproar was ugly and contentious.

I was somewhat confused about this uproar until I heard my friend Jim Gill speak to the Friendly Sons of St. Patrick in New York. The organizers, he explained, are simply committed to keeping the parade from being politicized. No banner, save one proclaiming "England Out of Ireland," is allowed in the parade. It's the only political message allowed in the entire parade. There are many causes that concern the Irish in New York. Immigration reform is probably number one. U.S. immigration laws had virtually stopped all legal immigration from Ireland from 1965 to 1986. New York has thousands of illegal alien Irish men and women who would love to march under the banner of immigration reform. While the Catholic Church supports the right-to-life movement, it has never requested, or demanded, that placards proclaiming this position be carried in the parade. For years, the efforts to free Joe Doherty, who many consider to be a political prisoner of the English, have been of primary concern to many Irish in New York, but no "Free Joe Doherty" posters are allowed in the great parade.

For 231 years, the parade has been a festival, a celebration of the Irish, their emigration to New York and America, and their thriving success in their new land. It is also a religious festival, a saint's feast day—St. Patrick being the patron saint of both Ireland and the Archdiocese of New York. It also honors the church in America. Because of the religious nature of the parade, the organizers have strenuously fought to keep politics out of the parade.

For more than two centuries, then, the parade was kept free of political rancor. This was no small feat. The Irish gift for argument and politics probably equals or surpasses the Italian's passion for pasta!

The politicians who backed the gays and bashed both the parade organizers and the church reads like a who's who of New York's politically correct pols, who will do *anything* to curry favor with an influential voting block. In 1992, Democratic Senate hopefuls Elizabeth Holtzman and Robert Abrams, mayoral wannabe Andrew Stein, and Mayor David Dinkins all refused to participate in the parade.

The parade should be a day in the sun—even if it is often a chilly winter sun—for the Irish. All of New York's ethnic groups have their special day. And yes, there is a great Gay Pride parade too. That's what this country—and particularly New York City—is all about.

Courts have now held that the First Amendment protects the right of the Ancient Order of the Hibernians to keep politics out of the St. Patrick's Day parade. Imagine if the government forced the Israel Day parade to accept a float from the PLO? What if the state insisted that Anita Bryant march in the Gay Pride parade? Ridiculous? Of course. The government cannot force a private or religious institution to do anything it does not want to do. That's what freedom of speech, freedom of assembly, and freedom of religion are all about.

MARIO
AND ME

I have always liked and respected Mario Cuomo. He is a thoughtful man and an eloquent speaker. Although I disagreed with most of the rhetoric in his now famous address to the 1984 Democratic Convention, I was moved by the passion of his words. As the first Italian-American senator from New York, I was proud when Mario was elected governor two years later. During the Senate Ethics Committee investigation, Governor Cuomo defended me and professed his sincere belief in my innocence. I was moved by his generosity.

While I admire Mario the man, New York suffered under his leadership. By every indicator—from crime, to jobs, to quality of life—New York declined in the 1980s. For too long, Governor Cuomo defended his record by claiming that he was fighting a valiant rearguard action against Reaganism. But that excuse wore thin. With Bill Clinton in the White House and Democrats in control of Congress, Mario had no one left to blame for New York's plight.

New York State's government is too big and taxes too much. New York used to be the Empire State. Under Cuomo, we became a tax-hungry Vampire State, ready to tax the life and enterprise out of every business and individual until they flee to New Jersey, the Sun Belt, Asia, or Mexico. I made up my mind that this had to stop.

Until 1991, Mario Cuomo and I had worked together for New York. Throughout the 1980s, I constantly went to bat for the state with the Reagan and Bush administrations. When the Reagan administration proposed eliminating the tax deduction for state and local taxes—an act that would have devastated New Yorkers—I was among the first to protest. The governor publicly appreciated my efforts, and I was never shy about helping my governor. The press even claimed we had a nonaggression pact. I did not break the peace between us. To my surprise, and disappointment, our cordial relationship ended abruptly and distastefully in the summer of 1991.

CROWN HEIGHTS

The Crown Heights riots were a turning point for New York City. On the night of August 19, 1991, a car in the motorcade of Rabbi Menahem Schneerson skidded out of control and killed a seven-year-old boy named Gavin Cato. Tragedy quickly gave way to hysteria, rumor, and violence. For days, roving gangs of street thugs held the community of Crown Heights hostage. Some posted anti-Semitic signs praising Hitler. But these gangs did not stop at signs and taunting. One unfortunate young man, Yankel Rosenbaum, was chased for three blocks by a gang shouting, "Kill the Jew! Kill the Jew!" He was surrounded and stabbed repeatedly, and he later died. In the 1990s, a lynching took place on the streets of Brooklyn.

Now this horrible story would be astonishing enough if it did not occur while New York City police had their hands tied behind their backs. The mayor, hoping to score political points with black voters, ordered the police to placate a rampaging mob. The mayor, to quote Governor Cuomo, had given the black community a "day of grace" to vent their rage over the death of Cato. The Jewish community learned that their civil rights, their safety, and their very lives were secondary pawns to the political maneuvering of New York's timid and calculating mayor, David Dinkins.

This was not the first time that David Dinkins had waffled under the pressure of New York's racial politics. In 1990, only months after his inauguration, Dinkin's faced a violent and illegal boycott of a Korean grocery in Flatbush, Brooklyn, led by the agitator Sonny Carson and a band of other shakedown artists. This racist boycott continued for months without a peep from Gracie Mansion. Dinkins ignored a court order and refused to take on Carson to protect the store owner. This cowardly act gravely disappointed many voters who had supported Dinkins. He had been elected, by a tiny margin, as a healer. Jerry Nachman, the *New York Post*'s editor, had endorsed him wholeheartedly as a mensch–a man of decency and integrity. Unfortunately, what New York got was a man of expedience, who showed the backbone of a marshmallow when the streets of Brooklyn exploded with the shouts and signs of "Kill the Jew!"

Crown Heights caught the Jewish, liberal establishment off guard. There has always been an uneasy relationship between the largely Hasidic community in Crown Heights and the Jewish establishment. The Hasidim–with their old-world garb, public passion for religion, and their conservative, family values–are a bit of an embarrassment to those Jews who live in Manhattan or the suburbs.

The Hasidic community is one of the few large white communities who have made a very pointed decision not to abandon Brooklyn. While many suburban Jews speak fondly of memories of Ebbets Field and Flatbush Avenue, the Hasidic Jews have stayed. Their stubborn persistence to survive in Brooklyn has often caused friction with their black neighbors.

Crown Heights was a wake-up call that few heeded. Where were Geraldine Ferraro, Elizabeth Holtzman, Mark Green, Bob Abrams, and Mario Cuomo when Yankel Rosenbaum was murdered? It is not "politically correct" to criticize a black mayor. Where were they when David Dinkins did nothing, and the New York Police Department was forced to sit on its hands? I did not remain silent. These riots violated everything I believe in. The government had failed to do its most basic job–protect its citizens. To make matters worse, while the city was still simmering in the aftermath of Crown Heights, David Dinkins was going to lead a delegation on a trip to South Africa. On Bob Grant's afternoon talk-radio show on WABC, I said that the trip was a mistake, but "if the mayor wants to take a sabbatical, maybe we could get someone who could run the city."

The media and Dinkins's allies seized upon this tongue-in-cheek comment. Deputy Mayor Bill Lynch, Dinkins's political guru, called me a racist. He said that I might as well have said that "we should all send the jungle bunnies back to Africa." The *Daily News* published more racially charged remarks that I never made. Their subsequent retraction did nothing to cool the explosion of righteous liberal indignation aimed at me. I had legitimately criticized the mayor's failure in the face of a crisis, but the media focused on remarks I never made. Too many reporters and publishers are consumed with white liberal guilt.

I was disappointed when Governor Cuomo joined in the chorus, saying that my comment "had a racist tinge." I did not expect such political opportunism from him, so I contacted a mutual friend, Vincent Tese, a close confidant of the governor. I told Tese that I was disappointed by Cuomo's statement. "As far as I'm concerned," I said, "the matter is closed. I will not respond to Mario's statements." But not more than a week later, the governor again accused me of racism. He publicly said that my remarks were tantamount to urging the return of all Italians to Venice. Suddenly, it seemed, Mario Cuomo had decided that there was some political advantage in attacking me. I was heading into a tough reelection fight while he was a potential presidential candidate. Maybe it would enhance his reputation if he could help finish me off. I was hurt. We had worked hard together for New York. Now, he said, "D'Amato delivers the baloney but not the bacon."

I concluded that the time for turning the other cheek was over. Three months later, in December 1991, I traveled to Albany to speak on behalf of an effort by Republicans in the legislature to submit their own version of the state budget. Cuomo was furious to see me take part in Albany politics. He put out the story that I was trying to disrupt his bid for the White House. This was nonsense. I was simply articulating the weariness of New Yorkers with Mario's tax and spend politics. Did he think that the voters across the country would *not* size up his record in Albany if he ran for the White House? I said as much on the capitol steps in Albany: "If people can't run their own budget here in the state, obviously people will wonder how you can handle that situation nationwide." The governor called me President Bush's attack dog and lamely responded that he could not enter the presidential race while a budget battle raged in Albany. He had not yet left Albany and was already starting to wilt in the spotlight.

When Mario Cuomo announced on December 21 that he could not enter the presidential race until the budget battle was resolved, Democratic leaders blamed me. State Democratic Chairman John Marino raved, "I'm going to make Al D'Amato pay for this. The gloves are off. He's through." I had definitely hit a nerve.

> Their very lives were secondary pawns to the political maneuvering of New York's timid and calculating mayor.

As Mario's wheels spun in the upstate winter snows, he got testier and testier. On January 8, 1992, I challenged him to a debate. He responded with personal venom, joking about my debating skills and blasting me as a "terrific talker," who had "talked myself out of a lot of trouble in Washington."

FOR THE LOVE OF THE MIKE

The next month, on February 17, Senator Moynihan and I attended the Association of Towns Convention at the Hilton Hotel in Manhattan. The room was filled with almost a thousand local officials from all over the state. There are more than 900 towns in New York, varying in size from a few hundred people to more than 700,000 (in my own town, Hempstead). Town supervisors and councilmen were having a very tough time. Try as they might to maintain local services like police, sewage disposal, garbage collection, and parks without raising property taxes, they were constantly saddled with mandates from the state and federal governments. Towns, villages, and counties became little more than tax collection agencies. In many suburban communities, it is not uncommon for middle-class taxpayers to pay more than $7,000 in property taxes a year on a modest home. This tax burden devalues property, rightfully infuriates homeowners, frustrates local officials, and has resulted in an exodus of people. The opportunity for young families just starting out to buy a house and to raise children in a community with safe neighborhoods is no longer a reality. As a former Town Supervisor, I understood the plight of these communities. We needed to cap spending, to cut taxes, and to privatize. I also proposed the introduction of workfare, not welfare, in New York and received thunderous applause.

After speaking, I went to the back of the room to listen to Senator Moynihan's remarks. Governor Cuomo was next. As soon as Mario took the podium, he began to lambaste me. He thought that I had left the room. He arrogantly sneered at my challenge to his policies. "Al D'Amato wouldn't dare say what he said if he knew I was here. He wouldn't have the nerve." To Mario's great surprise, I called from the back of the hall, "I'm here, Mario. Listening to your nonsense."

When the governor signaled for me to join him at the microphone, the whole room erupted. The place was in an uproar, with close to a thousand local officials eagerly anticipating the fireworks between Mario and Al. As I approached the stage, I saw that there was no place to sit, I grabbed a folding chair and took it with me. When my mother saw the events on the news, she later told me, "Al, when I saw you pick up that chair, I thought you were going to use it on the governor!"

The governor turned to me and asked me if I wanted to speak. I told him, "Not until you're finished. I don't want to interrupt." He then told me he was done and invited me to the microphone. Hundreds of officials shouted, "Give him hell, Al!" Many wanted me to let the governor know how bad things were and how the state and federal bureaucracies had lost touch with reality. I told Cuomo, "I'm not singling you out personally, but we need a spending cap and a tax cut at the state and federal level."

The reference to the federal budget obviously rankled him.

Even at that moment, a plane was waiting to fly him to New Hampshire for the announcement of his candidacy. There were dozens of cameras everywhere and reporters from every news organization hoping to get a scoop on a Cuomo run for the White House.

The governor rather testily tried to wrest the mike from me and to distort my words. Usually, people are afraid to debate him. He seemed shocked that I had accepted his challenge. He tried to bully me by asking questions and then misinterpreting my answers as he saw fit. He also personalized the debate, as if every point I made about the state and federal government was a slight directed at *him*. I wouldn't let him get away with this tactic.

Instead of retreating, as anticipated, I told Mario, "I never mentioned you by name. If there is anybody here who says that I even said 'the governor,' I'd like you to play back the tapes. But I did say, that at the federal level and at the state level we have got to cap spending, we have got to make workfare and not welfare and we have got to cut the fat out of the bureaucracy that is choking our educational systems and failing to deliver the services to the people of this state. Now that is what I said."

The governor then tried to take back the mike. I chastised him by mockingly saying, "Now Mario, I thought you were done, that's what you said to me, 'I'm done.' " The crowd was now delirious. They'd never seen anyone take on the governor before and they were enjoying it.

Cuomo could see that the crowd was not on his side. He said, "Let me ask you. Let's have a real discussion." To which I replied, "Good." But his idea of a debate meant distorting my positions. "You suggested that you would like to cut federal spending," he growled. But I did not let him get away with it. "No," I replied. "Cap, cap. You cap the spending. You cap the spending in the state too."

To which the governor responded, "Does that mean, Al, that you will not give us any more help than you are now giving us at the state and local level?" "Mario," I explained, "it means that across the board we can't say, 'Cut spending but don't cut my favorite program,' because that is what we have been doing." The crowd broke out in applause, and that only made Mario madder. "No, no, no," he protested, "you didn't answer me. Are you saying when you reduce the spending?" I came back with my best line of the morning. "I did answer you, Mario, you just didn't like the answer.... I didn't say reduce, I said cap."

But Mario continued to distort: "Cap–does that mean you are not going to give the state or the locals any more money? Are you also going to cap the aid to foreign governments? Just tell us clearly. We need more help. Are you going to give us more or less or the same?"

"Mario," I explained again, "if we are going to cap spending, it means across the board for everyone. We've got to hold the line on spending. That's my answer." Those assembled broke out in cheers again.

And so it went. Mario and I bantered back and forth, and every time I presented my case, he tried to distort it. Maybe he and I speak a very different brand of the English language. When I say "cap spending," I mean just what I say. He jumps through so many Jesuitical contortions just to avoid the obvious. This was never so clear as when he talked about welfare.

I received wild applause for supporting workfare. The governor lectured the assembled for having the nerve to challenge the current system: "Senator D'Amato just told you that what we need is a change in the welfare law and you all cheered.... But Senator D'Amato didn't answer the question, I don't blame him–welfare is one percent of the federal budget. Eighty-seven percent [of the recipients] in this state are women and children ... if you took them all off the welfare rolls, it would have nothing to do with the help we need to give you. What are you going to do with your friends, the bankers? What are you going to do with your friends in the Pentagon? What are you going to do with all of that corruption? What are you going to do with foreign aid? You come here and say to these people–and what's worse, they cheer you– you say to them I know the answer. It's not savings and loans, it's not defense, it's not entitlement. That's too tough for me. It's welfare. Get those women with children. That will solve our problem. I think it's a lot of baloney, and I think you ought to know it.

Thank you for your patience. God bless you."

Those were his parting words. He never responded to my criticism of mandates or capping spending. When he didn't like the way the local officials—many of whom were Democrats—cheered my remarks about welfare, he left in a huff.

Mario's appearance at the Association of Towns Convention was a flop. It was a harbinger of things to come. He never took that airplane to New Hampshire. It would have been fascinating to see him run against Bill Clinton, a candidate who campaigned on the promise (as yet unfulfilled) to "end welfare as we know it."

The question remains, Why didn't Mario Cuomo run for president in 1992? It wasn't the budget battle. Mario's woes in Albany were only a fig leaf. The fact is, you need a thick hide to survive a national campaign. While a great orator, he's always had trouble taking criticism. The media is brutal on presidential candidates and always has been. They called Lincoln an ape and a baboon. Grover Cleveland was taunted about an illegitimate child. They hounded Al Smith with scurrilous remarks about his Catholicism. Dirty tricks didn't start with Watergate and "bimbo eruptions" didn't start with Bill Clinton. Mario Cuomo did not want to jump into that kind of rough water.

Our debate at the Association of Towns meeting was great copy. *Newsday*'s headline blared, "Mario's Regret: Wishes he was campaigning in NH; Instead, he's at home arguing with Al D'Amato" The *Post*, characteristically, was more irreverent: "For the Love of Mike." Both reported that when the going got tough, Cuomo left the room. Mario's presidential dreams were done, and our fight to replace him in Albany had just begun.

GEORGE
PATAKI

After my comeback win over Bob Abrams, the press immediately began to speculate about a possible D'Amato vs. Cuomo battle in November 1994. In June 1993, I indicated that the chances were better than 50–50 that I would run, and many polls showed me running a strong race against Cuomo. That month, the press reported that the World Trade Center bombers had targeted me. At the same time there was talk that the Yankees would move to New Jersey. I quipped that New York was exporting its jobs and businesses to New Jersey while New Jersey sent us terrorists. This remark did not sit well with folks in the Garden State. But it served notice to Mario that I would not sit on the sidelines while his policies drove out business and the governor's opposition to the death penalty made a mockery of justice.

In the fall of 1993, the full extent of Mario Cuomo's arrogant stance against the death penalty was exposed for all New Yorkers to see. Thomas Grasso was convicted of murder in both Oklahoma and New York. He was sentenced to die for his Oklahoma crime. But instead of letting Oklahoma carry out its sentence, Cuomo had the gall to have him extradited to New York State where he would be imprisoned for twenty years before being returned to Oklahoma. Cuomo's rationale was completely out of touch with reality. Grasso's incarceration would cost taxpayers more than $600,000. Even more obscene, some violent criminals would be paroled to make space for him in our overcrowded prison system. Incredible.

In November 1994, New Yorkers elected George Pataki, who promised to send this killer back to Oklahoma. The new governor fulfilled this promise in his first weeks in office, and Thomas Grasso was executed in March 1995.

On October 19, 1993, I informed State GOP Chairman Bill Powers that I would not run for governor in 1994. I could have won. But, as a three-term senator, I was in a much better position to serve New York from Washington than Albany. I assured Powers and all members of my party that we could beat Cuomo if we ran a fiscally conservative Republican, someone who was committed to cutting spending, to cutting taxes, and to privatizing government. With my trial balloon candidacy over, the job of replacing Mario Cuomo had officially begun.

My flirtation with the governor's race had served its purpose. As long as I was a possible candidate, the field would not fill up with dozens of would-be nominees, dividing the party before we even had a chance. I was convinced that, more than anything, we needed a united Republican Party and an alliance with the Conservative Party to unseat Cuomo. Although the governor had won easily in 1986, the 1990 election, in which Republican and Conservative votes were divided, exposed his weakness. Cuomo had managed to get only 52 percent of the vote against Pierre Rinfret, a pathetic and wacky Republican candidate, and the Conservative Party candidate Herb London, who nearly outpolled Rinfret. Cuomo would be vulnerable against an articulate Republican candidate with Conservative Party backing. But I knew the media and the liberal establishment would do everything in their power to preserve Mario and destroy his opponent.

After I announced my withdrawal, many Republicans rushed to enter. Most were carbon copies of candidates Mario Cuomo had already beaten. Richard Rosenbaum, Nelson Rockefeller's old state party chairman, had the backing of Rocky's brother

David and former Governor Malcolm Wilson, but few of the rank and file. Former Manhattan Congressman Bill Green also threw his hat in the ring as a representative of "moderate" Republicans. But, if he couldn't win among his Silk Stocking district's voters, how could he prevail statewide?

On the conservative side, Herb London was more formidable. He had run an impressive campaign for governor in 1990. But I thought that London's 24 percent showing in 1990 was the best he could do. He would alienate many voters and galvanize support behind Mario Cuomo. In a London-Cuomo race, London would become the issue, and Mario would face an easy race.

The only Republican with the right stuff to beat Cuomo was State Senator George Pataki. The tall, handsome, Yale-educated former mayor of Peekskill had the right politics and credentials to beat him. I like George Pataki. We have certain things in common. While no one will ever accuse me of being a handsome Ivy Leaguer, we both began our political careers on a local level working our tails off to save our own small towns from decay. When George was elected mayor in 1981, Peekskill was considered "dead" by many. Its main streets were filled with boarded-up buildings. People were moving away. George fought to turn it around and instilled pride and hope in his home town. Within a few years Peekskill was thriving, and the same people who had written the town off were talking of a "miracle."

As much as I admired George, when he sought my support in September 1993, I could not commit. Ralph Marino, the majority leader of the State Senate, was openly hostile to George. It did not seem wise to back a candidate who would alienate the most powerful Republican in Albany. But George did not back down. "I'm still running," he said, and thanked me for my time.

For most of the brutal winter, I conducted a very public search for a gubernatorial candidate. Many names were trotted out—mogul Donald Trump, entrepreneur David Cornstein, and Jack Hennessy, chairman of First Boston. At one point, I tried to round up support for Frank Zarb, President Ford's Energy Czar and Smith Barney's chairman. But at the last minute Zarb decided not to run.

I pleaded with Senator Ralph Marino to drop his irrational opposition to George Pataki's candidacy. But Marino would not budge. With the Republican convention less than a month away, we still had no candidate. I decided to support Pataki come hell or high water. I admired George's willingness to run against all odds. All of those critics and writers who say that George Pataki is "D'Amato's puppet" have short memories. George ran in spite of the fact that I undertook a very public search to find another candidate. George began his race as his own man, and he will govern as his own man.

Once I decided to support George Pataki's candidacy, I worked with state chairman Bill Powers to ensure that Pataki would emerge from the convention with overwhelming support. No one wanted the party divided from May to September by a bloody primary campaign that would benefit only Mario Cuomo. I contacted virtually every county Republican leader on George's behalf.

Some accused me of heavyhanded machine politics. This was nonsense. I was simply trying to unite the party around the strongest possible candidate. Ironically, my biggest critic, Richard Rosenbaum, had used some pretty heavyhanded tactics when he was running Rockefeller's party in the sixties and seventies.

The Republican Party nominated George Pataki by an overwhelming majority. No other candidate received more than 25 percent of the delegates, and so we were spared a bloody primary. Herb London, George's most formidable rival, agreed to run as the candidate for comptroller. After nominating my friend Bernadette Castro to run for the U.S. Senate, we tapped the scholar Elizabeth McCaughey for lieutenant governor and prosecutor Dennis Vacco for Attorney General.

Our balanced, attractive ticket wasted no time driving home the theme "It's Mario Cuomo's Fault."

The Democrats never knew what hit them. Many dismissed George Pataki as "George Who?" My most persistent, albeit inconsequential, critic, the weekly *New York Observer*, claimed that I supported George because I was sure he would lose and wanted to prserve my position as the number-one Republican in the state.

The *Observer* even predicted that Cuomo would win in a cakewalk.

Nothing was further from the truth. Within weeks of his nomination, George Pataki was running neck and neck with Mario Cuomo. By July, the proud governor publicly was musing that he might lose. Speaking before the State Democratic convention, Cuomo could not make a credible case for four more years. At one point in his speech he pointed to the new rest stops on the New York Thruway. Was this the crowning achievement of Albany's fighting liberal? The would-be president? The man who turned down a seat on the Supreme Court? Rest stops?

Even though Cuomo's heart was not in his speech, I knew that George Pataki faced a tough fight. But George presented the governor with his first strong challenge since 1982, when he beat Lew Lehrman by less than 200,000 votes.

I thought Mario Cuomo would lose. But I didn't expect that the race would turn so nasty and that so much venom would be directed at me. It didn't come from Governor Cuomo alone.

RUDY GIULIANI

My stormy relationship with Rudy Giuliani goes back more than ten years. We have been friends and foes, but I sincerely believe that the city and the state have been best served when we have worked together. I was delighted when Rudy was elected mayor in 1993. David Dinkins had failed to lead. A Mayor Giuliani would never have allowed Crown Heights to get out of control.

I first met Rudy in 1981, when he was the Associate Attorney General, the number-three man in the Reagan Justice Department. I was then fighting for more drug enforcement agents and customs officers for New York, and Giuliani immediately impressed me as someone who could make a difference.

New York was being overrun with drugs. Narcotics traffickers laughed at our pathetic efforts to stop them. The Reagan administration talked tough about drug enforcement, but did little to fight for the money necessary to get the job done. While Ed Meese, who became attorney general in 1985, posed as Mister Law and Order, he didn't do much to get funding for customs agents. Some of the Reagan administration accused me of demanding "pork" when all I was asking for was decent enforcement of our borders against drug smugglers. Jim Baker sneered at me when I held up a vote on chemical weapons to get more drug enforcement money, but I felt that drug enforcement is just as important to our national defense.

Giuliani shared my feelings about the drug epidemic. We worked on legislation to allow the confiscation of drug dealer's cars, boats, and homes. It hit the gangsters where it hurt and raised countless millions of dollars for the war on drugs. Rudy gave criminals no quarter. I was impressed.

In 1983, the position of U.S. Attorney in New York's Southern District became vacant. My judicial screening committee– headed by Paul Windels and including former Secretary of State William Rogers, Conservative Party powerhouse Tom Bolan, Serphin Maltese, and my friend and attorney Mike Armstrong–interviewed dozens of prospective candidates for the job. After careful deliberations, they strongly recommended John Keenan, a former special prosecutor and longtime assistant D.A. in the Manhattan office of the legendary Frank Hogan.

Just days before I was to recommend John Keenan, Rudy Giuliani came to see me. He wanted to return to the Southern District as U.S. Attorney. I thought he was crazy. Many would consider such a step to be a demotion. In fact, Rudy later joked that his mother had said just that. But he explained that he was eager to return to New York. He had just become engaged to TV reporter Donna Hanover, who was moving to New York for a job with WPIX-TV. While Washington–New York power couples did exist, he did not consider such a commute a scenario for a happy marriage, and I respected that. As the associate attorney general, he knew of some exciting cases, including the long-awaited "Pizza Connection" drug bust, about to break in the Southern District.

I considered Rudy's request intriguing. My screening committee, however, was stunned. They had spent time and effort on their recommendation. Some members warned of Giuliani's personal ambition and told me I was making a decision I would regret.

Ultimately, I went ahead and recommended Rudy for the post. There were no protests from the Reagan administration.

Rudy had already cleared the idea with Attorney General William French Smith. On my recommendation, John Keenan was appointed to the federal bench in the Southern District, where he today serves with distinction.

Initially, at least, I was proud of Rudy's record as U.S. Attorney. He brought an intensity and zeal not seen since the days of Thomas Dewey in the 1930s. He went after drug dealers and organized crime bosses. He captured the city's imagination. He had a bright political future ahead of him.

Rudy and I were political allies and, for a period, friends. His wife, Donna Hanover, is a sharp, professional woman who is also very warm and down to earth. I still think the world of her. Rudy's mom reminded me of my mother. I invited Rudy to my daughter Lisa's wedding, and I attended his wedding. We had shared values and brought a sense of energy and adventure to public service.

Perhaps the highpoint of our alliance occurred in 1986, when we donned undercover disguises to demonstrate how easy it was to buy crack cocaine in Washington Heights. While both Rudy and I took a lot of heat from the press for grandstanding during that event, I must set the record straight. The idea for us to go undercover came from Bob Stutman, the Drug Enforcement Agency's special agent in New York. He was passionate about publicizing the scourge of drug dealing on our streets, and Rudy and I obliged him. I admired Rudy's willingness to take the extra step and above all to show *passion* for his job.

Now it's no secret that Rudy and I have had our differences. Two intense, Italian politicians with big egos and ambitions will butt heads sooner or later. We fell out over something that never should have happened. When Rudy considered leaving his post in 1988, he recommended his assistant, Howard Wilson, to replace him. Rudy assured me, "Al, you'll like him." Wilson came down on a weekday afternoon, and we had coffee in the Senate dining room. I mentioned that Rudy had been recently criticized for having three prominent investment bankers arrested at midday and led out of their office in handcuffs. Wilson almost laughed and told me, "As head of the criminal division, I ordered the arrest." He went on to explain that under the pressure of this arrest technique, some suspects "break down," and provide damaging information they might not give if their lawyers were present.

I was taken aback by Wilson's brazen admission. He seemed genuinely proud of this ploy. This was clearly a case of looks being deceiving, for despite his zeal for extreme methods, Wilson was one of the most bland people I have ever met. Perhaps he thought I would applaud his tactics. Not only wasn't I impressed, I made up my mind that he would not get my support to be top federal prosecutor in New York.

I later told Rudy that I just wasn't that impressed with Wilson. Nor was my committee. Rudy implied out loud that I could not be trusted to replace him, that I was too close to some of the cases he was prosecuting. I then took the unprecedented step of offering Rudy the power to veto my choice of his successor. I asked Judge John O'Mara, a member of my search committee, to travel to a criminal justice convention in Syracuse where Rudy was speaking, to let him know that he had veto power over my choice of successor. What more, I thought, could Rudy want?

Rudy's actions and statements during this episode hurt me. He wanted to handpick his successor, even though it was not his prerogative to do so. Even *Newsday,* no friend of mine, criticized Rudy's attempt to handpick his successor was way out of line: "[Giuliani's] attempt to blackjack a U.S. Senator is most unattractive. Whatever Giuliani thinks of D'Amato, the fact is that there's a crucial difference in their status: the junior senator was elected and he was appointed."

Not satisfied with my offer, Rudy launched a whispering campaign to impugn the reputation of the man that I picked to replace him, Otto Obermaier. The rumors circulated that Obermaier would go easy on the Wall Street traders that Rudy was investigating.

Things then got ugly between Rudy and me.

In 1989, when Rudy ran for the Republican nomination for mayor of New York City, I did not support him. I gave my support to my friend Ron Lauder, who came to me months before Rudy announced his candidacy. Ron had been one of my earliest supporters when I challenged Jacob Javits in 1980. Ron had stood with me when the odds were long, and I wanted to do the same for him. After Rudy won the primary, I supported him in the general election. I supported him again when he ran and won in 1993. I even raised more than $50,000 for his campaign.

After Rudy was elected mayor, I felt that the time for silence and acrimony between us had come and gone. I strongly supported his efforts to downsize city government, to rein in municipal unions, to improve the city's quality of life, and to enhance the business climate.

Yet I still could not help feeling that Rudy marched to the drumbeat of his own personal ambition. In August 1994, when House and Senate Republicans blasted President Clinton's crime bill, Rudy embraced this pork-laden legislation with great public zeal. He appeared with the President and attacked those who did not support the bill. I understand that, as mayor, he was salivating over millions of dollars of federal assistance, but he owed his fellow Republicans the courtesy of a "heads up"–a warning that he would be coming out strong for the bill. Little did we know that this was just the beginning of Rudy's rude behavior.

> ## We fell out over something that never should have happened.

As the race between Pataki and Cuomo entered the homestretch in October 1994, it became awkwardly apparent that New York City's Republican mayor had not yet endorsed the Republican candidate for governor. Many pols and pundits thought Rudy was waiting for the last possible moment to extract pledges of state money from George while maintaining cordial relations with the incumbent governor. Because the city depended on hundreds of millions of dollars in state aid, Rudy could not burn his bridges with Cuomo. As the days of October passed, Rudy's highwire act attracted more and more attention. At the Columbus Day Parade, he conspicuously marched with Governor Cuomo. I marched right behind the solid Republican ticket. The press did not let Rudy's cozy relations with the governor go unnoticed.

At this time, the Cuomo campaign began running what proved to be the most memorable ad of their campaign. Unable to make a case for the governor's twelve-year record, and sure most New Yorkers supported George Pataki's stand on taxes, workfare, and the death penalty, Cuomo's people chose another target–me.

Cuomo's campaign ran an ad that showed me leading George Pataki by the hand at a fund-raiser while Paul Simon's song "You Can Call Me Al" played buoyantly in the background. The ad claimed that Pataki was my puppet, and that we would turn the state government into a patronage nightmare. The ad was clever, but it did not respect the intelligence of New York voters. *I* was not running. The race was between Cuomo and Pataki. The Democrats knew that their man could not win a two-way race, so they tried to make *me* the issue.

The Democrats broadcast the "You Can Call Me Al" ad all over the state for almost a month. It was pathetic that the Cuomo legend had come to this. The voters were not fooled–the race was about Mario, not me.

On October 19, in endorsing George Pataki, the *New York Daily News* offered a scorching assessment of Cuomo's legacy: "After twelve years of Cuomo, New York confronts a struggle for survival. . . . Compared with the country as a whole, New York is an economic disaster area. . . . No sector of New York employment, with the exception of the government sector, has enjoyed growth in some time. During Cuomo's term, the state ranked forty-seventh in job creation."

While the Cuomo campaign danced to "You Can Call Me Al," the voters focused on Mario's sorry record.

Then Rudy dropped his bombshell. His announcement on October 24 that he was supporting Governor Cuomo was not so much an endorsement but a political temper tantrum. He called Mario Cuomo his "own man," and blasted George Pataki's campaign as "very much out of a political consultant's handbook. . . . There are clichés, there are slogans, there are sound bites." President Clinton was so tickled by Rudy's endorsement of a liberal Democrat that he personally called the mayor from Air Force One to thank him.

The immediate results were devastating for George Pataki. Before Rudy's endorsement of Cuomo, Pataki was running seven or eight points ahead. Over the next four days, he plummeted twenty-two points to trail by fourteen points.

While I tried to be measured and calm, Republicans across the city, state, and nation were outraged. As Senator Phil Gramm of Texas put it, "A lot of Republicans helped Rudy Giuliani when he ran for mayor. For him to turn around and support Mario Cuomo, who is an anathema to everything we want for New York and America, would be a disappointment." Alluding to Staten Island's pivotal role in Rudy's election, Borough President Guy Molinari exclaimed, "I've created a Frankenstein!" For the rest of the campaign, Republicans blasted Rudy as "Judas Giuliani."

The press lauded Giuliani's embrace of Cuomo as a political masterstroke. It was, they said, a rare act of principle and courage. Perhaps the only pundit to see clearly in the haze of Rudy-mania was the *New York Times*'s Bill Safire, who wrote in a column titled "Loyalty and Perfidy," dated October 29, 1994: "The mayor's maneuver has made him a citywide hero because the bumptious D'Amato has become anathema to the intelligentsia and a certified media villain. Sorry you D'Amato-bashers, there's a there there. Al was agitating for Baltic independence when most liberals were horrified at the thought of a breakup of the Soviet Union. He was scorned as "Senator Pothole" until more remote solons came to appreciate the virtues of what they now call 'constituent service.' D'Amato ferreted out the untruths in Treasury official's recent testimony, and, as banking chairman would bedevil Clinton cover uppers until the Whitewater scandal was exposed. . . . He gave me this deliciously malaproprietary reaction to Giuliani's double cross: 'Rudy's worried some Republican's gonna get ahead of him in the food chain.' "

Rudy's endorsement of Cuomo was an act of naked political ambition. If Rudy was so impressed with Cuomo's record, why did Rudy endorse Pierre Rinfret in 1990? It was obvious Rudy wanted to defeat Pataki and to wound me so he could run for statewide office in 1998.

After entering the ring, Rudy blasted away with real gusto–

with most of the shots aimed in my direction. On October 29, he erroneously charged that Pataki had entered into a "Faustian pact" to run a shadow D'Amato government. On November 5, with the election just three days away, Rudy very unfairly blasted Pataki as my stooge: "George Pataki is giving every indication that he will establish a government of D'Amato, for D'Amato, by D'Amato. If the D'Amato crew ever get control, ethics will be smashed." Even Governor Cuomo had to step back, saying, "I always said the same thing and always will and that's [D'Amato's] entitled to a presumption of innocence." Three days before the voters would decide his fate, Mario was still talking as if *I* were on trial.

After a brief media frenzy that improved Cuomo's poll numbers, Rudy's gambit proved too nakedly ambitious. His real motives had been exposed on November 3, when Senate candidate Bernadette Castro revealed that Rudy had asked her to join with him in sabotaging George's campaign.

Two weeks earlier, Bernadette had complained that I was too close to Pat Moynihan and had not done enough to help her campaign. Rudy must have thought that she would become his ally. He vastly underestimated Bernadette's character.

According to Bernadette, Rudy had told her that he feared he would be "destroyed" if Pataki won. He said to her that he had "a three-front war going" against Pataki and D'Amato. "Myself, [millionaire independent candidate] Tom Golisano, and Governor Cuomo. You could be the fourth front." To her credit, Bernadette blew the whistle on his plan.

In the end, Rudy's endorsement of Cuomo and his attacks on me proved to be both a betrayal of principles and bad politics. For one thing, Rudy moved too early. His surprise move clearly gave Cuomo a temporary boost in the polls. By endorsing Cuomo two weeks before election day, Rudy allowed Cuomo's numbers to rise and then to fall before election day. And while the press loved Rudy's gambit, would his embrace of Cuomo impress upstate voters? It turned out that upstaters feared that the governor had made a deal to funnel billions to his new ally in Gracie Mansion.

But this is all "inside baseball." On November 8, New Yorkers voted the way I expected they would if offered a strong, articulate alternative to Mario's tax and spend nightmare. Voters chose George Pataki by a slim but resounding margin of almost two hundred thousand votes. The battle that had begun at the Association of Towns Convention in 1992 was won. New York finally had a governor who understood that a government that taxed too much and spent too much had to go.

George Pataki has stuck to his campaign promises. He has signed a death penalty law and has moved to cut taxes and spending. On his first day in office he froze state hiring. George had asked Cuomo to do the same after the election, but Mario had forced through a thousand new hires for Democratic hacks. It's ironic that Cuomo left office acting like a serious political operator while George Pataki entered as a serious budget cutter, a man of his word.

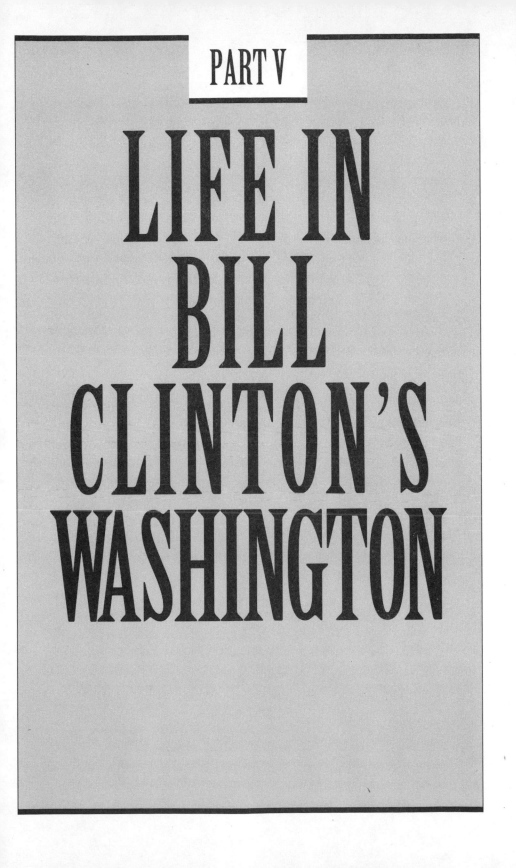

PART V

LIFE IN BILL CLINTON'S WASHINGTON

GAYS IN
THE
MILITARY

Bill Clinton is a master politician. He is smart, savvy, and hardworking. No one should ever sell him short. From a rocky start in New Hampshire to a triumphant convention in New York, a telegenic bus tour, and the TV debates, the Clinton campaign was impressive from start to finish. If he ran the White House with half the skill he displayed on the road, the country would be in much better shape.

Clinton impressed me when we first met in Borough Park in Brooklyn in April 1992. While running in the Democratic primary, he was under incredible attack. Buses of outsiders had been sent into this very Jewish district to taunt him. They shouted "Gennifer, Gennifer." Yet he never lost his composure or let the hecklers keep him from gaining a rapport with the mostly friendly audience of Orthodox and Hasidic Jews.

I told Clinton of my admiration for his toughness and his composure in the face of such vehement personal attack. He then looked at me with his infectious grin and replied, "You don't do so bad yourself, Senator." He was no talking head. He was schmoozing me in my own state. Eight months later, Clinton and I both carried Borough Park in landslides. Clinton and I both got 69 percent of the vote.

In January 1993, I got my next taste of Clinton's personal charisma when the President-elect addressed forty-two Republican members of the Senate. In a couple of minutes, he had the whole room charmed. His wit and grasp of issues was awesome. At one point, John Warner of Virginia made the case for spending cuts and handed Clinton a letter proposing cutting NASA's budget dramatically and killing the Supercollider project. Without missing a beat, the President responded, "I'm sure Senator Gramm [of Texas, home of NASA and the Supercollider] will support you on that." The whole room broke up. This was a politician of unusual charm.

As we now know, the savvy and charisma that put Clinton in the White House have not been enough. His presidency has lurched from one crisis to another. Many of his setbacks have been of his own making. Less than a week into his term, Clinton suffered his first major setback.

Candidate Bill Clinton had promised to lift the ban on gays in the military with the stroke of a pen. For this and other stands, he received the overwhelming support of the gay community. When he tried to put this promise into practice, however, all hell broke loose.

For a man with a reputation as a slick politician, Clinton blew this one. He didn't seek the advice or support of Colin Powell, the Chairman of the Joint Chiefs of Staff, or Sam Nunn, the powerful and respected chairman of the Senate Armed Services Committee. To his detractors, Clinton's announcement to end the military ban on gays, on the second day of his administration, reflected arrogance and naïveté. How could a man with a questionable draft record, who was elected with 43 percent of the vote, ram something so controversial down the country's throat? To his supporters, Clinton's choice of a first fight reflected confused priorities. He was elected, after all, with a campaign whose slogan was "It's the economy, stupid." He completely miscalculated the predictable firestorm. Sam Nunn, a moderate southern Democrat who probably thought *he* should be president, was an intractable foe. Just two days into his administration, Clinton's "honeymoon" was over.

I was surprised by Colin Powell's support for the ban. I was troubled that an African-American, who had directly benefited from the integration of the armed forces, was in effect stopping gay Americans from serving their country. When I mentioned this irony, one of my more astute colleagues, a senator on the Armed Services Committee, stressed that "Powell has his own constituency to satisfy." That may have been true, but after the Gulf War Powell presumably had the clout to stand up to his military constituency. Many think Powell could be an African-American Eisenhower and win either party's presidential nomination. But political capital is worth nothing if you lack the conviction to use it. After witnessing his reluctance to move beyond economic sanctions during the Gulf crisis and his political timidity on gays in the military, I wonder whether Colin Powell has either the courage or the convictions needed to lead the country.

I finally got tired of listening to all the nonsense and bull about how the military would be impaired by lifting the ban. Gays had served in the military with distinction. All of this posturing made me sick. So I decided to stand up for the President. I had never received any support from the gay community. In fact, the militant group ACT UP had regularly disrupted my New York office with sit-ins. Once they even offered to demonstrate safe sex techniques to a dismayed staffer. They had harassed my speaking engagements and fund-raisers by smashing garbage can lids and shouting profanities that would make even my good friend Howard Stern blush.

I knew that supporting Clinton's lifting of the ban would be very unpopular with many of my more conservative supporters. But I felt in my heart that this was a moral issue and not a political one, and that the government could not deny a citizen the right to serve on the basis of race, ethnicity, gender, *or* sexual orientation. Thousands of gay men and women had served in the military. It wasn't until 1981 that anyone was even asked to fill out a questionnaire swearing that he or she was not gay. The President was ending this hypocrisy, and I was behind him.

My stance on this issue hit close to home. The Sunday after I made my position known, I went to Island Park to attend a dinner for the Island Park Republican Club. When I went to my folks' house, my mother met me at the door in a rage. She had been in Evanston, Illinois, visiting my sister Joanne when I made my remarks and she hadn't had the chance to scream at me about it. She let me have it right away. I didn't have a chance to take my coat off.

"I didn't raise you that way," she said. "Like what?" I replied. "You know," she said. "I didn't raise you to support gays in the military . . . that whole thing."

Now, I knew that my friends in Island Park were probably just as mystified as my mother with my support for gay rights, so I knew I had to do a good job of explaining my position.

"Yes, you did, Mom. That's exactly how you raised me." As I saw her mouth drop, I began to tell her a story that I learned as a little boy. It seems that two brothers had studied hard to be teachers and had graduated near the top of their class. Even though they had good grades and outstanding recommendations from their professors, they couldn't get a teaching job. Classmates with poorer grades were getting hired. Then one of their professors told the younger brother, "You'll never get a job teaching in this school district because you're Italian." The younger brother then devised a plan to solve their problems. They would change their names to something more "American." He also found a lawyer who would do it for only $10. For $15, he'd change both of their names. A bargain.

The younger brother told the older that they could change their names and get jobs. When the older brother's wife heard about the proposition, she was enraged. "Out of the question," she roared. "I married you and I'm proud of our heritage and our family. I'm not hiding it, job or no job."

The younger brother went on to be a teacher and eventually an administrator. The older brother never changed his name, and never became the English teacher he always wanted to be. Instead he went into the insurance business.

I didn't have to tell my mother where I heard this story. The brothers involved were my uncle Michael and my father. The proud and angry wife was, of course, my mother, who was standing before me, proud and angry that her smart-aleck son had used her own words to argue against her. "You see, Mom, you taught me back then that it's just wrong to deny someone a basic right just because of their name, their color, or their sexual orientation. It's just wrong."

While I may have disarmed my mother for the moment, I knew that she was not alone in her outrage and her suspicion about letting gays in the military. My friends in New York's Conservative Party, the folks who gave me their faith and support when I was all alone in 1980, were outraged and dismayed. Many conservatives were devout Roman Catholics. It was one thing for Clinton to support gays, it was quite another for Al D'Amato.

While some of my closest supporters expressed dismay, the press unfairly dismissed my stand as a purely Machiavellian maneuver. D'Amato was not a man of principle. They denigrated my stand as a political ploy to curry favor with New York's liberal voters. Some said this was a sure sign that I would run for governor in 1994.

Several days after my announcement, Barry Goldwater, "Mr. Conservative," joined me. Barry said, "Anyone who wants to fight for their country should be allowed to." But Goldwater's support did not change people's minds. When I appeared on Bob Grant's talk-radio show, the phones rang off the hook. Most callers argued that this was only the first step in promoting the "gay lifestyle"–whatever that means–in the military. I countered that the current system actually compromised national security. If you have a career officer who is gay and who fears that he might be dismissed if discovered, then that officer is an easy target for blackmail. The history of both British and American espionage is filled with such cases. Why jeopardize security for such hypocrisy? Why make people who want to serve their country live a lie?

It seems to me that the real issue is conduct–not whether you are gay or straight. The Tailhook scandal demonstrates that heterosexuals have no monopoly on virtue. If a person's conduct does not conform to military codes, he or she should be punished. If, as some say, gay officers try to seduce young enlistees, they should be punished. But so should heterosexual officers who abuse their position. All should face the same rules, regardless of sexuality. The military has the right to enforce special rules of conduct for living in close quarters or battlefield conditions. But conduct–not sexual orientation–should be the criteria. Anything less is more than unfair, it's un-American.

In February 1993, while I was skiing in Windham, New York, the White House operator tracked me down. At first I thought this was just another hoax, but after my incident with Guy Molinari, I didn't say anything. It was indeed President Clinton. He was calling to thank me for my support of gays in the military. I told him he was absolutely right, and that he shouldn't compromise. I had heard that the administration was floating feelers about not permitting gays in combat or even segregating gays and straights in separate barracks. This would have been absurd, and much worse than the current situation.

The President accepted my support, but apparently didn't listen to my advice. In the first of a series of backtrack, flip-flop, waffles, that characterize his presidency, Clinton and the military finally agreed on a policy of "don't ask, don't tell." While the military would no longer ask enlistees if they were gay, nothing would protect a recruit from being discharged for being gay. The unfairness remained. The threat of blackmail was undiminished. Despite the support of Massachusetts Congressman Barney Frank, who is openly gay, I considered the policy a lot of drivel and obvious window dressing. The President ended up with the worst of all possible worlds: a bad policy, a disgruntled gay constituency, and a leery military establishment. He won nothing and had squandered much capital. Even worse, he demonstrated no political backbone or moral convictions. There's no doubt in my mind that the Supreme Court will finally rule–as Judge Eugene Nickerson, the former Nassau County Executive who now sits on the bench of the Eastern District of New York, did in March 1995–that our Constitution does not permit the military to discharge soldiers just because they say they are gay. Clinton should have stuck to his guns. His original proposal will eventually prevail.

My stance on gays in the military continues to have strange reverberations for me. Many have wrongly assumed that my stance on this position means that I support the radical agenda of some gay groups. Nothing could be further from the truth. My friend Dick Torykian illustrates this confusion. A proud former marine, he graduated from Chaminade two years behind me. He has helped raise hundreds of thousands of dollars for our school over the years. His son Richie and my son Chris were classmates at Chaminade. We are the closest of friends.

When I made my stance on gays in the military clear, Dick went into orbit. It was a mixture of shock and embarrassment. His old marine buddies put him through endless grief about his pal the senator and asked him, "Are all the gays now lining up behind D'Amato?" It took Dick several months before we could even speak without his blurting out how gays would destroy the military.

The Tailhook scandal demonstrates that heterosexuals have no monopoly on virtue.

But Dick Torykian's reaction was mild compared to a memorable encounter with one of my neighbors. Since 1982, I have lived in a two-bedroom condominium in Virginia, about twenty-five minutes from my office. It isn't the most luxurious place, but it was what I could afford. My sons, Dan and Chris, liked its recreation facilities, the security is good, and until my stand on gays in the military, I had never been hassled by my neighbors.

That all ended on October 5, 1993. While walking to my car, I saw a big guy wearing shorts and sneakers complaining loudly, too loudly, to his neighbors about the shuttle bus being broken down again. I had not gone more than thirty feet past him when he began to bellow at the top of his lungs, "There goes the faggot lover. There goes Al D'Amato, the faggot lover."

Various scenarios ran through my mind. My first thought was to blow him a kiss. The second was to reply with some obscenity. But since I still had a way to go to reach my car and didn't know if I could outrun this gorilla, I simply replied, "You're a class act." He didn't run after me, but screamed back, "You're a disgrace to your people." When I had a chance to think about it, I supposed "your people" meant my Italian ancestors.

Two nights later, I was waiting for an elevator when my loud critic appeared from out of nowhere. This time, I had no place to run, and only my assistant Chris Fish to protect me. My critic continued to mutter how disappointed he was with me, but seemed to lack the intensity and venom of the last encounter. Since we were going to share an elevator, I tried to reach out as diplomatically as I could.

He told me his name was Joe. I could tell from his taste in military fatigues that he was a veteran. I then asked him if he had known any gays when he was in the military, and he told me yes. Had any of them been good soldiers, I inquired. To his credit, he told me they had. So I continued, "All I'm saying, Joe, is that if a person is doing his job, it's none of our business what he is. No one should be thrown out of the military because of how they were born. We should judge people on their conduct alone. If they don't obey the rules, then they're out—gay or straight—and that's all there is to it."

To my surprise, Joe didn't have a problem with my position, but he quickly launched into a tirade, shouting, "I can't stand to watch the SOBs going into St. Patrick's and throwing the blessed sacrament on the floor!" Joe was pretty upset. I told him I agreed with him 100 percent, that anyone who desecrated a house of worship should be locked up. Joe was pretty taken aback with my position. Because the media had so simplified the issue to being pro-gay or anti-gay, Joe had just assumed that I had signed on to the whole gay agenda.

I've bumped into Joe a couple of times since, and he has been cordial, almost friendly. He's not a bad guy really, just a little scary when he's mad at you.

I'm glad I never threw him the kiss.

TERROR
STRIKES
HOME

On May 1, 1993, my phone rang at 1:38 in the morning. Who could be calling me at this godforsaken hour? As a parent and as the son of elderly parents I dread to think what news a late-night call might bring. I was tired and groggy, having just gotten to bed after attending an NBA play-off game earlier where the Knicks had almost blown a 20-point lead to the Pacers, but hung on to win by 3 points.

Lieutenant Matt Brady of the Nassau County Special Investigation unit was on the line informing me that FBI Director William Sessions had told him that I was the target of a terrorist threat. Needless to say, it was some time before I could sleep again. I was concerned for myself, my family, and my staff. Death threats and crackpots are part of life in public office, but terrorists were something else. After my initial shock, I cynically wondered, why this couldn't have happened when I was running against Bob Abrams. It might have been worth a quarter of a million votes.

The next day I met with Nassau County Police Commissioner Donald Kane and a special agent from the FBI who explained the situation. I immediately suspected that the group responsible for the February 1993 bombing of New York's World Trade Center

had targeted me. I had run into this murderous bunch years earlier during the trial of El Sayyid Nosair, the man charged with
murdering the founder of the Jewish Defense League, Rabbi Meir
Kahane. Nosair lived in Jersey City and was a follower of Sheikh
Omar Abdel Rahman, the blind Muslim cleric who emerged as
the guru of the radical clique responsible for the World Trade
Center bombing. During Nosair's trial, Mahmud Abouhelima,
one of those arrested for the World Trade Center bombing,
demonstrated outside of the courthouse and carried posters denouncing and threatening me. His posters called me a "racist"
and told me to "Kiss My Seat Good-bye."

Kahane had been assassinated at Halloran House, on the corner of Forty-eighth Street and Lexington Avenue on November 5,
1990. In a shocking decision, Nosair was acquitted of murder on
December 21, 1991. He was found guilty only of gun possession
and received a sentence of only seven years.

The Jewish community was shocked by the government's
handling of Nosair's prosecution. Kahane was murdered in an
obvious bias attack. Because a postal inspector, a federal employee, was also wounded in the attack, I asked U.S. Attorney Otto
Obermaier to investigate Nosair and his murderous entourage on
civil rights charges. This was never carried out. But law enforcement officials stuck to their conclusion that Nosair had acted
alone. If Obermaier had looked into the matter, I suspect the cell
that eventually bombed the World Trade Center would have been
exposed.

After the May 2 meeting with the FBI, my security detail was increased. This put a real cramp on my mobility and freedom. I was
expected to go about my business and not let on that I was a target. These lunatics would not keep me from speaking out. With
my friend Alaska Senator Ted Stevens, I proposed legislation to
impose capital punishment for terrorist acts resulting in deaths. I
was also very vocal about the outrageous fact that Sheikh Rahman, an Egyptian citizen, was still free. He was here illegally.
Under our immigration laws, the Justice Department could hold

him while he appealed his immigration status.

On three separate occasions, I wrote to Attorney General Janet Reno asking that Rahman be held in prison. I received no reply. The Sheikh's lawyer William Kunstler spread the rumor that the government would not touch the Sheikh because he was a CIA operative. Egyptian President Hosni Mubarak made similar noises. It was getting ridiculous. The longer this guy remained at large, the more people wondered about some peculiar conspiracy. It was sickening to watch our law enforcement agencies stand by impotently while this radical creep walked the streets a free man.

Secrets aren't good for long in politics but mine kept for a little over a month. Meanwhile, on May 25, the *New York Post* revealed that my friend Dov Hikind, an outspoken Democratic assemblyman from Brooklyn, was a target of the terror cell. On June 2, CNN called to inform me that they had a reliable source had indicated that I was on the same target list, and that reporter Charles Feldman was going to go with the story.

This put me in a bit of a jam. The last thing I wanted was to jeopardize the FBI's case. But I didn't want to issue an outright denial and look like a liar if the truth came out. We took the middle course and held a press conference. I was uncharacteristically vague, stating, "I've made some enemies by being outspoken about [the terrorists'] presence, and how they have been allowed to stay here, and how they have been allowed to use this country in a manner that is totally inappropriate. I'm not going to keep quiet about these terrorists." Charles Feldman and the other reporters present were skeptical and certain that I wasn't telling everything I knew about the plot.

Three weeks later, on June 24, my secret was revealed in a far more dramatic fashion. In a spectacular raid, the FBI arrested eight radical Muslims who were plotting to blow up the Lincoln and Holland Tunnels, the United Nations building, the FBI headquarters in Manhattan, and the Statue of Liberty on July 4. It was also publicly revealed that they wanted to assassinate me, along with President Mubarak, Dov Hikind, and U.N. Secretary General

Boutros Boutros-Ghali. The whole city of New York breathed a sigh of relief. But there was outrage that Sheikh Rahman was still a free man.

The next morning, Bill Clinton called me. "Al," he jokingly fumed, "I saw you on the Senate floor yesterday sticking me with that big pencil. I don't appreciate it." He was referring to a speech during which I had poked "Taxasaurus"—a picture of a giant dinosaur—with a three-foot-long pencil. We had a good laugh over what was an obvious spoof and then his voice got serious.

He said, "Al, I'm calling to express my concern over the ordeal that you had to go through with this assassination plot." I thanked him. It was very decent of him to call me. Then he lobbied for my support. "Let me tell you, Al, I want you to know that I'm going to take some pretty tough actions on countries sponsoring terrorism, and I want you to be on my side." Two days later, he launched a missile strike against Iraq in retaliation for a plot to kill former President Bush.

Before the President could get off the phone, I piped in with a quick suggestion. "Mr. President, I hope I'm not presumptuous, but I have written to Janet Reno about Sheikh Rahman. Under the law, the Attorney General can have him arrested pending the appeal of his immigration case. Mr. President, it's both good government and good politics to have the Sheikh taken into custody." He told me he'd look into it.

The President was as good as his word. Less than three days later Janet Reno asked to see me. Up until this time, we had not even received an acknowledgment of my letters. She showed up on Tuesday evening June 29, at 6:45. To my amazement, she walked in all by herself. In Washington, almost everyone—even an assistant secretary—travels with a gaggle of aides. I was impressed.

Not one for small talk, Reno got right down to business. "For law enforcement reasons," she explained, "I am not going to have the Sheikh held in custody." She didn't try to snow me. Her decision was based on close consultations with U.S. Attorney Mary Jo White.

By July 1, however, Reno had a change of heart. It had nothing to do with a change of circumstances. The White House had simply decided that it had to be done. I was giving them just too much heat. ABC News leaked the story that the Sheikh would be detained. I applauded Reno's decision. That evening I appeared on ABC's *Nightline* to discuss her decision to arrest the Sheikh. I was joined, via satellite, by the Sheikh's radical lawyer William Kunstler. His story that the Sheikh was a CIA operative had been given credence in the press. By asking us to appear together, *Nightline* obviously expected the sparks to fly. Viewers were not disappointed.

Bill Kunstler has made a career of representing anti-American radicals. Some of his statements have crossed the line. He once said that the country was better off that both Kennedy brothers had been assassinated. He asserts that all black defendants are innocent in a white racist society. I was not surprised for a second when he took on the case of Colin Ferguson, who killed six Long Island Railroad commuters in 1993, and argued that Ferguson was innocent by reason of "black rage," a kind of mental illness that released him from moral responsibility for his crimes.

I'm proud of standing up for the forgotten middle class against such liberal horse manure. I naïvely thought that Kunstler would stick to the issue of the Sheikh's detention when we appeared on *Nightline*. But he instead broadsided me with a personal attack. I didn't let him get away with it. Every time I attempted to make a legitimate point about the Sheikh, Kunstler tried to make the debate personal and nasty. Chris Wallace, the *Nightline* host that night, had a tough time breaking it up between us, as these excerpts show:

> WALLACE: Mr. Kunstler, did the feds cave in to public pressure from Senator D'Amato and from others?
>
> KUNSTLER: I think they did, and Senator D'Amato—who roared to the skies when he was accused of ethics violations and said, "I haven't had a hearing yet. How can you accuse me?"—I think he's really doing a shameful act here. He's say-

ing they ought to jail this man before there's any determination of even his guilt under the immigration laws of this country.

D'AMATO: That's nonsense and let me tell you something. I object to that.

KUNSTLER: You may object all you wish.

D'AMATO: Wait a second. Don't you get into that personality crap with me. The fact of the matter is the Sheikh did have a hearing. The fact of the matter is the court found that he was deportable. So don't tell me that he hasn't had a hearing. It was after that hearing and the determination that he was found deportable that the Attorney General then has the authority under the law—not just for the Sheikh, but for anyone in that status—to hold him. So all I said is make sure that the law is applied.

WALLACE: All right, Senator.

D'AMATO: For you to attempt to impugn me with that kind of nonsense is uncalled for. You may disagree, but I had a hell of a lot more respect for you intellectually in terms of the law than for you to try that nonsense. It's a cheap trick. You keep that for your trial antics–

KUNSTLER: Let me respond. All you're doing is butting in and getting your own piece off for your own press purposes–

D'AMATO: Why am I butting in when I say follow the law? . . . Does the law–

WALLACE: Senator, you haven't allowed–

D'AMATO: It's a personal thing and I'm going to answer it–

WALLACE: Let's give Mr. Kunstler an opportunity to finish his comments–

KUNSTLER: I'm quoting you quite exactly. I read what you said when you were first accused. And secondly–

D'AMATO: Where does that have anything to do with regard to this, Kunstler?

KUNSTLER: Will you butt out?

D'AMATO: I'm not going to butt out. You start talking about me in a personal way and I'm going to answer you.

WALLACE: Mr. Kunstler–

KUNSTLER: You know what you are. You're totally impolite.

D'AMATO: And you are a character besmircher. How do you like that?

WALLACE: In the interest of this discussion can we keep it to the Sheikh.

Words cannot express the joy I felt in sticking it to that sanctimonious creep. After three years of unfair ethics charges and two months under terrorist threat, I wasn't going to sit back and take it. I had been bottled up for so long. It felt great to be fighting again.

After making the correct decision to seize the Sheikh, the Justice Department spent the next twenty-four hours trying to find him. It wasn't pretty. The FBI was now engaged in a very public game of hide-and-seek. At one point dozens of FBI agents and reporters descended on a car in Jersey City containing the Sheikh, but its occupant turned out to be a decoy. Finally, the Sheikh agreed to surrender at a Brooklyn mosque. The FBI used great discretion in arresting him. The Branch Davidian compound in Waco, Texas, had gone up in flames just three months earlier. The last thing anyone wanted was an armed siege of a house of worship in the middle of Brooklyn. With the possible exception of William Kunstler and some other wackos, America breathed a sigh of relief when the Sheikh surrendered.

I later learned that the Justice Department's reluctance to pick up the Sheikh was based more on political than legal maneuvering. Just two days before calling for the Sheikh's arrest, Janet Reno claimed that she was holding off because U.S. Attorney Mary Jo White still wanted to use the Sheikh to observe and possibly capture other terrorists. But law enforcement officials had long since given up on the Sheikh as a source. I later learned that the State Department was leaking disinformation to keep the Sheikh out of jail. Our bureaucrats were more concerned about possible unrest in Egypt than protecting the streets of New York. It was shameful.

Even after the Sheikh's detention, columnist Mike McAlary repeated the old line about the Sheikh's usefulness as a source and blasted me for urging his arrest. I later learned that McAlary wrote this piece after having lunch with the head of the FBI's New York office, Jim Fox, who paraded him around New York FBI headquarters on a chummy tour.

After the arrest of the World Trade Center bombers, and the detention of Sheikh Rahman, many thought that my security problems were over. Not quite. Sheikh Rahman had plenty of followers who were now even more angry at me. The Sheikh's spokesman, Dr. M. T. Mehdi, singled me out as enemy number one. While I was proud that these creeps hated me, it did not make my life any easier. Security was tightened at both my New York and Washington offices. Every package was checked and X-rayed. One particularly suspicious package was dismantled. When it was revealed to contain only cookies from a constituent, my nervous staffers breathed a sigh of relief and devoured the batch. Then my assistant Mike Giuliani (no relation to the mayor) wondered out loud if the cookies were poisoned. The threats took their toll on my usually good-natured staff. With two men protecting me every waking hour of the day, I feared becoming every bit as much a prisoner as the Sheikh.

After two months of terror and tension, I looked forward to returning to Island Park for the July 4 recess. I was invited to spend the holiday afternoon at a backyard picnic of my old friends Geraldine and Doc McGann. We would be joined by old neighbors and friends, including "Nene" Russo. When I had first moved to Island Park, Nene had rescued me from the neighborhood bully, Jimmy Marsden. My grandmother had seen this kid beating me up day after day and called her friend to see if her son, Nene, could stick up for me. The very next time Jimmy Marsden showed up, Nene got a hold of him, smacked him around and told him that the next time he laid a finger on "my cousin Tippy," he'd get the beating of a lifetime. Suddenly Nene was my cousin. We have remained close friends ever since.

The afternoon gave way to evening, and we looked forward to watching the fireworks from New York. Still, it seemed odd that Nene had not shown up. I told Geraldine "it wouldn't be a Fourth of July without him." All of a sudden, a lunatic came running into the backyard screaming, "Death to the infidel!" He was wearing a turban and a white sheikh's robe. He shouted, "Where's Al D'Amato! Death to the infidel!" Gus, one of my bodyguards, drew his pistol. Suddenly, the intruder pulled off his turban and screamed, "Don't shoot. Don't shoot. It's me, Anthony."

I suspect that Gus knew all along that this was a joke, but he never let on. As the sun set and the fireworks began, we were still laughing about Nene's stunt. I'm sure we will all be laughing about it till the day we die. As Island Park stories go, it's got all the makings of a legend.

STOPPING CLINTON'S LIBERAL AGENDA

By the summer of 1993, most Americans had seen enough of Bill and Hillary's plan for America. The man who had been elected with 43 percent of the vote was not the real Bill Clinton at all. He won by borrowing the theme of my 1980 campaign: "I'm a fighter for the forgotten middle class." But most of his first term has been spent trying to bring about the big government, Great Society–type programs that have hurt the middle class. He may have been elected as a new Democrat, but he has governed as a tax and spend liberal. Clinton is more interested in redistributing wealth than in creating economic growth.

I have warmly supported two of the President's best appointees, Judge Louis Freeh to head the FBI and Judge Ruth Bader Ginsburg as a justice of the Supreme Court.

Louis Freeh is a remarkable public servant. I am proud to have helped along his career. We first met in the early 1980s, when we traveled together to Italy with Rudolph Giuliani. The two of them wanted to extradite an infamous Italian drug dealer in the famous "Pizza connection" case, and I went to explore measures for making it harder for drug dealers to launder money. Louis Freeh's perfect prosecution of the "Pizza connection" case brought him national acclaim. He convicted sixteen of the seventeen defendants. The trial lasted fourteen months. It was the largest and most complicated criminal investigation ever undertaken by the U.S. Attorney for the Southern District of New York. Freeh was thirty-two when the "Pizza connection" convictions came down. The *New York Times*'s Ralph Blumenthal described Freeh as "one of the government's toughest investigators, a ramrod-straight and ferocious crusader against the mob." I was impressed by Freeh and more than that, I really liked him. He was a down-to-earth guy from Jersey City who loved his job. He had wanted to be an FBI man from the time he was seven or eight years old. Ultimately he became an agent and went to law school. He set an example by working harder than everyone else. In 1991, I proudly nominated Freeh to become a federal judge. He arrived at his office every day at 8:00 A.M. and almost always ate a brown bag lunch so he could work at his desk. While many judges complain of a huge backlog, Judge Freeh worked through his caseload of four hundred to five hundred cases a year. He actually took on other judges' cases.

When the rumor mill started that Judge Freeh might replace FBI Director William Sessions, I was delighted. No one was better qualified. About six weeks before his nomination, Judge Freeh phoned. He was of course delighted to be considered, but didn't want to be hung out to dry. After watching the cruel spectacles of Zoe Baird's and Kimba Wood's public humiliation, I can't say I blamed Judge Freeh. At the same time, I told him he was crazy to say anything but yes. After all, he was a born FBI man and had worked with and for the agency for more than fifteen years. He couldn't say no. Happily, the Clinton people and Janet Reno were just as impressed by Louis, and the screening process proceeded without a hitch.

The day of the official announcement of Judge Freeh's nomination was hectic. Senator Moynihan and I already planned to introduce Judge Ginsburg to the Senate Judiciary Committee. My schedule was in flux. Oddly, the White House kept deleting my name from the invitation list for Judge Freeh's introduction. Each time we asked, we got a different excuse. Finally, Judge Freeh told the White House in no uncertain terms that if room could not be made for all of his invited guests including Senator D'Amato, then he would not attend the ceremony.

It was a beautiful day. I arrived at nine for the 9:45 A.M. ceremony. Many of the prosecutors and agents from Louis's past attended, including his first boss, Bob Fiske, and Barbara Jones, who had first brought Freeh to my attention. It was a special day for New York. Two nominees from our state were taking their place at the forefront of justice.

Senator Moynihan and I have long coordinated the selection of judges. Our tradition is unique in the Senate. Normally, the senator whose party controls the White House suggests all of the federal judgeships to the President. In the 1970s, Senators Moynihan and Javits had agreed that the senator whose party was not in the White House could nominate every fourth judge. From the start, I wanted to continue New York's tradition of selecting judges. This system keeps both senators involved in the critical process.

Judge Ginsburg arrived in my office with Senator Moynihan's aide Dick Eaton. I said, "Judge, I want you to know that I will do whatever I can do to support you. Whatever. Whether you want me to endorse you or oppose you, I will do as you please." She was amused by my offer. Sometimes, nonendorsements or downright opposition from certain quarters can be of great advantage. In the wake of the recent bitter confirmation hearings of Robert Bork and Clarence Thomas, I wanted to make things easy for her. I showed her the highlights of my office—the Taxasaurus monsters and the piano my mother and staff had bought me for Christmas. She later told the Senate Judiciary Committee that she had the most fun visiting my office. I had a great time too.

My other dealings with the Clinton administration have not been as pleasant. In April 1993, the President's short-lived attempt to jam an economic "stimulus" package through the Congress revealed his willingness to be an old-fashioned, pork-dispensing Democrat. This program wouldn't have had the slightest positive effect on a multitrillion-dollar economy. Its sole purpose was to funnel money to reward the politicians who had made Clinton's slim victory possible. The president proposed funding warming huts in skating rinks and $800,000 bike paths. It was a bad bill.

Clinton's "stimulus" bill did serve one positive purpose. It united Senate Republicans. Bob Dole led the rallying cry that brought unity back to our dispirited party. Every Republican senator voted against the bill.

The President did not learn his lesson. He kept trying to jam quasi-socialist programs down the throats of an unsuspecting public. Sometimes he got away with it. His National Service Volunteer Act is a blatant Trojan horse. Volunteerism is a wonderful concept. I have been a member–though inactive–of the Island Park Volunteer Fire Department since 1963. Such volunteerism is the backbone of our nation. Over 38 million Americans volunteer in organizations from the Lions Club to the Boy Scouts. *That's* volunteerism.

> He may have been elected as a new Democrat, but he has governed as a tax and spend liberal.

Clinton's idea of volunteerism is very different. His program provides a paycheck and tuition benefits for each "volunteer." That costs $22,600 per volunteer. This hidden boondoggle will bloat future budgets. If we have only 150,000 "volunteers," that will cost taxpayers more than $10 billion over five years. After reading Clinton's "volunteer" proposal, I called Senator Dole. This was more than just a pork program–it would fund a political army of loyal Democrats paid for by taxpayers. It was ludicrous, and a dangerous threat to the very notion of volunteerism and to the separation between public service and patronage.

With all of these arguments–we still lost the vote. It's hard to vote against anything that has to do with volunteer work, and Clinton is a good spin doctor. I tried to convince Bob Dole to make it a spending issue. Nancy Kassebaum of Kansas had already offered a very much pared-down version, and she had obtained 37 votes. After this vote, I persuaded Dole to present the Clinton plan as a budget buster and to present his colleague's version as a reasonable alternative. This time we received 42 votes. The Democrats then decided to play hardball and successfully moved to cut off debate. The program was then passed by a narrow margin, and an expensive new government boondoggle was born.

Two months later, the President's budget, containing the largest tax increase in history, passed only because Vice President Gore cast the deciding vote. Not one Republican voted for this bill.

We may have lost the White House in 1992, but by 1993 we were already winning back the country.

WHITEWATER

To me, Whitewater has always been a simple matter. This affair, like all presidential scandals since Watergate, boils down to two central questions: Was there wrongdoing and was there a cover-up?

The Whitewater scandal is murky business. A savings and loan, Madison Guaranty, went bust and was bailed out by the U.S. government's Resolution Trust Corporation (RTC). Madison failed, in part, because Clinton friend and crony Jim McDougal, who ran the S&L, had turned it into a personal piggy bank. McDougal allegedly diverted funds to Clinton's campaigns in the 1980s and, in a separate scheme, paid the mortgage on a failing Arkansas land deal now known infamously as Whitewater. McDougal's partners in Whitewater were Bill and Hillary Clinton. Whitewater involves more than the President's ties to Ozarks land development. David Hale, a former Arkansas municipal judge and businessman, has accused Clinton of pressuring him to make an improper Small Business Administration–backed loan to McDougal's wife. Another troubling charge involves the President's misuse of the Arkansas Development Finance Authority to pay off supporters, including one Dan Lasater, a convicted cocaine dealer who hired the President's brother, Roger as a driver.

Presidential aide Bruce Lindsay is implicated in charges involving the failure to report (as required by federal banking law) several transactions of Clinton's 1990 gubernatorial campaign.

The next question is: Did the President or his aides use his office to obstruct criminal or civil investigations?

Learning the answers to these questions is more complicated. There are allegations that the President improperly briefed Arkansas Governor Jim Guy Tucker about RTC criminal referrals. After Deputy White House Counsel Vincent Foster committed suicide in July 1993, files relating to Whitewater were withheld from investigators and taken to the First Family residence. Other officials, including former Associate Attorney General Webster Hubbell, may have impeded ongoing criminal investigations of Whitewater and Madison.

Many have argued that I became a leading spokesman on this issue for solely partisan reasons. If you'd like to know the real reason, it's simple.

It was my job.

As the ranking Republican on the Senate Banking Committee, it was my job to look into Whitewater. It was in the President's interest to have this matter investigated, and if possible, to put it behind him. Lord knows, I know what it is like to be under Senate investigation. My House colleague from Iowa, Jim Leach, also called for an investigation by the House Banking Committee. We both made every effort to ascertain the facts. But we were both confronted by stonewalling, evasion, and outright deception.

The White House raised more questions than it answered. Time after time, with dreary consistency, the Clinton people turned routine inquiries into convoluted cover-ups that overshadowed the original subject of inquiry.

WHITEWATER—A BRIEF CHRONOLOGY: DECEMBER 1993–MARCH 1994

In December 1993, I called for an official congressional probe of Whitewater. I wrote to the Senate Banking Committee Chairman Donald Riegle: "This is a cloud that could eventually rival Watergate. You already have [the suicide of Vincent Foster], the removal of paper from his office, a lack of enthusiasm on the part of investigators in the Justice Department. . . . This really cries out for a full hearing." I explained that Clinton's partner and fellow investor, James McDougal, may have received special treatment from bank regulators and that federally insured bank funds might have been used to pay debts from Clinton's 1984 gubernatorial campaign. "I believe we owe it to the American people to clear the President of any cloud of suspicion. Since much of the conduct in question involves financial institutions and federal agencies within the committee's jurisdiction, I believe we should commence hearings without delay."

When Jim Leach also requested hearings, House Banking Chairman Henry Gonzalez, in a partisan manner, responded that hearings would be "a waste of the committee's resources."

As the Democrats in Congress continued to stall, the controversy continued to swirl. On December 28, 1993, the *Wall Street Journal* published a scathing article examining the complexity and possible ramification of the scandal. On January 7, 1994, the *New York Times,* usually friendly to the President, speculated on the first page that Clinton was "willing to pay a price to keep files on land deal private and would rather bear the political consequences than allow all of the facts to become public."

I was alarmed. Even though the Clintons claimed to have turned all relevant files over to the Justice Department, the investigation into the Madison Guaranty's failure was being conducted by the RTC, which was then headed by Roger C. Altman, a longtime friend of Bill Clinton. Some investigation. At the same time, the statute of limitations on any criminal charges arising from the Madison matter would expire on February 28, 1994. I suspected that the White House would do all it could to stall so the statute would run out. I began a public campaign to defer the statute. Each day I went to the Senate floor with a large calendar counting down the days left until the statute expired. Each day I released a statement complaining that the clock was still ticking.

On January 10, 1994, Senator Pat Moynihan became the first Democrat to call for the appointment of a special prosecutor.

Presidential aide and spinmeister David Gergen pooh-poohed Whitewater as partisan politics. Gergen, who had worked for Presidents Reagan *and* Clinton, seemed a fine one to talk about partisan politics. My good friend Hal Madden once borrowed a line from the film *The Best Man* to describe Gergen: "He has all the attributes of a dog–except loyalty." But by January 12, even Clinton speculated that perhaps a special prosecutor might be a good idea. All the while, I continued my public cry to defer the statute of limitations. The clock was still ticking.

On January 13, the President called for the appointment of a independent counsel to conduct an inquiry on Whitewater. Two days later, Senator Dole, Congressman Leach, and I requested hearings on the scandal. On January 20, Attorney General Reno appointed Robert Fiske as the special prosecutor. I called Fiske "a man of unflinching, uncompromising integrity."

On January 31, Senator Don Riegle again rejected my call for special Banking Committee hearings on Whitewater, claiming that we should wait for the independent counselor's report. But everyone knew that might take years–the Iran-contra independent counsel had taken more than six years to conclude his investigation. No one wanted to wait until the year 2000. With public outcry mounting, on February 2, Chairman Riegle finally agreed to Senate Banking Committee hearings on the RTC's handling of Madison Guaranty. RTC head Roger Altman informed me in a letter that he would "vigorously pursue all appropriate remedies to recover more money from Madison, including seeking an extension of the civil statute of limitations." All the same, I continued to appear on the Senate floor with my countdown calendar.

At a February 3 meeting of the Banking Committee, my colleague Lauch Faircloth of North Carolina and I questioned Ricki Tigert, Clinton's nominee to head the Federal Deposit Insurance Company (FDIC). Here was another key regulatory position being filled by a Clinton friend. Lauch, in his inimitable North Carolina drawl and fatherly style, questioned Tigert about her friendship with Hillary and Bill and read published accounts indicating that Tigert had "hung out with the Clintons" over the preceding new year's holiday. He asked whether she, a friend of the First Family, could objectively investigate Madison: "Doesn't it present an almost impossible situation ... here you are investigating any possible violations [which may result in] extreme embarrassment ... of your favorite 'hanging out' friend."

When I asked Tigert if she would recuse herself from any such investigation, she refused to provide a straight answer. Five days later, she announced that she would, in fact, recuse herself. On February 4, *Wall Street Journal* columnist Paul Gigot had blasted Tigert for being part of "a pattern of regulatory cronyism from Little Rock days."

On February 10, after two months of my calendar announcing "the clock is ticking," the Senate passed by a vote of 95–0 a measure giving the government an additional two years to take civil action on matters relating to Madison Guaranty. I said that this sent "a strong message that the House as well as the Senate will not tolerate gross fraud or negligence at the taxpayer's expense—no matter who the culprits are. Those responsible for bilking the taxpayers will not be able to hide behind the calendar. Despite weeks of obfuscation, the bell has tolled for the administration's foot dragging." The House passed a similar amendment by a vote of 390–1, and the conference committee adopted my version.

By February 22, notwithstanding Roger Altman's promises to be cooperative, the RTC was dragging its feet. I promised "to fully explore the actions of the RTC and its interim leader in the Madison/Whitewater controversy, including delayed and incomplete responses to congressional requests for information as well as the question of Mr. Altman's recusal."

On February 24, in response to questions by Senator Phil Gramm, Roger Altman made a startling admission. He informed the Banking Committee of a meeting with White House Counsel Bernard Nussbaum, Deputy Chief of Staff Harold Ickes, and the First Lady's chief of staff, Margaret A. Williams, to discuss the Whitewater inquiry. This admission blew the lid off the White House's claims that it had not tried to interfere with the investigation.

More than any other event or admission, Altman had created the impression that the White House was involved in a cover-up.

Representative Jim Leach blasted Altman's meeting as a "thoroughly unseemly" act which "compromised the integrity of the regulatory process."

While Altman soft-pedaled his meeting as an unremarkable briefing on pending business, I had an entirely different view: "Can you imagine if I or another senator brought someone to the RTC to ask for an update of a lawsuit? What would they think of us? It is totally inappropriate and presents the worst of appearances. And these were not the Clinton's personal lawyers. They were Nussbaum, Ickes, and Williams." Senator John Kerry of Massachusetts wasted no time in attacking me for "piling on in a political fashion."

On February 28, the *New York Times*'s lead editorial blasted "Slovenly White House Ethics" and stated that "it was only through Senator Alfonse D'Amato's efforts that the government released any RTC documents." The *Times* continued: "It is time for the Democratic Congressional leaders, Thomas Foley and George Mitchell, to try to educate this White House about the normal protocols of governance. . . ."

That same day, Roger Altman finally rescued himself from matters related to Whitewater. I also received praise from another unlikely source that day: a *Newsday* editorial entitled "It Smells Bad." The newspaper wrote, "We're unaccustomed to applauding Senator Alfonse D'Amato on matters of ethics, but in this case, he did a real service by focusing attention on the Altman meeting."

Taking Heat from the Democrats

With the liberal press singing my praises and hammering away at the Clintons' ethics, the White House began to lose its cool. Within hours of Altman's "heads up" revelation, the President personally attacked me. With his voice filled with sarcasm, he remarked that "the Republicans have decided to make Senator D'Amato the ethical point man" on Whitewater. Democratic National Chairman David Wilhelm chimed in with some low personal blows. Rather than respond to legitimate questions about the integrity of the White House, the President's people began to attack me and my record.

I quickly dashed off a rebuttal to Wilhelm:

> I am in receipt of your letter from this afternoon. It only reconfirms my suspicion that there is something rotten in Little Rock. You can be sure that I will now redouble my efforts to get to the bottom of this Whitewater/Madison scandal.
>
> P.S. Your attempt to interject political intimidation into this process is despicable.

After reading Wilhelm's letter, I could not help but notice a familiar refrain to the charges being hurled against me. I later discovered that Mark Waldman, a former researcher for Mark Green, was a special assistant in George Stephanopoulos's office. Waldman had appeared on *60 Minutes*' 1991 hatchet job on my reputation. He had apparently moved up in the world. I guess, in a perverse way, I should be flattered. While I used to be smeared by small-time operators like Mark Green, now I was the focus of a presidential assault.

Although I fully expected the White House and Wilhelm to take me on over Whitewater, I did not think that my Democratic Senate colleagues would be as rude and unsenatorial in their attacks. But I was wrong. At a March 14 political rally in Boston (at which the President had a minor tantrum and called the Republicans the party that always says, "No, no, no, no, no" to his proposals), Senator John Kerry took a shot at me. Noting his amusement that I was the Republican leader on Whitewater, he quipped, "I guess Bob Packwood was busy."

This low blow was surprising coming from Kerry. We had worked hard on drug interdiction and Manuel Noriega. I thought we had a professional, even friendly relationship. In Kerry's defense, he later approached me on the Senate floor and apologized, explaining that his comments made in the heat of a partisan rally. I accepted his apology on the spot and told him to make no more of it. Senator John McCain of Arizona was not so forgiving, however. He personally chided Kerry for his cheap shot. He wanted Kerry to apologize in public. McCain, a veteran of the Vietnam War and former POW, is a gutsy and considerate guy. I appreciate John's standing up for me.

Wendell Ford of Kentucky has also attacked me. Ford, then the majority whip, shares none of former Majority Leader George Mitchell's graces. Even though Mitchell could be as partisan as they come, he was always a gentleman. Ford is entirely different.

During March 1994, with Whitewater at a rapid boil, I asked Senator Hollings if he would yield the floor so I could make a brief statement. Hollings politely gave me the floor and I completed my remarks. Instead of graciously concluding the order of business, Wendell Ford took to the floor and offered a blistering and personal broadside against me. He actually said that my "mere presence" on the Senate floor aggravated him, and that New Yorkers would be better served if I spent my time in committee meetings and did not come to the Senate floor to make speeches. I reminded the senator from Kentucky that the people of my state had decided who was serving their interest, not Wendell Ford.

I paid a price for pursuing Whitewater. Phil Donahue insulted me on his talk show. Clinton political consultant Mandy Grunewald sneered at me on *Nightline*. And *Crossfire*'s liberal Michael Kinsley subjected me to any number of energetic outbursts. I even appeared offscreen in Garry Trudeau's comic strip *Doonesbury* as an arrogant lout screaming, "It's payback time, Baby!" to the imaginary moderate Republican Congresswoman Lacey Davenport.

Once the Democrats and their friends in the media found that they could not shut me up, they began to circulate stories that the Republicans were embarrassed by my position as a leader on the Whitewater scandal. The *Washington Post*'s Mary McGrory wrote a ridiculous column entitled "Attack Dog D'Amato Gets a Watchdog," which erroneously stated that Senator Dole had called in Senator Bill Cohen of Maine to watch my handling of Whitewater. McGrory wrote that "for both sides of the seething Senate D'Amato epitomizes the excesses of the whole Whitewater saga.

[They] are acutely aware that the Émile Zola *(J'Accuse)* role that D'Amato has seized for himself is a bit of a stretch." This column was a complete fabrication of events. It was *my* idea to seek Senator Cohen's counsel on possible Whitewater hearings. I knew he had the experience from both the Iran-contra and the Watergate hearings. Any correspondent or columnist could have asked Senator Cohen or Senator Dole directly, but that would have ruined their story.

One of the more disturbing attacks came from the *New York Observer,* which published parts of classified testimony from my 1991 Ethics Committee hearings. Senate rules do not even permit *me* to have a transcript of my own testimony. I have no doubt that the *Observer* obtained these documents from Justice Department sources friendly to the White House.

THE 1994 WHITEWATER HEARINGS

After months of foot-dragging by the Democratic leadership, the Senate Banking Committee finally began hearings on Whitewater on July 29, 1994. In a partisan move to limit political damage to the President, Senator Mitchell succeeded in severely limiting the scope of our hearings to questions about the circumstances surrounding the death of Vincent Foster and about improper contacts between the Treasury Department and the White House on RTC referrals involving Madison Guaranty.

Even with such limitations, the hearings revealed a White House consumed by what *Time* called a "culture of deception." More than one hundred hours of testimony by twenty-nine current and former members of the Clinton administration revealed that the White House was desperate to keep Roger Altman on board as head of the RTC to shield the Clintons from an investigation of Whitewater. It also became painfully evident to all concerned that Roger Altman had deceived the Banking Committee on February 24 when he told us that he had held only one "heads up" meeting with Clinton's advisers. By that time, he had held more than twenty such meetings.

The entire nation watched with intense discomfort as bright

young Clinton aides seemed to engage in a chorus of lies and equivocation to cover for the White House. The Treasury Department's top lawyer, Jean Hanson, had an entirely different recollection of events than Roger Altman about his desire to recuse himself from the Madison investigation and the White House's pressure to keep him at the RTC. Roger Altman's testimony utterly defied logic and belief. Both Democrats and Republicans were outraged at his incredible habit of deception. I was being gentle when I accused him of being "at the least disingenuous." Senator Phil Gramm called his testimony "totally unbelievable," and Senator Richard Shelby, a Democrat from Alabama, got to the heart of the matter when he called on Mr. Altman to resign, asking, "Mr. Altman, do you think when someone asks you a straight question, you should give a straight answer?" The answer was painfully obvious to all concerned. And then there was poor Josh Steiner, a twenty-eight-year-old Treasury official. Steiner's diary entries revealed a series of meetings between Altman and the White House. Obviously coached, he was reduced to the pathetic role of denying his belief in his own words.

It was obvious that these Treasury aides were left to twist in the wind to protect the White House. Roger Altman's testimony was directly contradicted by the testimony of nine other Treasury officials. Josh Steiner had to contradict himself. George Stephanopoulos, who has a reputation for a steel-trap mind, had to use the phrase "I don't remember" an amazing thirty-one times during his Senate deposition.

Despite their limited scope, the hearings succeeded in educating the public about Whitewater. To return to my initial two questions about Whitewater—was there wrongdoing and was there a cover-up?—it is now abundantly clear that a cover-up was going on. The question remains, just what is the White House so intent on covering up? Based on a pattern of deceit that has continued for more than a year, I find it increasingly difficult to believe that the Clintons have nothing serious to hide. As the *New York Times* observed as early as January 1994, the Clintons are willing to pay an extremely high political price to keep *something* under wraps.

Perhaps the most pleasant aspect of the Senate Whitewater hearings was their bipartisan nature. Despite the obvious damage done to a president of their party, my Democratic colleagues conducted themselves in a spirit of inquiry free from political gamesmanship. In the Democrats' own report on Whitewater, they urged the President to issue an executive order requiring Executive Branch officials to provide testimony that was "forthright, complete and timely." Apparently they were as aghast as the rest of us.

For me, the most surprising and rewarding moment to come out of a whole year of Whitewater were the unsolicited words of praise from my colleague Senator Phil Gramm:

> I want to say something about Al D'Amato. We don't talk much about profiles in courage very much anymore. Maybe there's not as much of it as there used to be; maybe we don't recognize it when it's in front of our eyes. But I think Al D'Amato is one person who has exhibited so much of it that people have seen it. . . .
>
> It took a lot of guts for him to stand up on this whole issue. . . . Al knew that he was going to be attacked personally, that old accusations against him which had been looked at and rejected were going to be dredged back up, that everything that he did in this hearing was going to be challenged and personal attacks were going to be leveled against him.
>
> Yet I think it would be fair to say that we would not be here . . . and the public would not have been served had not this guy from New York—who talks funny, who has a little flare of temper, who speaks in a loud voice occasionally—been so courageous. I'm proud to have been sitting here next to him and to have simply watched it all occur.
>
> And I want to congratulate him for his leadership on this matter.

Thanks, Phil. Our work has just begun.

Now that the Republicans have taken control of the Senate, I am now chairman of the Banking Committee. The committee will conduct a full investigation into all matters relating to Whitewater. On May 17, 1995, the full Senate voted 96–3 to authorize Whitewater hearings. Our pursuit of this matter must be fair, thorough, and responsible. The American people expect and deserve no less.

MEXICO: WORSE THAN WHITEWATER?

The Mexican peso, not Whitewater, dominated the first months of my tenure as chairman of the Banking Committee. I once again found myself taking on the establishment in defense of the middle class.

When the full story is told, the central question of the 1996 campaign could be: "Who lost Mexico?" We know that the Clinton administration fed the American public a false line about Mexico all during 1994—that Mexico was an economic model for the developing world. President Clinton even said so on December 9, just eleven days before Mexico devalued the peso and set off a world financial crisis.

All during 1993 and 1994, the Clinton administration praised its Ivy League friends from south of the border. But something else was going on behind closed doors. Treasury officials knew that Mexico was on the verge of financial collapse. In the summer of 1994, the CIA had warned Treasury that Mexico was living well beyond its means. By September, Treasury officials were privately warning their Mexican pals to shape up. Publicly, however, the administration's spin doctors told American investors to keep sending money to Mexico. No one said anything to Congress.

When Mexico's currency collapsed, on December 20, 1994, the administration came to Congress for a $40 billion bailout. When Congress balked, the administration turned to an obscure fund—the Exchange Stabilization Fund—over which the President had sole control. This fund was intended to stabilize the dollar, not the peso. Without any objection from most of my colleagues, the administration arrogantly ignored the will of the people. It was wrong.

I argued that "the President had rewarded a corrupt, dictatorial Mexican regime and saved global speculators from massive losses." Now, in my view, when Congress had to cut domestic programs to balance the federal budget, was not the time to bail out rich investors in speculative investments paying 20 or 30 percent interest. We don't even know who those investors are. I would rather spend the money to help New York, [California's] Orange County, or the District of Columbia. The administration claimed that our money was secured by Mexican oil revenues. But what would the United States do if the Mexicans ran out of oil or refused to send their revenues to us. Were we going to send the 82nd Airborne to Mexico to get our money back? As former FDIC Chairman William Seidman told the Banking Committee, the solution to the crisis was for Mexico to negotiate its debt with its creditors. That's the capitalist way. After the dollar—which had now been contaminated by the peso—plunged 15 percent in the first months of 1995, I

> These Treasury aides were left to twist in the wind to protect the White House.

asked: "Who will bail us out if the dollar continues to fall? The Japanese, the Germans, the Mexicans? I doubt it."

Make no mistake about it, Mexico is a quagmire. The Mexican people resent our bailout. They will blame us for their hyperinflation, 100 percent interest rates, and severe unemployment. By March 1995, after his brother was arrested for masterminding an assassination, former President Salinas had left Mexico for Boston. The Mexican army was still fighting rebellion in the Chiapas region. Mexico is a narco-dictatorship. Sixty percent of the cocaine shipped to our shores passes through Mexico. The administration itself admits that corruption is "evident at almost every level of the Mexican government."

The final chapter in the Mexico saga has not yet been written. In March 1995, I introduced an amendment, sponsored by thirteen other senators, to require the administration to obtain congressional approval before sending more than $5 billion to Mexico. Predictably, the *New York Times* and the *Washington Post* accused me of mischief. Only time will tell if Al D'Amato is right about Mexico, but my track record is pretty good. While I hope for the best for the Mexican people, I continue to predict that the bailout will go down as one of the biggest mistakes of Clinton's presidency. We simply cannot afford to be the world's banker.

THE
FUTURE OF
THE REPUBLICAN
PARTY

Georgeorge Bush was buried in 1992. Beaten by a young, relatively unknown governor from Arkansas, George Bush barely managed to get 38 percent of the vote, less than George McGovern received in 1972 when he carried one state against Richard Nixon. After twelve years of Reagan-Bush landslides, how did George Bush, a man of great intelligence, urbanity, good looks, and charm, manage to lose so disastrously?

You can point to Perot. You can blame the economy. You can say, as many conservatives already say, that Bill Clinton is an "accidental president," a man who won with 43 percent. You can also stick your head in the sand and hope somebody doesn't kick you in the behind. The fact is, the ground has moved under us. The world is a changed place for all of us—Democrats, Republicans, Conservatives, and Liberals. The rules have changed, and the strategies and coalitions that the Republicans used to own the White House from 1968 to 1992 are as dated and out of touch as the old Roosevelt coalition that preceded it. That Republican lock on the White House is history, and if we don't learn from that history, it could be another generation until we get back in.

Let's look at what has occurred. Five years of American history produced forty years of American presidents. Every president from Eisenhower to Bush was shaped by World War II. From the great general of the great war to the youngest fighter pilot, each of our presidents shared World War II as the central experience in his lives. From 1941 to 1945, every movie you saw, every paper you read, and every day of your life was devoted to winning the war. I was just a little kid at the time, but even from my sandbox I could feel the intensity of the period. My father and all of his brothers were fighting the enemy. My mother and all of her girlfriends were working at defense plants. We rationed gas, we saved tin foil, and we grew vegetables in a victory garden. It was a total economic, political, personal, and emotional experience unlike any other that we have seen before or since.

After the war ended, the intensity of that period defined much of American social and political life for the next two generations. The supreme value of American patriotism, so ingrained in all of us during the war, would remain the central focus of politics until 1992, when Bill Clinton, a child of the sixties and a product of the Vietnam generation, defeated George Bush, the last president to serve in World War II.

From 1953 to 1992, every president shared in the common triumph and sacrifice of that war. Service to country, allegiance to the military, and unity before a sworn enemy were simply assumed by all Americans who lived through that war. By 1952, when Dwight D. Eisenhower wrested the nomination from the isolationist Republican Robert A. Taft, he ensured that the Republican Party would stand for a strong America, ready, able, and willing to defend itself and the free world against the Communist menace. By 1952, the same emotional patriotic quality that had united most Americans against Germany and Japan now united most Americans against the Communist menace emanating from Moscow and Peking. In 1952, the Republican Party stood for strong, resolute anticommunism and patriotism—and it won by a landslide. The unifying theme of patriotism would unite Republicans and constitute a powerful electoral force for the next forty years.

Patriotism, love of country, and a strong anti-Communist platform kept together some of the disparate and often warring factions of Republicans. The party included both economic liberals like Nelson Rockefeller and free market theorists like Milton Friedman, but patriotism kept them together. The party included socially conservative evangelicals as well as social liberals, but belief in a strong defense and patriotism kept these differing groups pulling in harness.

With patriotism as its central theme, the Republican Party changed and grew from a minority party to a majority party encompassing overlapping and occasionally contentious coalitions. In fact, two of the losses on the presidential level during the last forty years occurred when the Republicans were outperformed on this issue. When John F. Kennedy ran as more of a hawk than Richard Nixon, with his talk of a missile gap, he won. When Gerald Ford made the outrageous gaffe that the Soviets did not control Poland, he lost. From 1952 on, the unifying issue of anti-communism kept the Republicans together and made them stronger with each election. They were helped enormously by the fact that, from 1964 on, the Democrats seemed to abandon the issue of patriotism. In fact, Nixon probably had a stronger civil rights record than Kennedy, while Kennedy ran as a stronger cold warrior than Nixon. Democrats could still count on class identification to win over the working-class ethnics in the cities and the poor and working class in the still "solid South." With memories of FDR and Hoover still in the air, Kennedy, the multi-millionaire, had more pull with the blue-collar workers than Nixon, who had been born dirt poor and struggled to put himself through school.

In 1964, however, much of that changed. The Republican convention resulted in the victory of the ideological conservative Goldwater over the middle-of-the-road to liberal Nelson Rockefeller. If there were ideological differences between Nelson Rockefeller and Lyndon Johnson, you could find them only with a magnifying glass. The conservatives carried the day at that convention, calling for a "choice and not an echo." Liberal Republicans like New York's Senator Kenneth Keating stormed out of the convention while the former president of the Screen Actors Guild brought the convention to its feet with a stirring proclamation of conservative values. His name was Ronald Reagan.

While Goldwater's landslide defeat looked like a disaster to the pundits at the time, it was the beginning of the party's reinvigoration. No longer dominated by liberal, rich Republicans of the *New York Herald-Tribune*–Wall Street variety, the party became a true conservative party. The liberal Republicans who walked out of the Republican convention left for good and joined the Democratic Party, which was becoming increasingly liberal. As Great Society Democrats became increasingly associated with a welfare state and the crime and rioting in America's cities in the 1960s, white conservative Democrats from both the deep South and the industrial cities deserted the party of Roosevelt in droves.

In 1968, Republicans nominated Nixon, who, with a history of staunch anticommunism and a promise of returning law and order, ran as a conservative standard bearer. George Wallace bolted from the Democratic Party. His third-party candidacy served as a way station for those disaffected Democrats not ready to vote Republican. Many of his supporters were working-class ethnics in the north and Democrats from the South who were solidly behind the economic benefits of FDR's New Deal but were increasingly turned off by the party's mindless lurch to the left on social issues and its dominance by antipatriotic politicians who seemed to be tearing America down. Hubert Humphrey was nominated while outside the Democratic convention on the streets of Chicago rioters brandished Molotov cocktails and Vietcong flags. A solidly liberal candidate with a strong record of pro-union and civil rights activism, Humphrey was hooted and insulted by an increasingly left-wing Democratic Party that seemed more interested in satisfying the media than its longtime voters and constituents.

Although the fashionable media portrayed the demonstrators sympathetically, the overwhelming majority of Americans were outraged. And they were doubly outraged that the party of Roosevelt, Kennedy, and Johnson no longer had the guts or the common sense to condemn anarchy in the streets, anti-American demonstrations, and the overwhelming spiral of rioting, crime, and welfare in its cities. In 1968, only four years after the landslide defeat of Goldwater and the ideological definition of both political parties, a conservative Republican, Richard Nixon, and a conservative Democrat, George Wallace, together won nearly 60 percent of the vote, demonstrating that the vast majority of Americans were looking for a president and a party that put patriotism first. For the first time in more than a generation, Americans were voting not on class differences but on ideology—conservative versus liberal—and the Republican Party had successfully defined itself as an institutionally conservative party. As such, our party quickly lost the likes of John Lindsay while gaining John Connally. This made the Republican Party narrower in focus, but deeper in real support. At the same time, the Democrats became more narrowly liberal and watched their real support shrink day after day.

The Democrats were voted out of the White House because they became increasingly associated with the antiwar movement. Once out of power, they became even more associated with the congressional efforts to hamper Richard Nixon's ability to conduct the execution of a war he had inherited from Lyndon Johnson. While pandering to the antiwar movement might have made points with the radical chic of the media and the Hollywood crowd, on a grassroots political level it was a disaster for the Democrats. I know this from personal experience.

When I was running for reelection as the Receiver of Taxes for the Town of Hempstead, I gave out little flag decals at every rally. We blasted the protester and stood up for our fighting boys. I ran with the flag and I won by a landslide. I won because patriotism wasn't just a gimmick, it was something that my generation and my parents' generation knew to be fundamental about being an American.

Like all immigrants and second-generation Italians, my parents and neighbors were grateful to this country for the opportunities it gave them and proud of what they had accomplished here. Like many ethnic Americans of their generation, many were Roosevelt Democrats in the thirties and forties. They were union members and union leaders. But by the seventies, they were Republicans and they were sick and tired of watching people tear the country down. And, whether they were union Democrats or Republican shopkeepers in the 1950s, they shared basic conservative values of thrift, hard work, patriotism, and religion.

Now don't get me wrong, there were plenty of other issues that divided people within both parties. There were conservatives in both parties who opposed school busing and liberals who supported it. Likewise on issues like abortion and women's rights. And, as ideology came to mean more than class or party, conservative Democrats, working-class Democrats, and middle-class Democrats left the party of their parents and their past to become Republicans. These voters would later be known as Reagan Democrats, a term that is only partially accurate. Ronald Reagan did not *make* them Republicans, they already were.

With the Wallace voters permanently estranged, the Democratic Party careened leftward and over the cliff into extremism in 1972, when they nominated George McGovern, the most left-wing candidate offered by any major party in American history. Nixon won all of the Republican vote and all of the Wallace vote and clobbered McGovern as he received almost 62 percent of the popular vote. The difference between the parties had now boiled down to pure ideology, and that ideology was most clearly defined by the Republicans as patriotism and anticommunism.

There were two factions to Republican conservatism held together by shared patriotism, a desire for a strong national defense, and a fervent anticommunism. The two factions were very different: the traditional free market, probusiness economic conservatism that had been the party's hallmark since the days of Calvin Coolidge and before, and the religious, moral, and conservative wing of the party that was newly energized by their strong reaction to the moral and social permissiveness of the 1960s. Thus the strong belief in patriotism and anticommunism provided the glue that kept these very different groups with very different agendas together in the Republican tent.

The victory of 1972 and its lesson was quickly obscured by the Watergate mess. But Watergate had nothing to do with the ideological shift that was moving in the Republicans' favor. Gerald Ford looked like a sure loser in 1976 when Ronald Reagan came within an eyelash of wresting away the Republican nomination. I think it can be said with great certainty that had Ronald Reagan won the nomination in 1976, he would have won a comfortable victory, and we would have been spared Jimmy Carter's horrible presidency.

Sensing a real opportunity, in 1976 the Democrats returned to their old FDR coalition and nominated a southern agrarian, a born-again Christian who could appeal to liberals and play the old class card. Yet with everything going for him, Carter still managed a narrow victory over a bumbling, stumbling Jerry Ford, a former congressman who could probably not prevail in a statewide race, never mind a national campaign. Yet, with a weak economy and with all the baggage of Watergate, Ford really lost the election because he could not convince the voters that he was serious about anticommunism. Totally intoxicated by Henry Kissinger's failed policy of détente, Ford embarrassed himself at the presidential debate when he blurted out that he felt that the people of Poland were not under Soviet domination. Carter, an Annapolis graduate, convinced enough people that he would be tougher on the Soviets than Ford. While Ford had a lot of negatives going into 1976, the fact that he did not hold the upper ground on the key issue of patriotism and national defense was a key factor in his defeat. As Kennedy had proved in 1960, when a Democrat was a tougher cold warrior than his opponent, he won.

By 1980, Jimmy Carter faced the electorate with one of the sorriest records imaginable. A waffling foreign policy had resulted in disgrace abroad while his inept handling of the economy resulted in 20 percent inflation and 20 percent interest rates. The national mood was sour, depressed even, and it cried for strong leadership. It was clear to the electorate that a liberal administration had ruined the economy, had given a green light to the Soviets, and had resulted in social malaise.

On a national level, the election of 1980 completed the ideological polarization of the parties that had been in process since 1964. Ted Kennedy led true-believing liberals on a crusade to unseat Jimmy Carter. Amazingly, he felt that Jimmy Carter was not liberal enough. He found, as Reagan had in 1976, how impossible it can be to wrest the nomination from a sitting president. All the same, Kennedy's race helped energize the left wing of the party and helped many liberal candidates (like Liz Holtzman) succeed in local primaries. The 1980 Democratic convention might have nominated Jimmy Carter, but it was emotionally dominated by Teddy Kennedy's long-winded speech praising traditional liberalism. It was clear that the true heart of the party was way left of center and out of touch with most middle-class Americans.

On the Republican side, many of the party's more establishment leftovers considered Ronald Reagan too old and too radically conservative to win the nomination or the election, but they were 100 percent wrong. John Anderson, a liberal Republican from Illinois, dazzled the media in some early primaries and then bolted the party to form a third party when Ronald Reagan's nomination was all but assured. Anderson's candidacy provided a way station for those liberal Republicans who could not abide the Republican Party that was narrowing its focus under Ronald Reagan. Just as Wallace's 1968 candidacy cleansed the Democrats of their conservative base, Anderson led the exit of the last liberals from Ronald Reagan's party.

Uniting the main Republican constituencies with his message of more economic freedom, more personal responsibility, and a solid core of patriotism and anticommunism, Ronald Reagan ran as the most conservative candidate in American history and won decisively in a tidal wave that also made the Republicans the majority party in the Senate.

The election of 1984 proved to be the high-water mark of the ideological polarization between the parties. The Democrats nominated Walter Mondale, a Minnesota liberal of the Hubert Humphrey school. His convention *promise* was actually to raise taxes! Incredibly, he thought this was a good idea, and the Democrats present stood and applauded, demonstrating live and on television just how out of touch they were. The party was now completely under the control of its left wing, which truly believed in more taxes, less personal responsibility, and a weak and compromising foreign policy. With this gang of experts behind him, Walter Mondale went down in flames, barely carrying his own state and losing every other state in the Union. His choice of Geraldine Ferraro as vice presidential candidate was a transparent act of political correctness and was seen for the gimmick that it was. Once again, when faced with a clear choice between a true conservative and a true liberal, the people voted about 60–40 to give Ronald Reagan four more years.

It was at the 1984 Republican convention that Jeane Kirkpatrick, a former Democrat herself, made the most persuasive and eloquent description of the difference between the parties on foreign policy and America's standing in the world. She brilliantly, and quite accurately, labeled the Democrats as the party that "blamed America first" for the problems in the world while the party of Ronald Reagan was one that stood tall and had returned America to a position of power and pride in foreign affairs. Her taunt—that "the Democrats always blame America first"—effectively haunted the Democrats until the end of the cold war.

In all honesty, the Reagan administration simply lost its bearings and ran out of steam in the second term. The ideological true believers who gave the Reagan revolution so much energy and inspiration were on the way out, and the pragmatists and power brokers who would come to dominate the failed Bush administration were on the ascent. Meese, Deaver, Kirkpatrick were on the way out. The philosophical excitement of passing the largest tax cut in history was over. Infighting replaced innovation. Jim Baker and Donald Regan switched jobs and both of them proved disastrous. Jim Baker never had any loyalty to anyone but himself, and Donald Regan was completely over his head. He owed his job to CIA Director Bill Casey's intervention. His public infighting with the President's wife was a complete disgrace and demonstrated what kind of man he was, a fool.

We lost control of the Senate in 1986 after the party moved from ideology to pragmatism. Once the Democrats regained the Senate, they had the ability to block the President's legislative initiatives, to thwart his nomination of Robert Bork to the Supreme Court, and to initiate the Iran-contra investigation, which put the once ideologically innovative Reagan administration on the defensive in its final years. With Iran-contra, the press and the liberals thought they might have a rerun of Watergate. Since scandal and not ideas was the only way that they had regained the White House since 1964, they were anxious to give it a go, even if it meant impeaching the most popular president in a generation. In spite of all his troubles, Ronald Reagan left office with one of the highest approval ratings ever. While I believe that much of this can be attributed to Reagan the man, it is also a factor of the natural conservative bent of the voters who twice elected him. His patriotic appeal to the key conservative constituencies—economic and social—made him unbeatable. In spite of his age, I am certain he would have won a third term in 1988 if constitutionally allowed.

With Reagan out of the picture, it looked as if the differing key Republican constituencies might all go their separate ways. Alexander Haig, Kirkpatrick, and Dole represented hard-line anti-Communists; Jack Kemp appealed to the economic conservatives with his free market theories; and Pat Robertson, the TV evangelist, spoke to the social conservatives. No one, it seemed, could unite the party as Ronald Reagan had.

George Bush was in a very strange position. Everything about his record and background reflected the moderate to liberal Republicanism that the party had long since expelled. In a party increasingly dominated by grassroots conservatives, he was a blue blood whose father had been best friends with Thomas Dewey. His Yale education (including a Skull and Bones membership) and his work with the United Nations, the diplomatic community in Communist China, and the Trilateral Commission and other internationalist organizations made him a dubious choice to represent hard-line anti-Communists. His 1980 presidential bid as a prochoice moderate Republican who referred to Reagan's promised tax cuts as "voodoo economics" hardly endeared him to either the social or economic conservative constituencies.

But give George Bush credit. Some have said that the vice presidency isn't worth a bucket of warm spit, but he made it work. He remodeled himself as Ronald Reagan's heir apparent. He ran as "Son of Reagan." He trudged through the snows of New

Hampshire with a "No New Taxes" pledge sheet and asked every candidate to sign it. My good friend Bob Dole couldn't, in good conscience, sign something he might regret in the next four years. He told the truth in New Hampshire, and he stumbled. "Son of Reagan" beat Bob Dole with his no-new-tax pledge and repeated it over and over again as he won primary after primary. He repeated it at the Republican convention when he delivered Peggy Noonan's wonderful speech. He repeated it again and again and he beat Mike Dukakis's brains out. He repeated it so many times that the country believed that he *was* "Son of Reagan." And just to make sure, he ran a strong campaign that underscored his belief in the narrow, conservative focus that Ronald Reagan had brought to the Republican Party. For economic conservatives, he promised, "Read my lips, no new taxes." To underscore his allegiance to social conservatism and law and order, he reminded voters of Mike Dukakis's crazy liberal experimentation and his habit of paroling convicted killers like Willie Horton. And of course George Bush ran on patriotism—particularly on his allegiance to the flag and his service in World War II as the youngest pilot in the war. He spent weeks blasting Dukakis's veto of a Massachusetts law requiring students recite the pledge of allegiance to the flag. Mike Dukakis and the Democrats didn't know what hit them. They complained in the press: "This is 1988–is Bush really talking about the flag?" You're damn right he was. He knew people's belief in patriotism, in strong conservative values, still won elections. And just for good measure, they ran an ad showing Mike Dukakis looking like a dwarf popping out of the turret of a tank. Who would be stronger in defense of America, George Bush the war hero or little bitty Mike in the tank?

As "Son of Reagan," Bush wasn't exactly the Gipper, but he convinced enough voters that he would just have to do.

The problem is, George Bush never believed for a second that he was "Son of Reagan," and he started to deny his patrimony the second he took office. The first hint of this betrayal was all that talk about "kinder and gentler." Kinder and gentler than *what*? True conservatives had nothing to apologize for. What was he talking about? *Who* was he apologizing to? The Reagan era brought about unprecedented economic growth. We cut taxes and created jobs, opportunity, and hope. We restored our prestige abroad and were containing and defeating communism throughout the world. George Bush did not believe in the philosophy of Ronald Reagan. It's just that simple.

Bush began almost immediately to betray the economic conservatives by allowing the size of the government and the size of the deficit to balloon out of control. His economic advisers—Brady, Darman, and Sununu—were borderline incompetents, and by July 1990, when the first crunch came with a Democratic Congress, Bush and Co. made their move. Did they tell the Democrats to stuff it? To cut spending? Did they make the tough call? No, they raised taxes and tried to believe it was no big deal. This was Bush's defining moment. Ronald Reagan had toughed out the worst recession since the 1930s. Things were *rough* in 1982, but Ronald Reagan had convictions. It was not that tough in 1990. There was no earth-shattering crisis. A standoff with Congress of a few weeks or even a month would not have threatened the republic. On the contrary, it would have shown that the President had some convictions, some *cojones*. Instead, he waffled, and he lost all credibility.

He also lost his party. It was just George Bush's luck that his greatest failure (raising taxes) coincided with the end of the Soviet empire. *Both* of these events sealed his political doom. By raising taxes he lost the support of economic conservatives. Without a Soviet threat to contend with, the core concern of anticommunism that kept economic and social conservatives together was no longer there. For a brief, shining moment, when George Bush could return the focus to patriotism with his military triumph over the Iraqi army, his numbers were simply stratospheric. Once the focus returned to the economy in 1991–92, he faced an angry electorate with a Republican Party spinning out of control.

What could he do? When he gave a speech on the economy, no one believed him. When he talked tough on foreign policy, there was no one left to listen to him. Then one day he made a speech about family values and he got applause. Like any politician or entertainer, when you get applause, you do it again. Talk of "family values," contempt for the "cultural elite," and disdain for Murphy Brown became the one-note theme of the Bush-Quayle campaign. This was no accident. With the loss of two key constituencies, Bush was playing to the only sure voters he had left. And as he played to the social conservatives, he was unknowingly scaring the economic conservatives out of the party.

By 1992, the ideological 60–40 split that had given the Republicans a lock was dead and buried. The emergence of Bill Clinton as the Democratic candidate and Ross Perot as a third-party choice presented voters with a fascinating menu representing the whole spectrum of politics. While Bush had inadvertently alienated much of Reagan's economically conservative base, Clinton did his damnedest to put some distance between himself and the word "liberal." He was a "new Democrat" and he made the most of that. He

> **George Bush started to deny his patrimony the second he took office.**

was pro–death penalty, tough on crime. He promised to end welfare as we now know it. He was prochoice, but reluctantly so. He cleverly put some distance between himself and Jesse Jackson by personally rebuking the foulmouthed rap star Sister Souljah in the reverend's presence. He did a masterful job of distancing himself from the Democratic image that had proven so disastrous for the party—that of a weak-kneed liberal hopelessly pandering to the extreme wing of the party's antiwar faction (feminists, liberal black activists, and left-wing labor leaders). And, at the same time, without the Soviet threat to contend with, Clinton could successfully campaign as if foreign affairs hardly existed. Patriotism and anticommunism, the twin pillars of every Republican victory since 1952, no longer seemed to matter. It was a whole new ball game. In 1972, Nixon beat McGovern by a landslide when conservatives brandished the Democrats as the party of "acid, amnesty, and abortion." Well, here was Bill Clinton, an admitted pot smoker who willfully avoided service in the Vietnam War and who was certainly pro-abortion. All of the old strategies were thrown out the window.

How did this happen? Well, a whole new generation has come of age and are in tune with a very different beat than the patriotic message of World War II. The postwar generation has grown up with its own agenda. Issues like feminism, health care, the environment, day care, and gay rights—issues that did not really exist on the political horizon until the 1970s—have now taken their place at the table. Bill and Hillary Clinton, together with Al and Tipper Gore, did a much better job of addressing those issues and the millions of voters concerned with them than the Bushes and the Quayles.

Clinton and his wife also spoke to a whole new generation of voters. The contrast between Bush, the last of the World War II presidents, and Clinton, the first of the baby-boomer generation presidents, could not be more striking. The problem for Bush was that he was still following the same script that beat McGovern in 1972. Every time the Bush campaign bashed Clinton as a pot-smoking, draft-dodging, rock 'n' roll loving bum, it underscored the fact that Bush represented the past and Clinton the present and future.

But the differences between George and Bill were nothing compared to the huge generational gap between Barbara and Hillary. During the campaign, Hillary Clinton spoke to an entire generation of working women whom the Bush people never reached. The more the Bush people bashed Hillary, the more they alienated millions of voters—particularly young working women—and convinced them that the Republican Party just didn't have a clue.

Into this generational abyss walked Ross Perot. Neither a baby-boomer nor a World War II veteran, Perot spoke to my peers, the Korean War/fifties generation. For those voters not quite ready to hear rock 'n' roll blaring from the Oval Office, Perot offered a safe alternative. His computer literacy was in marked contrast to Bush, who couldn't recognize a supermarket scanner. As a multibillionaire, he was also attractive to those economic conservatives who didn't trust Clinton's dubious conversion from liberal economic redistribution. His unspecific aura of toughness spoke to those voters concerned with crime, drugs, and social disorder, and his prochoice stance appealed to those economic conservatives who were put off by the Republican's increasing strident stance on "family values."

George Bush walked into the Republican convention in Houston in August 1992 where only the social conservatives were at all enthusiastic about his candidacy, and that enthusiasm scared the hell out of many Americans. It scared the hell out of me. I left that convention in disgust, and that was covered on the first page of the *New York Times*. There were people at that gathering who said that Democrats had no family values. What idiotic nonsense. Do you mean to say that my friends and relatives who are Democrats, my parents, who happened to have been raised as Democrats, were less moral, less American than others? The Houston convention was a horror show, an orgy of intolerance that doomed Bush's already faltering campaign. Anticommunism and patriotism had held the party together for forty years, now moral intolerance was splitting it in two. The crack-up of the Republican Party was an ugly sight to behold.

We Republicans have to keep that convention in mind as we look toward 1996. Let's not kid ourselves. Beating Bill Clinton will not be easy. Without anticommunism as a unifying force, and without a common leader like Reagan to keep us together, the Republicans in 1996 cannot simply rely on Clinton's negative poll numbers and anti-incumbency. A new generation of voters has entered the picture, one that is looking for new ideas and new solutions. Who understands their needs and concerns? It's a very tough call.

The results of the 1994 November elections were heartening to every Republican and to all Americans who voted for smaller, more efficient government, lower taxes, and an end to business as usual in Washington. Clinton's enormous tax increase, Hillary's unwieldy health care proposal, and a pork-laden crime bill had given the American people a clear indication that this "new Democrat" was a champion of big government and all the taxes, programs, and bureaucracy that entails. Americans by the millions voted and said "enough is enough" to Bill and Hillary's way of doing business. Newt Gingrich deserves great credit for mobilizing Republican voters and making the battle for the House of Representatives a national referendum, instead of 535 individual races.

At the same time that we savor our great victory, we Republicans cannot afford to be complacent or to lose sight of the fact that this landslide was a vote for freedom, less government, and greater economic opportunity. It was not an endorsement of one culture and a condemnation of another. Newt Gingrich's remark immediately after the election to the effect that Bill and Hillary are "counterculture McGoverniks" is precisely the kind of rhetoric Republicans should avoid as we mobilize for 1996. We don't need that kind of name-calling nonsense to build a winning majority in America.

Here in New York, George Pataki unseated a three-term governor because he kept the focus of his campaign on freedom and opportunity. Pataki unseated Cuomo in a heavily Democratic state because the people rallied to his cry for commonsense government and economic freedom. Contrast Pataki's victory with Oliver North's experience in Virginia. North lost to a wounded Democratic candidate in a conservative state in the midst of a national Republican tidal wave—despite the fact that Ollie was telegenic and engaging and spent $18 million. The simple fact is that North and the people who supported him in the Republican primary scared the daylights out of a sufficient number of Virginians to put Chuck Robb back in the Senate. As we look toward 1996, we should remember that fact.

1996

The Republican presidential field for 1996 is impressive. All of the major contenders are my friends. If our party is to triumph in 1996, we must keep the focus on economic and personal freedom.

Phil Gramm will never win any prizes for congeniality, but he is a tenacious fighter who believes that every dollar of unnecessary government spending is a dollar stolen from poor and middle-class Americans. At a time when many hardworking citizens are having a tough time making ends meet, that is a powerful argument. No one should underestimate the appeal of Phil Gramm's message.

Senator Dick Lugar of Indiana is one of the most respected men in Washington. He is a master of foreign affairs, and his gutsy willingness to oppose farm subsidies shows that he is a serious budget cutter. Everybody knows George Bush should have selected Lugar for vice president in 1988. In terms of intellect, political maturity, experience, and stature there was simply no comparison between Dick Lugar and Dan Quayle.

Arlen Specter is a close friend. We were elected together in 1980, both among the "sweet sixteen" Republican senators who were swept into office with Ronald Reagan. When I was in political trouble, Arlen advised me well: "Alfonse, never let your face show how hard they're kicking your ass." Arlen's candidacy faces a very uphill climb, but at least, to quote Teddy Roosevelt, he's "in the arena" and fighting the good fight.

As someone who has been written off more than once, I appreciate how Pete Wilson has battled back from the brink of political oblivion. In 1990, he was given next to no chance against Dianne Feinstein in his race for California governor. After California's economy went into the tank in the early 1990s, and the state was hit with riots, floods, fires, and earthquakes, no one would have predicted that he would win reelection in 1994. Not only did he win, but he won by a landslide. Richard Nixon predicted that Pete Wilson would be president or vice president some day. Given Pete's indominatable political spirit and California's electoral clout, though he's gotten off to a late start, he's a serious contender.

One candidate who mystifies me is Lamar Alexander. With an inside-the-Beltway résumé dating back to the Nixon administration, why is Alexander pretending to be a populist insurgent? It will take more than a plaid shirt and a folksy road trip across the 50 states to convince America that he can bring real change to the city where he worked for so many decades. So far, Alexander's campaign is a long shot with a long way to go.

In 1988, I defied the conventional wisdom and backed Bob

Dole against George Bush. I said then that he had the guts, the experience, and the temperament to be a great president. I am sure if he had won the nomination in 1988, we would be enjoying Bob's second term instead of suffering through Clinton's first. As Bob said on David Letterman's TV program, "Every country needs a president." The electorate has serious doubts about Bill Clinton's political maturity. No one can have any such doubts about Bob Dole.

In March 1995, I again announced my support for Bob Dole for president. After working closely with Bob for more than fourteen years, I'm now more convinced than ever that he is uniquely qualified to be our president. He's a leader in the fight to reduce government spending, to control taxes, and to get government regulation off the backs of working men and women.

A candidate of the religious right or the socially conservative wing of the party will certainly run in 1996. Pat Robertson or Pat Buchanan will base their campaign on family values, cultural civil wars, and a battle for the soul of America. Remember, at the 1992 Houston convention, that message went over very well. It was wildly received. But the Republicans who applauded Buchanan's call for a cultural civil war were as out of touch with America as the Democratic liberals in 1984 who applauded Mondale's call for higher taxes. Buchanan provided the kind of message that excites true believers and inspires a populist volunteer political army. I believe that if a candidate of the extreme social right, like Buchanan or Robertson, gains control of the party through a primary insurgency driven by a grassroots force of Christian volunteers, the Republican Party will most certainly go down to defeat in 1996.

Now why do I say that? I am a conservative Republican. I'm a practicing, but hardly perfect, Roman Catholic who considers his faith and its culture very important. I am personally and morally opposed to abortion and have run on the tickets of the Right to Life Party and the Conservative Party. I consider my family to be a rock of strength and support and feel that the American family is the basis for the strength and stability of our society.

But—and it's a very big but—I part company with Buchanan

and Robertson because they seem to believe that the Republican Party should be an instrument of cultural domination and control. While I believe in many of the values of the social right, I part with them because they believe that their values are the *only* acceptable set of values and that those values should be imposed by the government. I believe the American people should be free to be who they are and that values should be taught by the family and the church and not by the government. In Iran, the mullahs outlaw music and movies they don't like and burn books they find unacceptable. I don't want—and I know that mainstream America doesn't want—an Ayatollah mentality in American culture. If you don't like Howard Stern, tune to another station. Don't ban him from the airwaves or use the FCC to harass him.

I believe that culture can never be dictated by political party or government. My family came to this country so they could be free to be who they were. There were many people in Newark and Brooklyn who were not happy to see Irish, Jews, Italians, or Poles coming into town, cooking their strange foods and speaking their strange language and sending their kids to their schools. But America was big enough and smart enough and free enough back at the turn of the century to accept all those disparate and foreign cultures, and America is a stronger, greater, and freer nation now because of it. We do not need a party of cultural coercion from either the right or the left telling people what they should do.

Just as many Americans were scared to death by the religious right at the Houston convention, millions more are frightened by the specter of liberal "political correctness" that has settled over so much of our national discourse. Politically correct liberals want to dictate what words you can say, what ideas you can talk about, and what you can eat, smoke, read, or enjoy. That's why I take such joy in befriending and defending Howard Stern, an outrageous man and a great family man who has such a good time lampooning the puritans on both the left and the right and who is now a victim of a ridiculous vendetta by the FCC, one that has made the government a big brother of censorship and social control.

I strongly believe that, like me, most middle-class Americans, when faced with the intolerant right and the politically correct left, will say, "A plague on both your houses," and tell them both to go stuff it. I contend that the vast, overwhelming majority of Americans are too smart, too practical, and too fair to succumb to either extreme. I firmly believe that if the Republican Party recognizes this and runs a fair and open-minded candidate in 1996, a candidate who concentrates on cutting government, streamlining bureaucracy, cutting spending, privatizing services, and getting Washington off people's backs, it will have a terrific chance of galvanizing a new and strong coalition of voters for the next generation.

Just as patriotism dominated the last forty years, I believe that freedom—the protection of individual rights from a coercive government—can be the issue that the Republican Party can succeed with for many, many years to come. Most people feel that the government is too big, too bloated, and too inefficient. The last thing they want is for that government to tell them what to read, what to think, or what movie to go to. That's outrageous. I don't want Pat Robertson censoring films and I certainly don't want Bill Clinton to do it either. The government can't even run the Post Office right, the last thing it should be trying to run is the culture. Culture comes from your family, from your mind, and from your soul. The only governments that try to dictate culture are dictatorships, and we don't want that here in America.

I would like to build a strong America and a strong Republican Party that put freedom first. The freedom to be a Catholic, a Jew, an atheist, or a Hindu. The freedom to run and start a business, free from excessive taxation, regulation, and government interference. The freedom to go to work, to church, to school, and to a neighbor's house without the fear of criminal assault. People who cower in their homes behind locked doors are not free. A government that stands for opportunity for all of its people must also ensure that criminals do not have free rein to terrorize the law abiding. Freedom from fear must be the cornerstone of our party.

When I was in my twenties, just a kid really, I took over the local Unity Party in my little village of Island Park. It was out of power and just about defunct, but within a few short years I worked to build up that party, so that it not only regained control of the village board but has now kept it for the last thirty-odd years. How did we do that? By keeping our doors open. By telling people they were welcome, be they Democrat, Republican, or former members of the rival Public Party. We were an inclusive party that stood for local control. We knew that if left to our own devices and our own common sense, we in Island Park could do the best job for ourselves.

I still believe in keeping the door open. The Republican Party at its Houston convention in 1992 slammed the door in the face of millions of Americans who rightfully rebel at any party or government who tells them what is right and what is wrong. We need to keep the door and our minds open as we enter the twenty-first century. We have to keep our eye on the ball and remember that we are the party of Lincoln, of freedom, and of economic opportunity. If we forget that, we are lost, and we deserve to be. If we remember, we can begin to build a solid majority party for the next generation.

INDEX

D'Amato, Alfonse Marcello (*cont.*)
Senate campaign of 1980, xv–xvi,
81–100
Senate campaign of 1986, 133–38
Senate campaign of 1992,
xviii–xix, 153, 217–36
and Senate filibusters, 147–53
on Senate personalities, 139–47,
154
as "Senator Pothole," 52–53,
128–29, 138
separation and divorce, 119–20
singing on Senate floor, 142, 151
surgery to correct sight, 36–37
terrorist threat against, 295–303
travels: to Israel, 200–7; to Italy,
xi–xii, 122–25, 304–5; to Kuwait,
208–12; to Lithuania, 184–85; to
Northern Ireland, 101–8
as Unity Party Chairman, 58–63
and Whitewater probe, 309–20
and WWII, 33–34, 48
D'Amato, Antoinette Cioffari "Ann"
"Mamma" (mother), xiii, 4, 29,
185
and Al's childhood, 31, 33–34,
37–39, 43
and Armand's prosecution, 244,
246, 251
birth of, 20
campaigns for Al, xv, xviii, 78, 95,
96–97, 100, 218, 230, 236
fiftieth anniversary, 10–11
and gays in military, 290–91
lunch with Reagans, 12, 14–16, 131
marries Armand, 9–10
and Rockefeller, 53–54
D'Amato, Armand (father), xiii
and Al's childhood, 31, 37–38
and Al's law school tuition, 46
and Al's Senate races, 78–79, 95,
235, 236
background, 7–9
doesn't change name, 290–91
fiftieth anniversary, 10–11
and Island Park politics, 51–53, 61
lunch with Reagans, 12, 14–16, 131
marries Antoinette, 9–10
names Alfonse, 4
travels to Italy, 122–23

Village Voice attacks, 95, 237
and WWII, 34
D'Amato, Armand, Jr. (brother), 78,
79, 99, 153–54, 180
prosecution and exoneration of,
237, 239, 240–51, 258
D'Amato, Christopher (son), 109, 293
D'Amato, Dan (son), 39, 109, 170–72,
236, 293
D'Amato, Dan (uncle), 33
D'Amato, Ettore (grandfather), 7
D'Amato, Mrs. Ettore
(grandmother), 7
D'Amato, Gilda (aunt), 94
D'Amato, Joanne, 290
D'Amato, Lisa (daughter), 4, 126.
See also Murphy, Lisa D'Amato
D'Amato, Lorraine (daughter), 39,
120, 170
D'Amato, Michael (uncle), 8, 33,
290–91
D'Amato, Penelope "Penny" (wife),
23, 47–48, 78, 84, 119–20
Danforth, John, 248
Daniels, Mitch, 129
Darby, Father, 41–42
Darman, Dick, 189, 190, 192, 334
Davis, Cheryl, 97
Deaver, Michael (Mike), 12, 13, 331
Defense Department, 157, 160, 180
DellaBovi, Al, 131
Delvalle, Eric Arturo, 159–60, 161
Democratic Party, 73, 83, 112–13
changes in, 325–30, 334–37
Convention of 1968, 326
Convention of 1980, 330
and Whitewater, 314–17, 319
Democratic Party of Nassau County,
54, 55–57
Democratic Party of New York State
and Senate race of 1980, 92–93,
98, 99
and Senate race of 1986, 133–34,
135–37
and Senate race of 1992, 222–25
DeSapio, Carmine, xv
Dewey, Thomas, 53, 332
Diaz Herrera, Colonel, 156, 158
DiCarlo, Dominick, 110, 131
Dill, Bob, 56–57